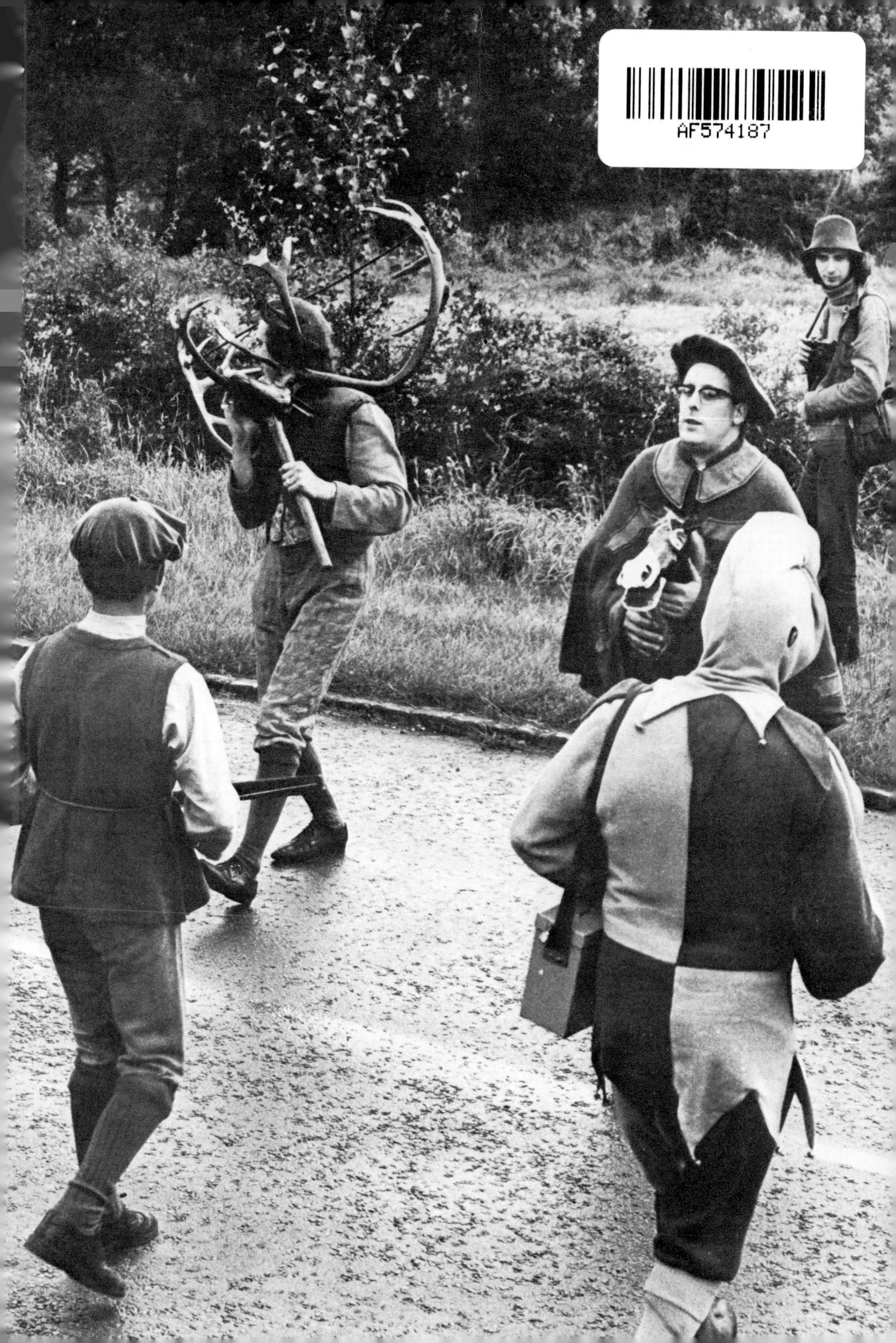

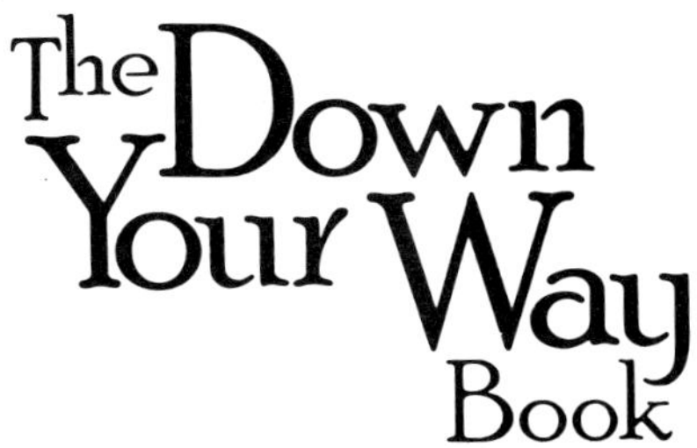
The Down Your Way Book

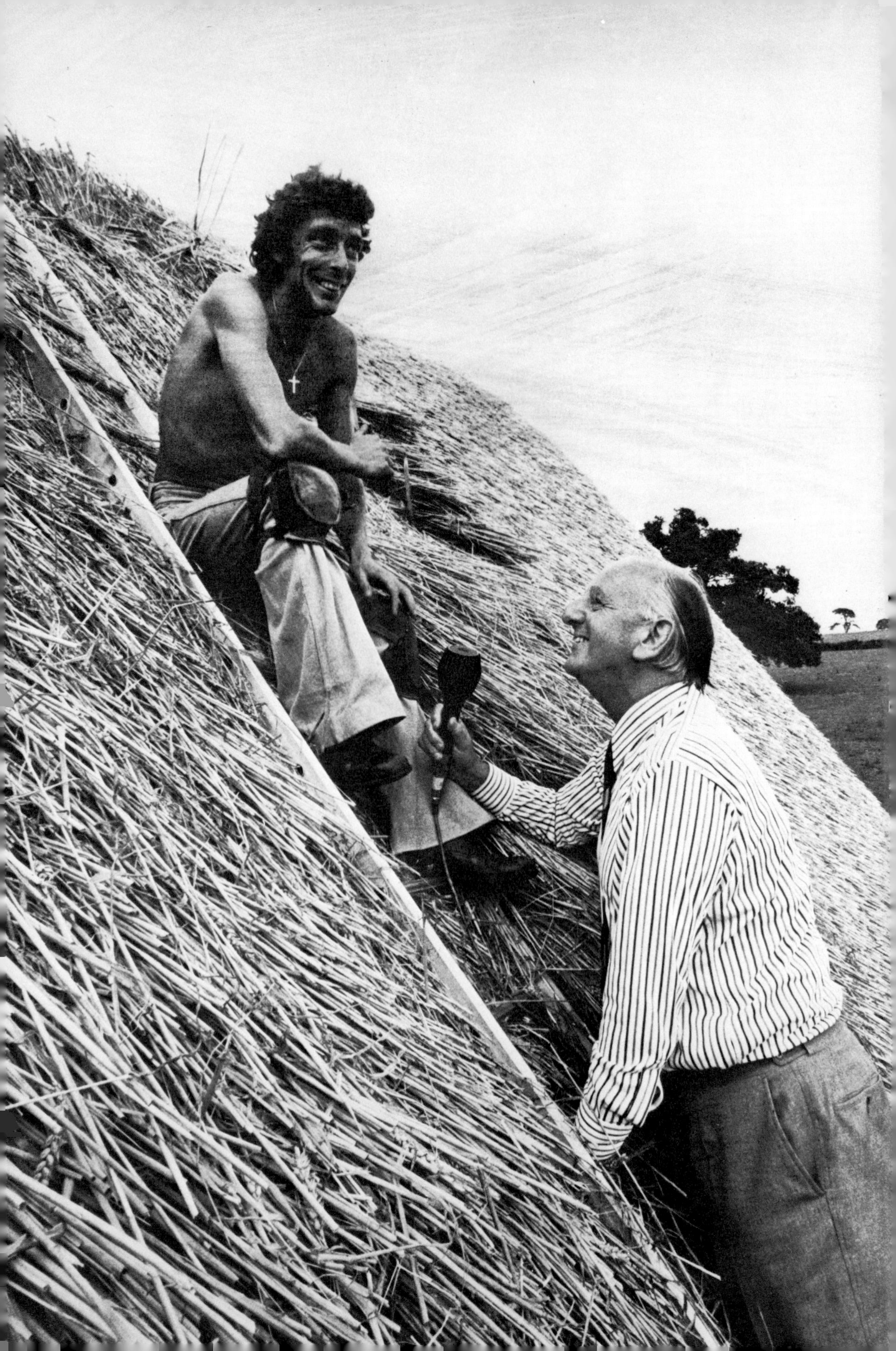

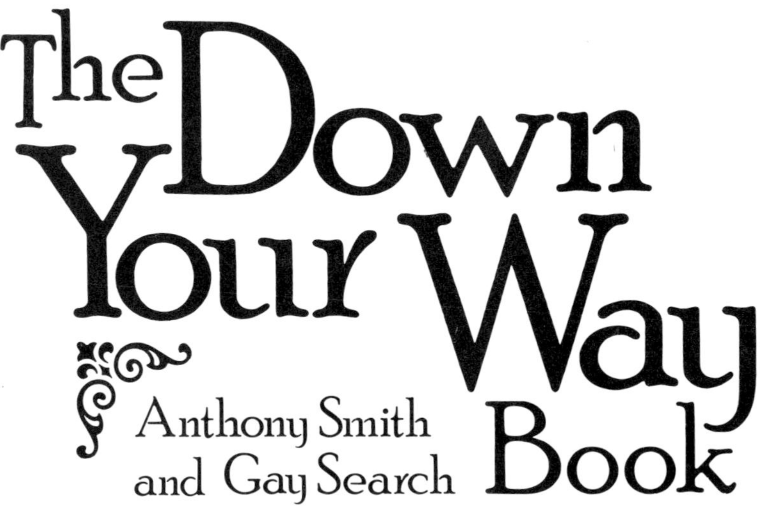

Introduction by Brian Johnston

Arthur Barker Limited London
A subsidiary of Weidenfeld (Publishers) Limited

Acknowledgements

The Publishers are very grateful to the following for kindly allowing them to reproduce the pictures in this book:

Aberdeen Journals: page 134; J. Allan Cash: 71; Barnaby's: 115; R. G. Barnett: 65; H. Beddington: 109(a); Ben Nevis Race Association: 153(a); Berwick Salmon Fisheries: 121; Biddenden Vineyards: 75; British Tourist Authority: 178; Walter Collins: 109(b); George Cross: 106(b); Cumberland & Westmorland Herald: 52(b); Cumbria Tourist Board: 150; Dartington Glass: 166(a); David Harris Consultants: 175; Harold Davies: 90; Hywel Davies: 89; Donnington Brewery: 73(a); Express & Star: 63; Glen Scotia Distillery: 67(a); Willie Gordon: 124(a); Grange Training Centre: 78; John G. Hall: 16; Herts & Essex Observer: 24; Len Homewood: 26; Isle of Man Tourist Board: 100, 101; J. Jeans: 95; Jonathan Products: 181; R. Jovanovic: 92; Margaret Lawson: 45(a); Maldon Crystal Salt: 137; J. McKeown: 147; Museum of Cider: 73(b); National Foaling Bank: 34; Queenie Newcombe: 52(a); Northamptonshire Evening Telegraph: 37(a); Oban Divers: 132; Oxford Mail: 160; Hugh Pasmore: 106(a); Pentangle Puzzles: 184; Petworth: 41; Portsmouth & Sunderland News: 153(b); Radio Times (Tony Evans): frontispiece; R. Rees: 118; R.F.D. Inflatables: 138; J. L. Roberts: 49(a); Bert Rogerson: 156; Rossendales Crematorium: 49(b); Royal Doulton: 166(b); Scottish & Universal News: 43; Brian Shuel: endpapers, 13 15(b), 17, 20(b), 22, 29, 142, 143; Skye Venture Knitwear: 180; Bill Smith: 163; Spectrum: 67(b); Suttons Seeds: 173; Homer Sykes: 8, 15(a), 20(a); Paul Taylor: 168, 169; Thomas Rivers & Son: 57; Tiptree: 59; Fiona Vigors: 37(b); Charlie Waite: 97; Wales Tourist Board: 45(b), 83; A. P. Wilson, Field, Stream & Covert (England) Ltd: 128; Dermot Wilson: 124(b); Woodmen of Arden: 87.

The Publishers have taken all possible care to acknowledge the ownership of all illustrations. If by chance an incorrect attribution has been made we will be happy to correct it in any future reprint, provided that we receive notification.

Published by arrangement with the British Broadcasting Corporation.

Published in Great Britain by Arthur Barker Ltd
91 Clapham High Street
London SW4 7TA

ISBN 0 213 16787 5

Printed in Great Britain by
Butler & Tanner Ltd
Frome and London

Contents

Introduction

by Brian Johnston

By the time this book is published *Down Your Way* will be celebrating its 1500th edition, and my own score will be 444 not out. I was sent in to bat at extremely short notice and in very sad circumstances. It all started on Thursday 2 March 1972. I was walking down a corridor in Broadcasting House, when someone popped their head out of a doorway and asked: 'Have you heard the sad news? Jingle has died.' 'Jingle' was Franklin Engelmann, and it seemed that after recording a *Down Your Way* as usual on the Wednesday, he had returned home and died of a heart attack during the night.

I was naturally very distressed at the news, but immediately had a funny feeling that his death was going to affect me in some way or other. And how right I was. Within a couple of hours I was asked if I would take his place – at least temporarily – and be prepared to record the next week's programme in six days' time at Hyde in Cheshire. After some thought I accepted, not just to help out the department, but because I knew that I would only have to do it for ten weeks until the cricket season started.

It was a daunting task. Jingle had presented *Down Your Way* 733 times since he took over from Richard Dimbleby in 1955. He had become *Down Your Way*. I felt very humble and apprehensive as I started to record my first programme in Hyde. I thought that the regular listeners would regard me as an intruder. But I need not have worried. I received nothing but kind letters, and during those ten weeks I became more confident and had the feeling that I was gradually being accepted. And, what's more, I was thoroughly enjoying meeting and talking to so many people.

During the cricket season four different broadcasters presented the sixteen programmes. But by the beginning of October I had retired from the BBC as a member of staff, and so was no longer the Cricket Correspondent. I was therefore free to accept the welcome invitation to do the programme on a regular basis. And I have enjoyed doing it ever since – with one slight hiccup!

It's a lovely programme to do, because we are non-knockers. We go to a place to find out the *nice* things about it. We never look under the carpet. We avoid all controversy, whether local or national. All right, it may sound square. But it offers a wonderful opportunity for listeners to visit so many beautiful and interesting places, and to learn about the many old crafts and customs which still exist all over Great Britain. Even more important are the characters we meet. Such as the dear old lady who had just celebrated her hundredth birthday, but was disappointed with the Queen's telegram, because 'it wasn't in her own handwriting'! Or the vegetarian who during the war was sent to India to look after mules. He took with him packets of mustard and cress seeds, which, at the end of a long sweaty day, he would plant in his hot wellies. Result – mustard and cress the next morning for breakfast! It really needs a book on its own to tell all about *them*. But one point I would like to stress. The papers these days are full of stories about criminals and vandals, and of how selfish and uncaring our society has become. But if you were to come with us round the country on our journeys for *Down Your Way* you would, I think, be pleasantly surprised to find how *many* people are doing things to help *other* people.

Down Your Way is the second-longest running radio programme of all time, after Roy Plomley's *Desert Island Discs*. Since it started in 1946 it has visited over 1500 cities, towns, villages, institutions and places of interest. The format has remained basically the same, with a few minor alterations. When Stewart MacPherson started in Lambeth Walk in December 1946, the programme was restricted to various parts of London. There was no preliminary research, nor any advance warning to the people to be interviewed. The producers, who were then Leslie Perowne and John Shuter, just chose a location, and knocked unannounced on people's doors. This method was quickly abandoned after Stewart had knocked on a door, and the man who answered mistook him for someone who had been molesting his wife – and slugged him one!

Luckily nothing as unpleasant as that has ever happened to me. But there have been one or two amusing greetings after we have knocked on peoples' doors. One lady opened her front door and said in an effusive and friendly way, 'Oh, Mr Johnston. How nice to see you. I've always wanted to meet you. I'm afraid I only have a very small house. Do tell me. How big is your equipment?' I only hope that she was referring to our engineer's recording gear!

On another occasion we were about to interview the wartime Commander-in-Chief Bomber Command Marshal of the Royal Air Force Sir Arthur Harris – nicknamed Bomber. In true Grenadier fashion I made sure we arrived five minutes before we were due! (In the Brigade of Guards, if a Parade is advertised for 10 a.m. it really means 9.55 a.m.) Somewhat apprehensively we knocked on his door. A moment or so later the well-known but rather terrifying figure of Bomber opened the door, looked us up and down and said in a gruff voice, 'You're early.'

And once, when Phyllis Robinson and I were visiting Kirby Lonsdale we got lost in the dark in a country lane on the way to do an interview late in the evening. The previous week I had appeared on television in Derek Nimmo's chat show, and at his request I had tucked my ears in. This is a rare and rather bizarre talent which I share with John Woodcock, Cricket Correspondent of *The Times*, and my son-in-law David Oldridge. I must admit, it looks quite funny and certainly created a lot of merriment amongst the studio audience. Anyway, Phyllis and I decided to knock on the door of a lonely farmhouse to ask the way. A lady opened the door rather suspiciously and looked at me standing there. After a slight hesitation she said, 'Oh, aren't you Brian Johnston? Please will you tuck your ears in for me to prove that you really can do it?' I did as she asked, and only then did she give us directions.

After that unfortunate doorstep incident Stewart returned to ice hockey and boxing commentaries, and *Down Your Way* spread its wings all over Great Britain. It was then that the producers started to go on ahead and research the chosen place before the arrival of the interviewer.

Stewart had done ten programmes, and Lionel Gamlin six, when in the spring of 1947 'an ex-wartime reporter' called Richard Dimbleby started his long stint of 350 editions. He stopped in 1953 because of his growing television commitments, and there was a two-year gap before the programme returned under a new presenter – Franklin Engelmann.

The length of each programme and the number of people interviewed have varied through the years. At one time there were as many as nine 'victims', as I usually call them! Then there were seven, later six, and now five. But each person has *always* been asked to choose a piece of music to be played at the end of their interview. This is one of the fascinating aspects of *Down Your Way* – guessing what will be chosen. A bishop may want the Beatles, or a blacksmith a Beethoven Sonata. We never know. It's *their* choice. The only exceptions are when what they choose has already been asked for in the same programme, or if it is being too regularly selected week after week. For instance during the past few years the theme tunes from 'Love Story' and 'The Onedin Line', as well as popular songs like 'Amazing Grace' and 'Annie's Song', have had to be rationed. In Richard's day it was 'Bless This House' and 'Now Is The Hour', while back in Jingle's time 'Jerusalem' and 'Stranger On The Shore' were the top favourites. Incidentally, in Richard's day the accent was more on the music, with the interview getting less time. But it was then realized that the people – and what they had to say – were the more important, and an average interview today consists of about four and a half minutes of speech and two minutes of music. One excellent rule has been handed down and still applies today. The producer only chooses five people to be interviewed and they are *all* broadcast. In some radio programmes as many as eight people may be interviewed and only five finally used, but with us no one is discarded. So they can safely tell their friends: 'I shall be in *Down Your Way* on Sunday.'

You will notice that it is the producer who chooses the victims, *not* the presenter, and it is impossible to stress too strongly the vital part he or she plays in the production of each programme. In fact they become so involved that *Down Your Way* becomes a major part of their life. Until 1975 the programme was produced in London and Phyllis Robinson and Richard Burwood used to do six weeks on and six weeks off. Nowadays the overall producer, Tony Smith in Bristol, is responsible for the whole operation, with Sarah Pitt doing the occasional programme to help him out.

First of all the producer has to choose the location. It is the policy of *Down Your Way* to give as fair a coverage as possible to the *whole* of the United Kingdom during the course of a year. So Tony studies the big map full of flags showing where we have already been, and selects an unflagged place in the area of the country where we are due to go. He is often able to accept one of the many invitations which we receive, asking us to visit a particular place.

The method of producing the programme has changed since 1975. Up to then one programme was recorded each week. The producer researched the place on Monday and Tuesday when he or she was joined by me and the radio engineer with his recording machine. We then did our interviews on Tuesday evening and during most of Wednesday. The producer then returned to London to edit the interviews and slot in the pieces of music, and the completed programme went out on the Sunday at 5.15 p.m. In those days Phyllis Robinson used to run tremendous risks – she never had a spare programme up her sleeve. So if the presenter fell ill or the engineer's equipment was faulty she had no stand-by programme. But remarkably her luck held, and she was never left with a blank.

Nowadays we are more cautious, and the recording procedure is different. Generally we record two programmes in the first week of each month, and two in the second week, leaving the last two weeks for the producer to edit and put the programme together. It's a great time and money saver, as the two places selected are normally between thirty and sixty miles apart, though usually in different counties. Because of my cricket commitments and my 'hols', we do have to do the occasional 'one-off', and normally we have at least three edited programmes 'in the can' as an insurance against illness, holidays, etc.

Here's an example of how it works now. One week we were visiting Tenbury Wells in Worcestershire and Newport in Shropshire, about fifty miles apart. Tony Smith left Bristol on Monday and went to Tenbury Wells, which he researched on Tuesday. He moved on that evening to Newport and researched there all Wednesday. I joined him in time for dinner travelling by car from London. An engineer from North Region also arrived, so that the team was now together. *Down Your Way* is very dependent on team-work, all three of us having an equally important part to play. After a briefing by Tony that evening, we spent Thursday recording our five 'victims'. It is a tightly timed but well organized affair. We go to people's houses, offices, farms, etc., and we always allow one hour for each interview. Without wishing to be immodest, we realize that for most of them it is quite an important and exciting day in their lives, so we feel that an hour in their company is the least we can offer, rather than rushing in and getting the job over as soon as possible. In this way I can get to know the person whom I am about to interview and try to gain their confidence over a cup of tea – or something stronger. I would say we probably take forty-five minutes on average before starting the actual interview. Some of this time is taken up by going round the factory, shop or farm. We then record something like seven or eight minutes of conversation, though we never look at a stop-watch. I simply go on asking questions until I feel that we have learnt everything relevant about the person, their job or their craft.

By about three o'clock we had finished and motored off to Tenbury Wells, arriving at tea-time. As far as I remember we did one interview that evening, leaving four to do on Friday morning, finishing soon after lunch. Tony then had five tapes from each place to take back to Bristol and we all made our separate ways home. My job – and the engineer's – was then finished. I have nothing further to do with the programmes once they are recorded, and have no say whatever in the editing. But for Tony the really hard part has just begun. He has the job of editing the programme down to its overall thirty-five minutes, which has to include the opening and closing announcement in the studio and also the music chosen, which Tony slots in between the interviews. This means tidying up a lot of the conversations, taking out the occasional 'er', the odd fluff and of course cutting out some of the seven or eight minutes recorded to bring it down to about five minutes. This can be a heart-rending job when a real character has given us a magical interview and some of his or her splendid stories have to be left out. It is equally difficult for Tony to cut the music down to approximately two minutes without offending music lovers, especially if it is a long piece like a symphony or concerto.

One other gratifying feature of *Down Your Way* is the great interest shown by the local press. More often than not we are followed round on our interviews by a reporter and a camera, so that our visit is featured in the next week's paper. From this and the number of requests to visit places which we receive, it is clear that a visit from *Down Your Way* is still regarded as a pleasant event in the life of a community.

As you can imagine the travel and timetables can be quite complicated but – touch wood – we have always met up at the right place at the right time. There was one minor exception at Godalming, where we were both waiting for our rendezvous in different car parks and it was over an hour before we caught up with each other. But considering the mileage we cover each year that is not a bad record, and we owe a great debt to Rosemary, the *Down Your Way* secretary, who works out our timetable and makes all the aeroplane, train and hotel bookings.

Earlier on I said I had been presenting *Down Your Way* ever since October 1972, *with one slight hiccup*. This was in April 1975 when the programme was temporarily taken off the air and, but for our faithful band of listeners, would have died altogether. It happened like this. The BBC (as usual) were having to make cuts, and Radios 3 and 4 had to share programmes at certain times of the day. The Controller of Radio 4 did not wish to lose a particular favourite of his called *Celebration*. So he picked on *Down Your Way* as the sacrificial lamb, and it was announced that the programme on Sunday 20 April would be the last one. I must say we were all staggered by the reaction of the press and public when they heard the news. We never knew that we had so many friends. The press really went to town on our behalf, and the listeners inundated the BBC with thousands of letters and telephone calls. There was even a letter from one of the Royal Palaces! To give credit to the BBC, they soon saw from this terrific reaction that they had made a misjudgement and quickly gave us six programmes during the summer in the *Any Questions* slot, when that programme had its annual holiday. But a new Controller had taken over – Clare Lawson-Dick – and she was particularly impressed with the pleas from blind people who claimed it was their one way of travelling around and getting to know their country. So for the first time ever the BBC publicly announced that they were bowing to the wishes of the listeners and that *Down Your Way* would restart on its usual weekly basis from October. There was, however, one major change. It was to be produced in Bristol instead of in London, which had been its home ever since it started in 1946. It was a sad blow for Phyllis Robinson, who had been with it almost from the start and who, with Richard Burwood, had produced it for the last thirteen years. I felt very sorry for her. But 'That's show business', as they say, and it's nice to know that since then she has continued to produce many successful entertainment programmes.

For me, of course, this switch provided a chance to work with Tony Smith, an old friend and colleague with whom I had done many sporting programmes. It's indeed lucky that we *are* friends, because we have to spend a lot of time together in strange places many miles from home. I am therefore delighted that he has been asked to write this book. It will, I am sure, help you to appreciate what a fascinating and interesting programme it is to present and produce. We never stop learning *something* new about our country, whether it be an old traditional ceremony or custom, an unusual craft or hobby, a local recipe or some industry where special skills are used. You too can now learn about these first-hand, from the people who told *us* all about them when we talked to them in their cities, towns or villages. My hope is that when you have finished the book you will feel, like us, that it was a programme worth creating – and worth preserving.

P.S. In July 1981 *Down Your Way* was extended from thirty-five to forty-five minutes and it now contains six interviews and six pieces of music.

Times Remembered

Our ancient traditions and customs

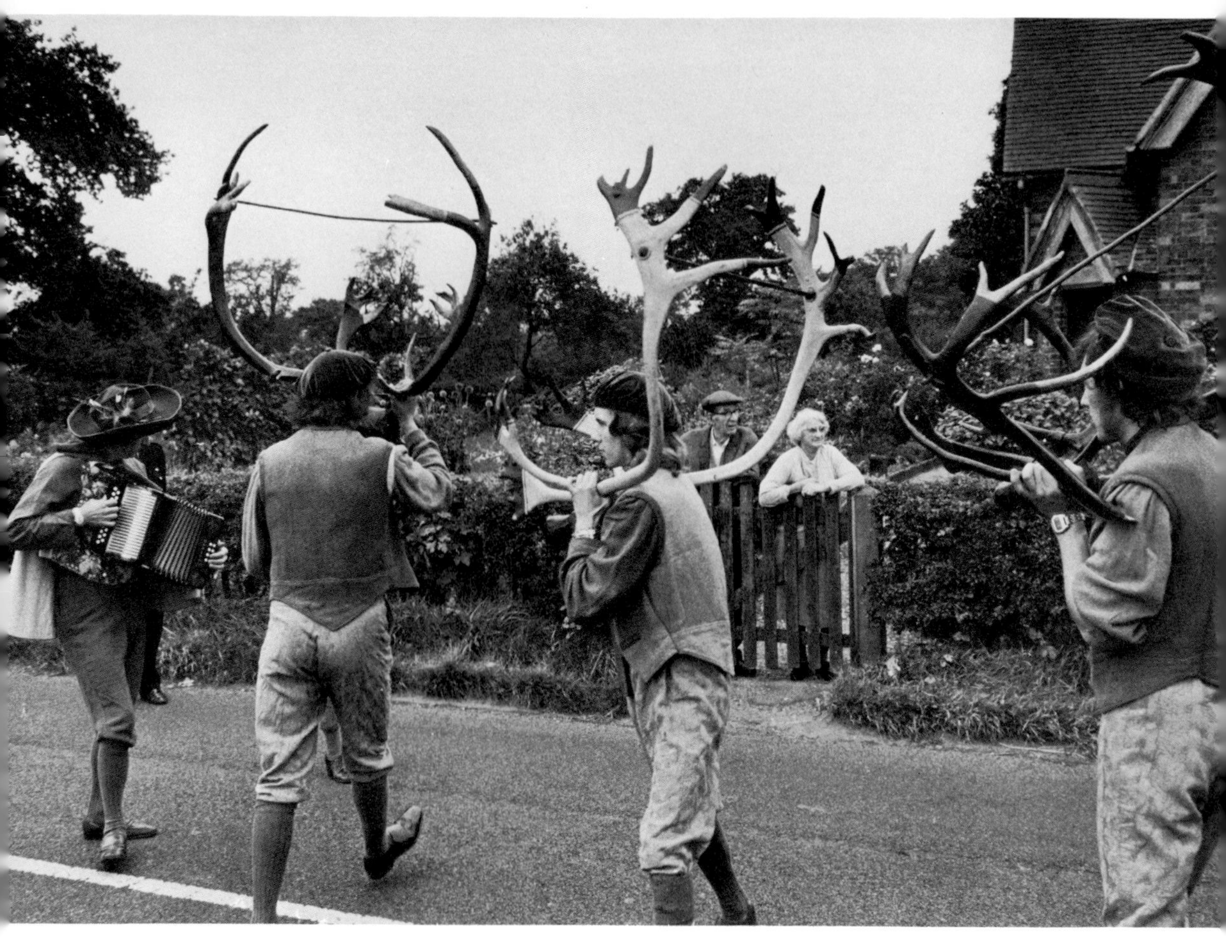

The Ancient Horn Dance is danced all over Abbots Bromley and at many of the outlying farms and houses.

The Ancient Horn Dance at Abbots Bromley, Staffordshire

Britain's many traditional ceremonies have long been one of our greatest tourist attractions. Some of them are extremely well known – the Trooping of the Colour, the Royal Maundy Service on the Thursday before Easter, and, Brian Johnston's favourite, the rain-making ceremonies performed on the hallowed turf at Lord's, The Oval and Old Trafford all through the summer. But many of our ancient ceremonies aren't so well known, and yet they are often even more intriguing. Some of them date back thousands of years to pagan times, long before any kind of record was kept. In many cases they have changed with the times – with the coming of Christianity, for instance. Working on the principle: 'If we can't eradicate them, let's incorporate them', our early Christian fathers gave many ancient, pagan ceremonies a Christian interpretation.

One of the oldest and most fascinating ceremonies we have come across in our travels is the Ancient Horn Dance at Abbots Bromley, a lovely old Staffordshire village ten miles east of the county town. It takes place every year on Wakes Monday, all that's left of the old St Bartholomew's Fair, which is the first Monday after the first Sunday after 4 September. It's danced throughout the day all round the village – outside the vicarage, in the marketplace, at Blithfield Hall, home of the Bagot family, for centuries one of the great families of the area, at outlying farms and houses – some twenty miles in all! The dance is performed by six local men, some of whom have long-standing family connections with the dance, in one case going back four hundred years, who each carry a set of reindeer horns, fixed to a carved wooden stag's head.

'They dance initially in procession as a straight line,' said Dr John Salter, who has been a local GP for thirty years. 'Then they break into a circle, and from the circle they turn into two lines, facing one another. Then the two lines come forward, like rutting stags, with their heads down, then go back a few paces, then pass through the line on the other side, turn round, come forward, then back, and then through again.'

Six other people take part besides the horn dancers. There's a musician who used to play a concertina or violin, but these days plays an accordion, and a boy with a triangle. 'If he's got a good sense of time, he hits it in time with the music,' Dr Salter said. 'Sometimes, though, they have no sense of time, and they hit it wildly, completely out of rhythm!' Then there is 'Maid Marian', who is always played by a man – usually a very tall or big man, Dr Salter told us, so that it's very obvious that he's a man dressed as a woman – and who carries a ladle to collect money from the passers-by. There's a Fool, complete with a pig's bladder on a stick, a Hobby Horse, and 'Robin Hood', a boy with a crossbow. These few characters show the influence on the dance of the Robin Hood legend, and of Morris – or 'Moorish' – dancing, which was introduced into the area by John of Gaunt, Duke of Lancaster between 1340 and 1399, to whom the Bagot family owed fealty.

The dance itself, though, is thought to be much older, though no one knows its precise origin. As Dr Salter says, all the books get round the question by simply saying, 'It's origins are shrouded in the mists of time!' One theory is that it began in Norman times, to celebrate the granting of hunting rights in the nearby Forest of Needwood to the local people, but that seems unlikely. As a former vicar of Abbots Bromley, the Reverend Ladell, points out, the Norman nobles guarded their own hunting rights so jealously that any villager who killed a deer on purpose or by accident lost a hand or an eye for a first offence, and was hanged for a second, so it would have been extremely unwise for anyone to boast of his success by parading round the village in his prey's antlers!

Another theory is that it is a fertility dance, and certainly it takes place during the deer's rutting season. But perhaps the most interesting theory is that it comes from an ancient belief, held by primitive peoples all over the world, that eating the flesh, drinking the blood, or wearing the skin or horns of the wild animal you hunted was the most effective weapon against it. There is a carving on a bone found in caves at Cresswell in Derbyshire, which shows a man wearing antlers very like the Abbots Bromley antlers, and the bone is at least eight thousand, if not ten thousand years old!

Dr Salter keeps an open mind. 'The only definitive date that can be given is by carbon-testing of the horns. A few years ago a portion of the horn was broken, and the carbon-dating of it suggests that it was about 1065. This does suggest that it's not a strictly prehistoric dance, but the horns themselves are reindeer horns, and reindeer have been extinct in Britain for a very long time. But it still begs the question of whether there was an earlier dance, or whether someone brought the horns here in that period of history, which isn't much recorded, and made them up at a later date, because the metalwork and the type of carving on the heads of the deer suggest a date nearer 1300 and 1400.'

The first written account of the dance is in Dr Robert Plot's *Natural History of Staffordshire* published in 1686, which states that the dance was performed outside the church on Christmas Day, New Year's Day and Twelfth Day, which implies that the church had given the dance a Christian interpretation, and indeed the horns are kept in the church today. There is no mystery, though, about the costumes the horn dancers wear. Until the middle of the last century they wore their own clothes, but according to the Reverend Ladell, for the celebrations following the restoration of the church in 1860, the vicar's daughters, the Misses Maria and Alice Lowe, designed and made costumes using the illustrations in their edition of Shakespeare as a guide. They were a great success, and are now very much a part of the tradition.

The Flora Dance at Helston, Cornwall

The Abbots Bromley Horn Dance has its own special, though probably not very ancient, tunes, but it's unlikely that you'd find anybody outside the immediate area of Abbots Bromley who could hum them. Ask people to hum the tune of the Furry Dance which takes place in the Cornish town of Helston each year, and it's odds on that the majority could oblige. Strictly speaking, though, they would all be wrong, as Edward Cunnack, chairman of the stewards who organize the Furry Dance, was quick to point out.

'I think it would be a good idea to scotch for all time the idea that the ballad entitled "The Cornish Floral Dance" has any real significance as far as the ancient Helston Furry Dance ceremony is concerned. Katie Moss, the composer of it, was staying in St Ives in about 1906 when she composed the words and the tune, but she never meant it to be a copy or a portrayal of Helston's ancient custom. She did use a part of the melody, but it was just a picturesque and imaginative little song which came out of what the composer saw and heard and felt when she visited Helston to enjoy our celebration!'

Edward Cunnack also put the record straight on the question of the ceremony's proper name. It's never been a 'Floral' Dance – it's either the 'Flora', the 'Faddy' or the 'Furry'. His father always called it 'the Faddy', which may have derived from an old English processional dance called the Fading, or from an Irish processional dance called the *Rincce Fada* – the long dance.

'"Flora", which is still traditional, has been going for quite two hundred years,' Edward Cunnack said, 'when it was fashionable in the late eighteenth century and early nineteenth century, to relate everything to Greek and Latin classicism! "Furry" came from the Latin word *feria* which means a feast day, so the dance has been known, more authentically I think, as the Furry Dance!'

No one knows exactly when the ceremony started. 'I would say we are justified in saying that it was pre-Christian,' said Edward Cunnack. 'Our primitive forefathers expressed their deepest emotions in rhythm. And the emotion our forefathers expressed on our festive day was unquestionably joy at the triumph of spring over winter, life over death, light over darkness, and this is what it's all about. When our Christian forefathers came to Cornwall, they didn't say, "Now, away with this rite, this processional dance these primitive chaps are doing!" They said, "There is something in this because they are celebrating the triumph of light, and surely Christianity is also the triumph of light, so we will connect this with a saint's day." And they connected it with the Feast of St Michael, Helston's patron saint, which is 8 May.'

The dance still has religious connotations, and the day begins with the church bells at six-thirty in the morning, followed by a special communion service. The first dance of the day – the Early Morning Dance – begins at seven. 'In the old days, say a couple of hundred years ago, the Early Morning Dance would have been the dance of the retainers, the domestic helps, the footmen and the butlers who, for the rest of the day, would have been waiting on the gentry,' Edward Cunnack told us. These days it's danced by the young people, and anybody else who won't be able to dance later in the day. Then, at half-past eight, the 'Hal-an-Tow' begins.

'It means "Haul on the rope", and it's an old sea shanty.' Some people believe it's probably the oldest part of the ceremony, though after becoming something of a drunken revel in the last century it was dropped from the day's proceedings until 1930, when it was revived.

'What happens is that the young lads go out into the woods, collect sycamore and beech, bring the branches back into the town, and sing this fine, rumbustuous song. It is really more *Merrie England* than Cornish, I would say, and the chorus goes,

> For summer is a come-O,
> And winter is a gone-O

and that's what it's all about!'

The children's dance, introduced in 1928, begins at ten o'clock, and is very popular. These days some nine hundred schoolchildren take part, the girls in white dresses, with distinctive garlands in their hair to show which school they come from, and the boys in white shirts and shorts, with bunches of lily-of-the-valley, the day's traditional flower, pinned to their shirt fronts. As the town clock begins to strike twelve, the Principal Dance sets off from the Guildhall. 'In the old days, the class distinction was quite defined. No one would be able to dance the mid-day dance unless they were the gentry! Today it's an invitation dance, and the invitations are sent out by the stewards to about a hundred and twenty couples. We limit it because, if the procession gets too long, it becomes unmanageable.'

It's a great honour to be asked to lead any dance, and Edward Cunnack pointed out that in every dance, the first set always consists of people born in Helston. Seeing the Principal Dance, the ignorant outsider could be forgiven for thinking that he had stumbled across a mass wedding, what with long lines of men in top hat and tails, and women in frilly hats and pretty, often long, dresses. 'We dress as we should dress if we went, say, to the Queen's garden party, an important occasion. You have to remember that, to Helston people, this is an enormously important occasion!'

The last dance of the day at five o'clock, used to be danced by the town's tradesmen, but now it is led by the Early Morning dancers, though in its last stages the spectators can – and usually do – join in. Everyone in the town is involved in the Furry Dance, willy-nilly. The streets and houses are decorated with flowers and greenery, and the route of the dance takes the dancers in and out of the shops, offices, banks and private houses – a nightmare for any houseproud householder who objects to dirty shoes on the carpet!

Naturally Edward Cunnack chose for his piece of music the Helston Town

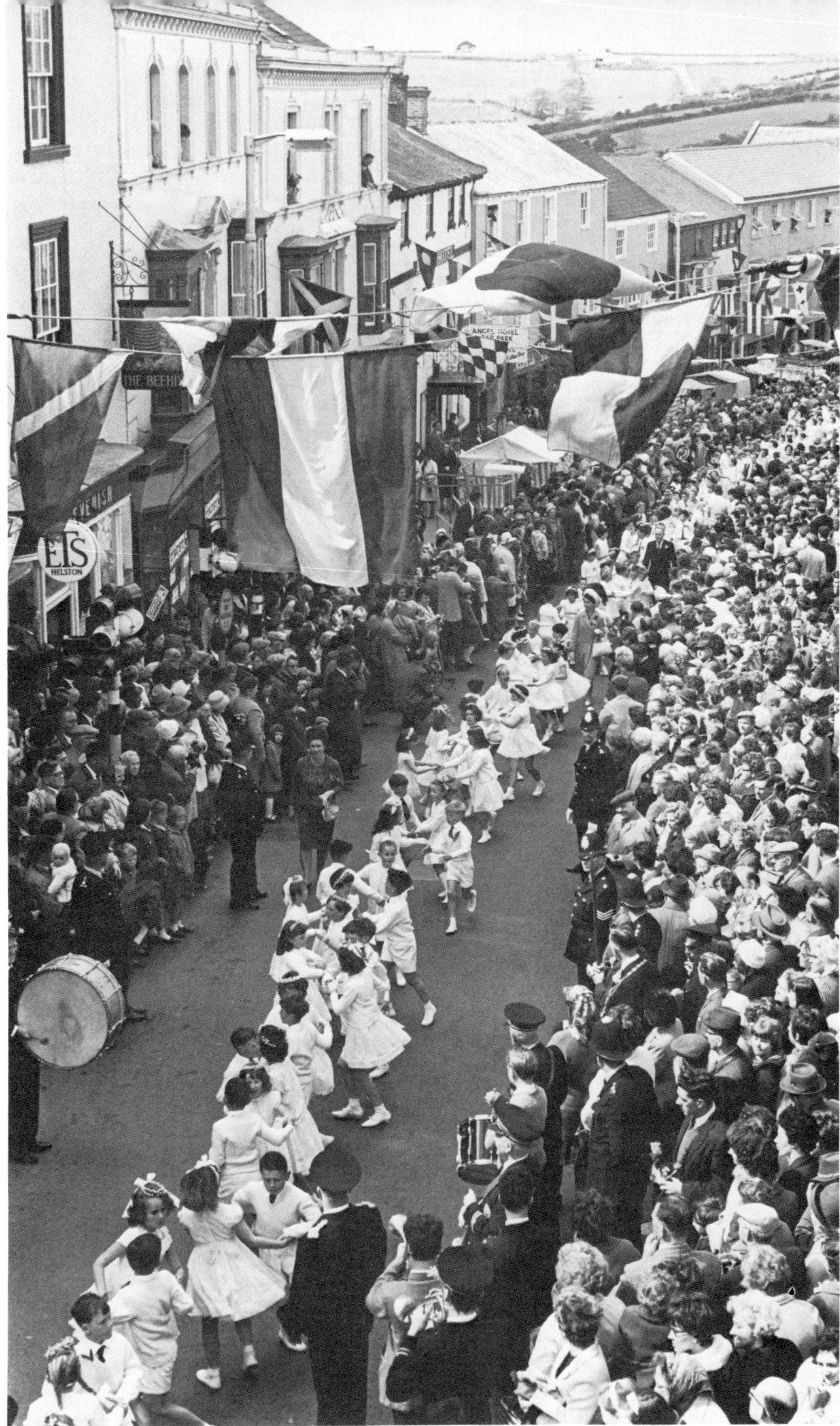

The children's dance was introduced to the Helston 'Flora' Dance in 1928. Nine hundred children take part in this very popular dance.

Band playing 'the real, genuine Helston Furry Dance, recorded on the day itself!' But he could equally well have chosen Stravinsky's *Rite of Spring*.

Garland Day at Castleton, Derbyshire

Grace Crookes, treasurer of the Garland Day committee in the village of Castleton in the heart of Derbyshire's Peak District could also have opted for Stravinsky, since the town's Garland Day is exactly that - a rite of spring. It takes place on 29 May, Oak Apple Day, which celebrates the escape of Charles II after the Battle of Worcester by hiding in an oak tree.

'Previous to the great day,' Grace Crookes told us, 'the children of the village go out to gather the flowers - both wild flowers and garden flowers — which make up the Garland. On the day itself the men of the village go to the public house where the actual ceremony is taking place from [the town's six pubs take it in turn], and start building the Garland itself in the shape of a beehive. They start from the top, with the small flowers, and then go down round the bottom with the biggest flowers - garden flowers, mostly, by that time. There are two eye-holes made in the Garland for the "King" to see through - usually depicted by paeonies, if we can get them. It's finished usually just after lunch, and then the "Queen" of the Garland - a small posy of flowers which sits on top of the beehive - is made on a pole by two ladies.'

About quarter to six in the evening the 'King' and his Lady arrive on horseback at the public house. Until 1955 the 'Lady' was always a man dressed in women's clothes, but since then she's been the genuine article. The finished Garland, which is over three feet high and weighs about six stone, is hoisted on to the 'King's' shoulders, covering his head and chest completely - hence the need for the eye-holes! Although the actual ceremony only dates back three hundred and fifty years, the 'Green Man' figure, covered in flowers and greenery, symbolizing rebirth and the arrival of spring, has been a central figure in European fertility festivals for centuries.

In the Castleton ceremony, the 'King' and his consort set off on a tour of the village, followed by the town band and the local children dancing to a tune which has more than a passing similarity to the Helston Furry Dance. 'We think the ceremony originated', Grace Crookes said, 'when the Cornish people came up here to do the lead-mining, and brought the tune with them.'

At each of the town's six pubs the procession stops for a drink all round, and then from the last port of call, traditionally the George, it makes its way to the churchyard. 'The "Queen", the small posy, is taken from the Garland, and then the "King" and his consort go to the church steeple, where the Garland is hoisted on a rope, up to the middle pinnacle. The tradition is that it stays there for three weeks, or until every flower is dead.'

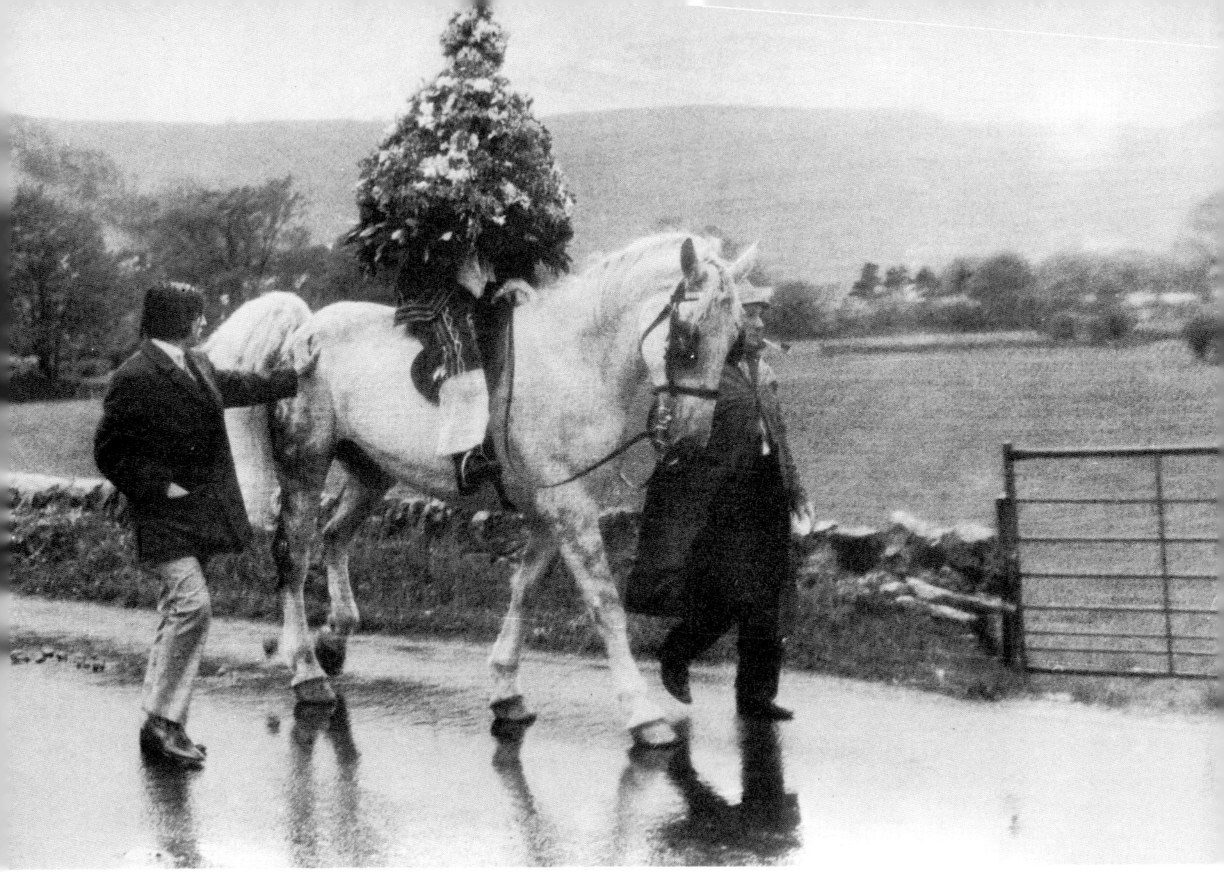

Two fine examples of the garland paraded every year through the Derbyshire village of Castleton to commemorate Charles II's escape from the Roundheads.

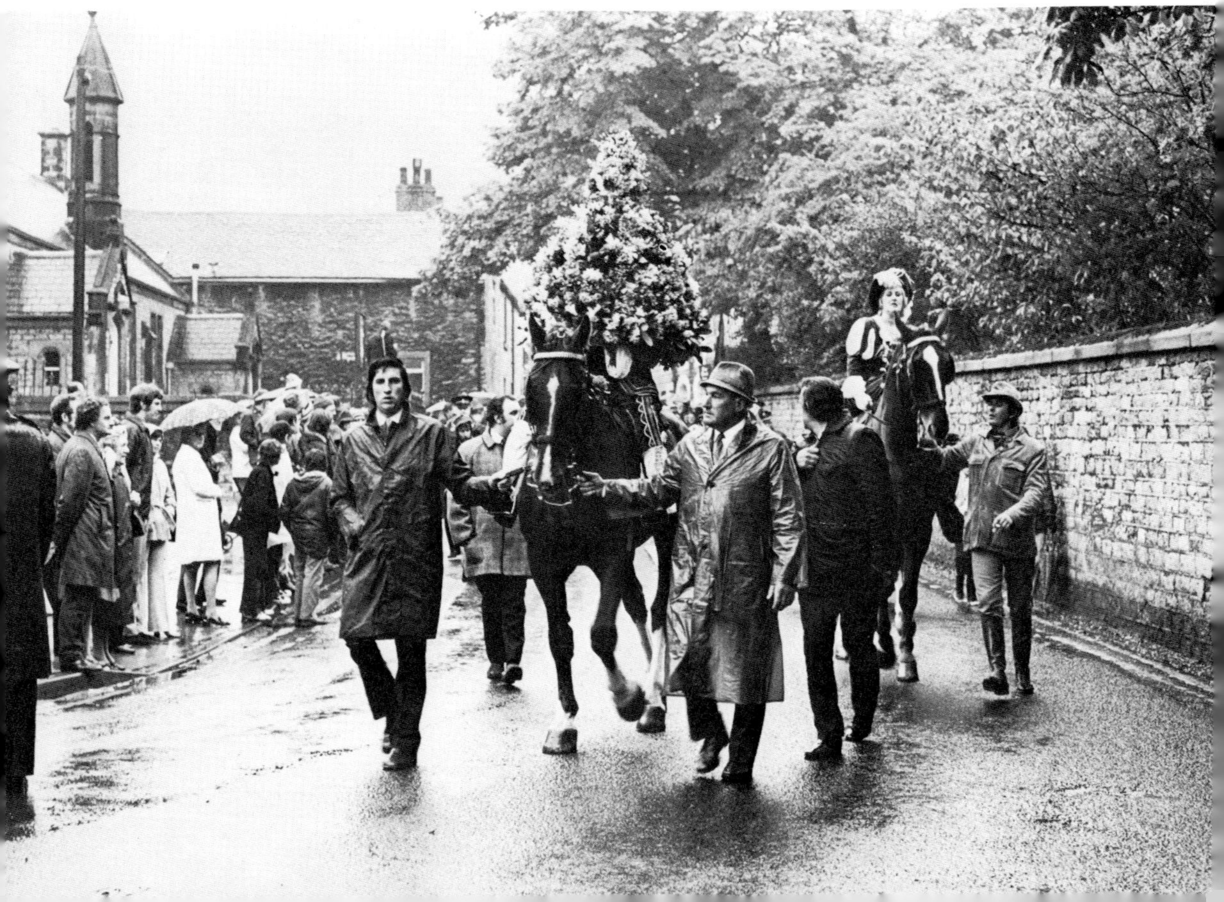

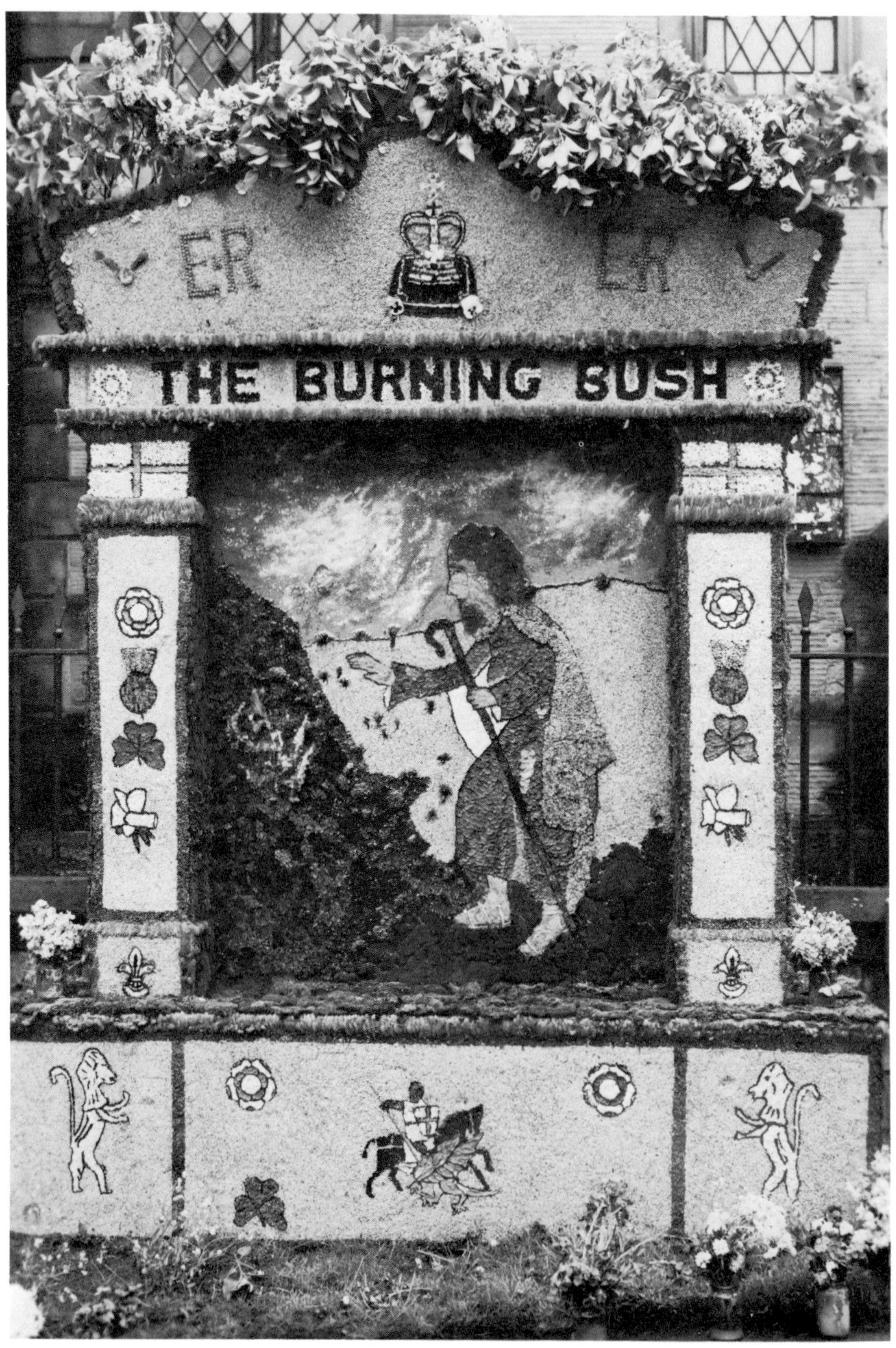

Prize-winning well-dressing at Wirksworth. The rules stipulate that only natural materials may be used. Petals and moss are the main ingredients.

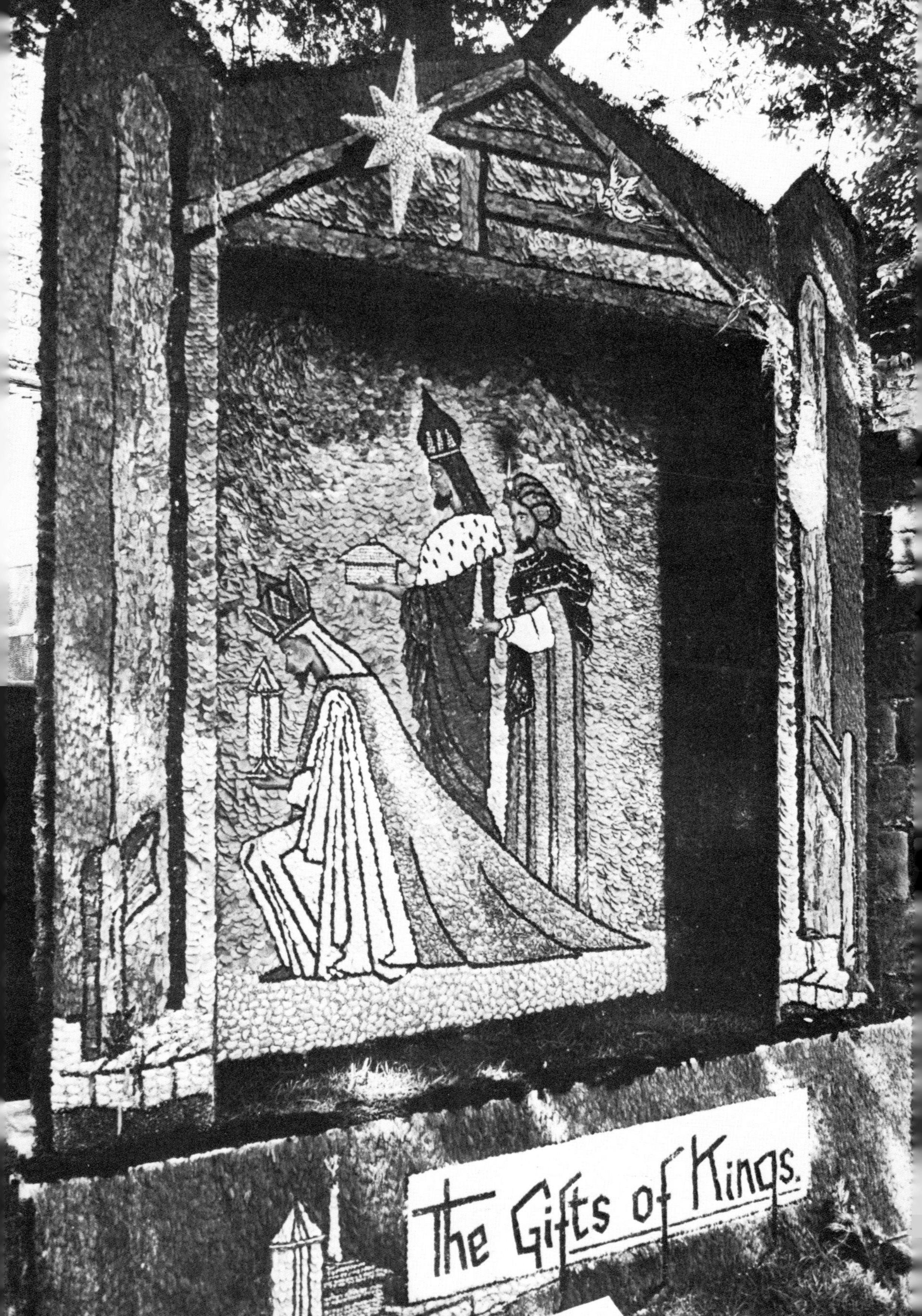
The Gifts of Kings.
SECOND

The first mention of the Garland ceremony in written records is in connection with this part of the proceedings. In the churchwardens' accounts for 1749 there is a reference to '... 8 pence for an iron rod to hang ye Ringers' Garland in'. It was called the 'Ringers' Garland' because until the end of the last century the ceremony was performed by the town's bell-ringers, who toured the streets with the Garland, performing Morris dances and making a collection for themselves.

There have been a number of changes since the First World War, too. A maypole, for instance, is now set up on the village green for the children to dance round, and instead of the 'Queen' being presented to the wife of a local dignitary, it is now laid on the War Memorial while the Last Post is sounded. After the ceremony is finally over, according to Grace Crookes, 'It's Mum's turn, Grandma's turn, anybody's turn, and we all dance with the children back down the street with the band, to the pub where it all started!'

Well-dressing at Wirksworth, Derbyshire

About twenty miles away, in the small town of Wirksworth, also in Derbyshire, they also have a spring festival involving flowers which has its origins in pagan times, but there the similarities end. It is called 'well-dressing', and it happens every Spring Bank holiday – what used to be Whit Monday.

The well-dressings themselves are quite beautiful, and require a tremendous amount of patience and skill, as John Hall, an expert on local customs who used to be Wirksworth's station-master until his retirement, explained.

'How it's done is, we have a frame, approximately eight feet high, made of wood which is covered with nails, protruding about three-eighths of an inch, over which is spread specially prepared clay until you've got a nice, smooth surface. And then, having already decided on the picture you're going to draw, you lay your paper with your drawing on it over the clay, and with a sharp needle you prick out every line on your drawing, take your paper off, and then you've got your picture in dots on your clay. To outline your drawing, you get lichen moss, cut it an eighth of an inch wide, turn it black side up, and line out all your picture. When you've got your picture drawn, the work begins. You get petals – no complete flowers, it's petals only – and you lay them on the clay in the same way a tiler lays his tiles, so that if it rains, the water washes straight off. And you gradually build up each particular part until you've got a complete picture which, when it's completed, looks something like a stained glass window.'

There are strict rules about what materials can be used – anything of natural origin, nothing that is man-made – and the subject matter has to be religious, like the Agony in the Garden, or 'Blessed are the merciful for they shall obtain mercy.' Any group or organization in the town can make a well-dressing if they choose to do so, and any money collected goes to the charity of their choice.

Several Derbyshire villages hold well-dressing ceremonies, and accounts of their origins vary. In one village, it is said to date back to the middle of the fourteenth century when the Black Death decimated the population. Their wells remained untainted and only a few villagers died. As far as Wirksworth is concerned, John Hall believes the ceremony dates back to pre-Roman times, and the lead-miners who worked in the area.

'When the miners were going through the hills, looking for lead, they very often came across water, and were in danger of losing their lives because of the water, and so naturally, as primitive people, they made their offerings to their god of water. Then we had the Roman occupation of Wirksworth and the Romans likewise decorated their well-heads every spring to their god of water – or rather, goddess of water. Then we had Christianity coming to Wirksworth in AD 653 and the Christian church, as was their custom, took this idea that was embedded in the people and said, "Well, have your well-dressing, but make it a thanksgiving to God for water!" We usually have somewhere around a dozen dressings, and they are placed anywhere in a strategic place around the town. In 1827 piped water was brought to the town, and the well-dressings were placed round the public taps. Even today, you can still find some of the old people who call them 'tap-dressings'. When the public taps were removed, then we simply put the well-dressings anywhere in the town so that they can be seen properly. But the best part of it is that, on the Monday morning, we have a united church service in the Market Place as a thanksgiving to God for water, and having had the main service there, the people go round the various well-dressings and sing a hymn at each one.'

The fact that there are no actual wells in Wirksworth does cause some confusion for visitors to the town, as John Hall recalled: 'When we came to Wirksworth, we restarted the scout group, and the group dressed a well. Two lads were standing against it when the District Commissioner, who was a stranger to these lads, came along and said, "I don't see a well here! Why do you call this a well-dressing?" It flummoxed the lads for a minute, but then one of them looked at him and said, "Well, sir, isn't it well-dressed?"'

•

The Fire Festival at Allendale Town, Northumberland

Like the worship of water, the worship of fire goes back thousands of years, and there are still a number of fire ceremonies in existence, all over the British Isles. Many take place on Twelfth Night, originally to celebrate the Midwinter Solstice and the fact that spring is on the way, but in Allendale Town, Northumberland, the exact centre of Britain, the ceremony takes place six days earlier, on New

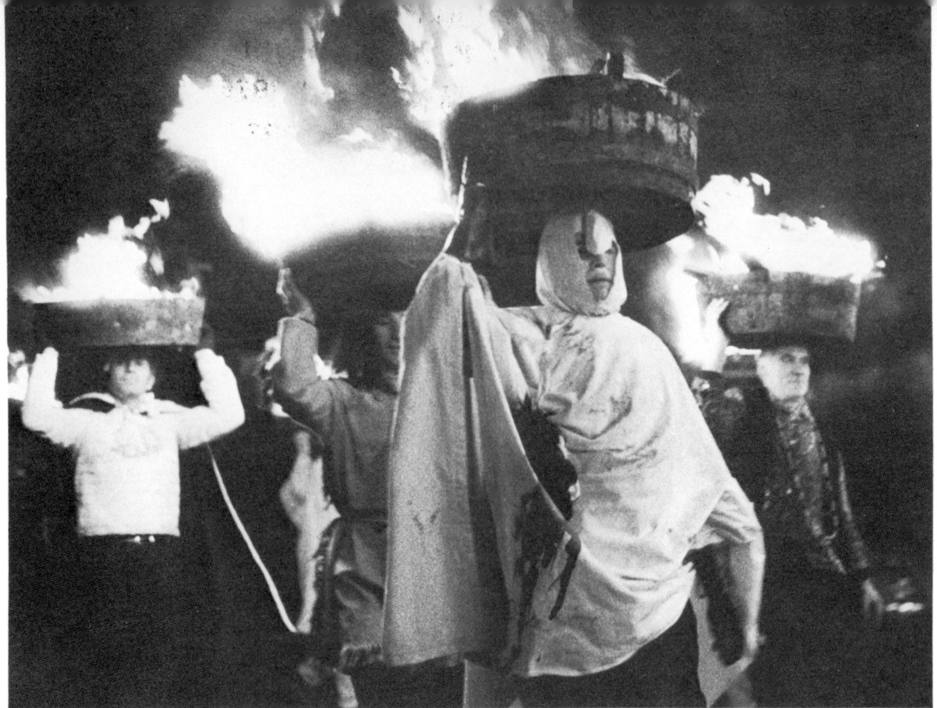

There can be few more dramatic sights than the Fire Festival at Allendale Town. The worship of fire goes back thousands of years, but no one knows the origin of this particular ceremony.

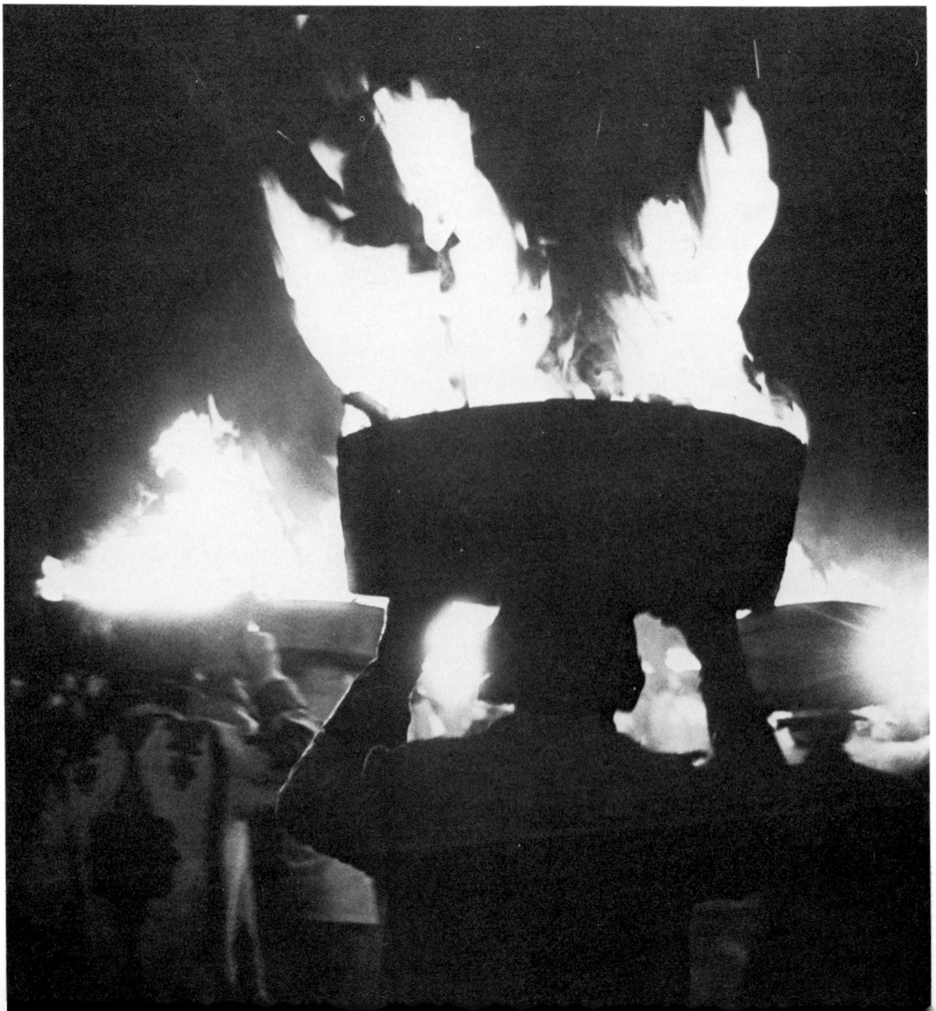

Year's Eve. And very dangerous it looks too, with forty or fifty 'Guisers' – thought to come from 'disguisers' since they all wear very colourful fancy dress – parading round the town with 'kits' – blazing tar barrels – on their heads. These are then hurled into the huge bonfire that's been built in the village square.

'There's quite a lot of work entailed in the "kits",' said Tom Shield, local hotelier and chairman of the council. 'The tar barrels are cut to a depth of twelve or fifteen inches, and then filled with wood and wood shavings. Then at the last minute about a pint of paraffin is poured into each one. Finally, about twenty to midnight, they're lit and carried round the village on the Guisers' heads in procession, led by the town band.'

The Guisers are all local men. 'You can't just come into Allendale and think you'll get a tar kit on New Year's Eve!' Tom said firmly. 'You won't! You've got to be born and bred!' No one knows when the fire ceremony started. 'The newspapers speculate every year as to its origin, but the locals don't know. I had an uncle who died before the war at the age of ninety-six, and he didn't know the origin!' For his piece of music for *Down Your Way*, Tom chose 'The Fireman's Gallop' – not a prophecy! It's just that he is also a part-time fireman!

The Pancake Race at Olney, Buckinghamshire

If you were playing word-association games, and someone said to you, 'Olney', chances are that you'd reply, as quick as a flash, 'Pancakes'! The town of Olney in Buckinghamshire is famous throughout the world for its annual Shrove Tuesday pancake race, in which local women, frying pans in hand, race from the Market Place to the church gate.

According to legend, it all began over five hundred years ago when a housewife was using up all her eggs and butter before Lent by making pancakes. She had started to cook them when the shriving bell began to ring, and without stopping to put the frying pan down she ran to the church to be shriven! After that, according to Sid Morgan, who's known locally as 'Mr Olney', the local women, '. . . just used to run across to the church with the pancakes to give them to the sexton, and to give him a kiss, but it wasn't really a race.'

Sid Morgan is currently one of the starters of the Pancake Race, for which he wears a resplendent, if somewhat historically cross-bred, costume of plumed helmet, red tunic and a pike. 'The tunic was worn at the Battle of Waterloo, and the helmet was worn in the Napoleonic Wars, as was the pike.' The competitors, who have to be over sixteen and have to have lived in Olney for six months, also wear a uniform, as triple champion Sally Faulkner told us, 'You have to wear a skirt and an apron and a headscarf.'

Sally's record for the 411-yard course is just under sixty seconds, tossing the pancake once at the start, and twice before the finish. The pancake, Sally said

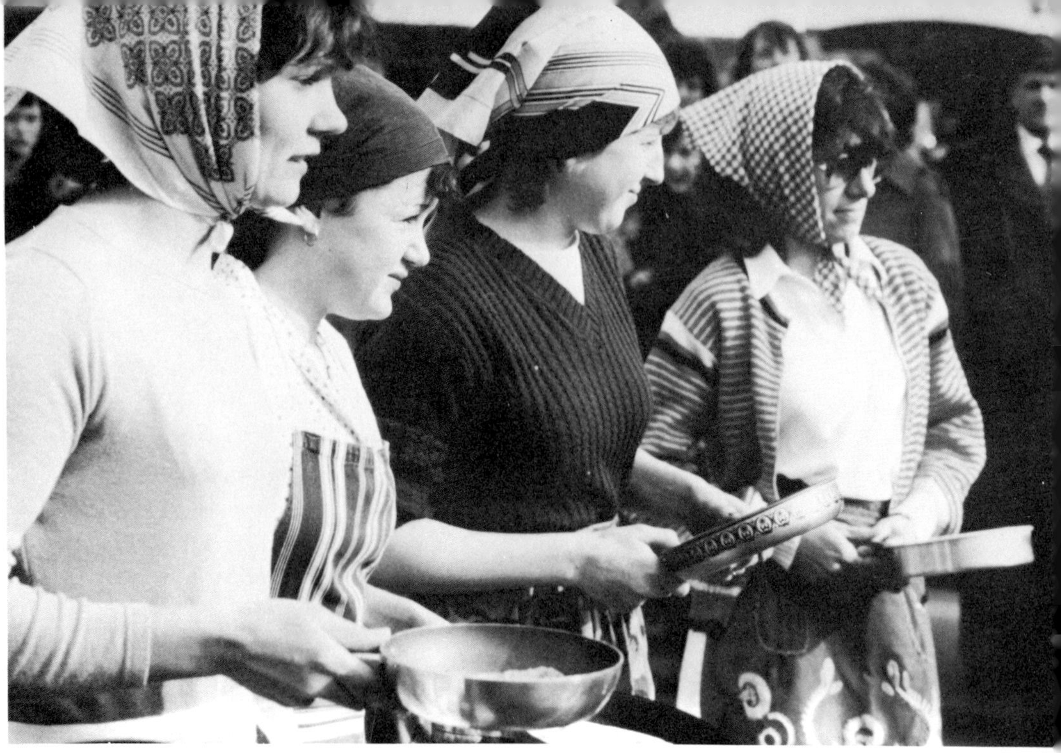

The Shrove Tuesday pancake race, which has made the Buckinghamshire town of Olney famous throughout the world.

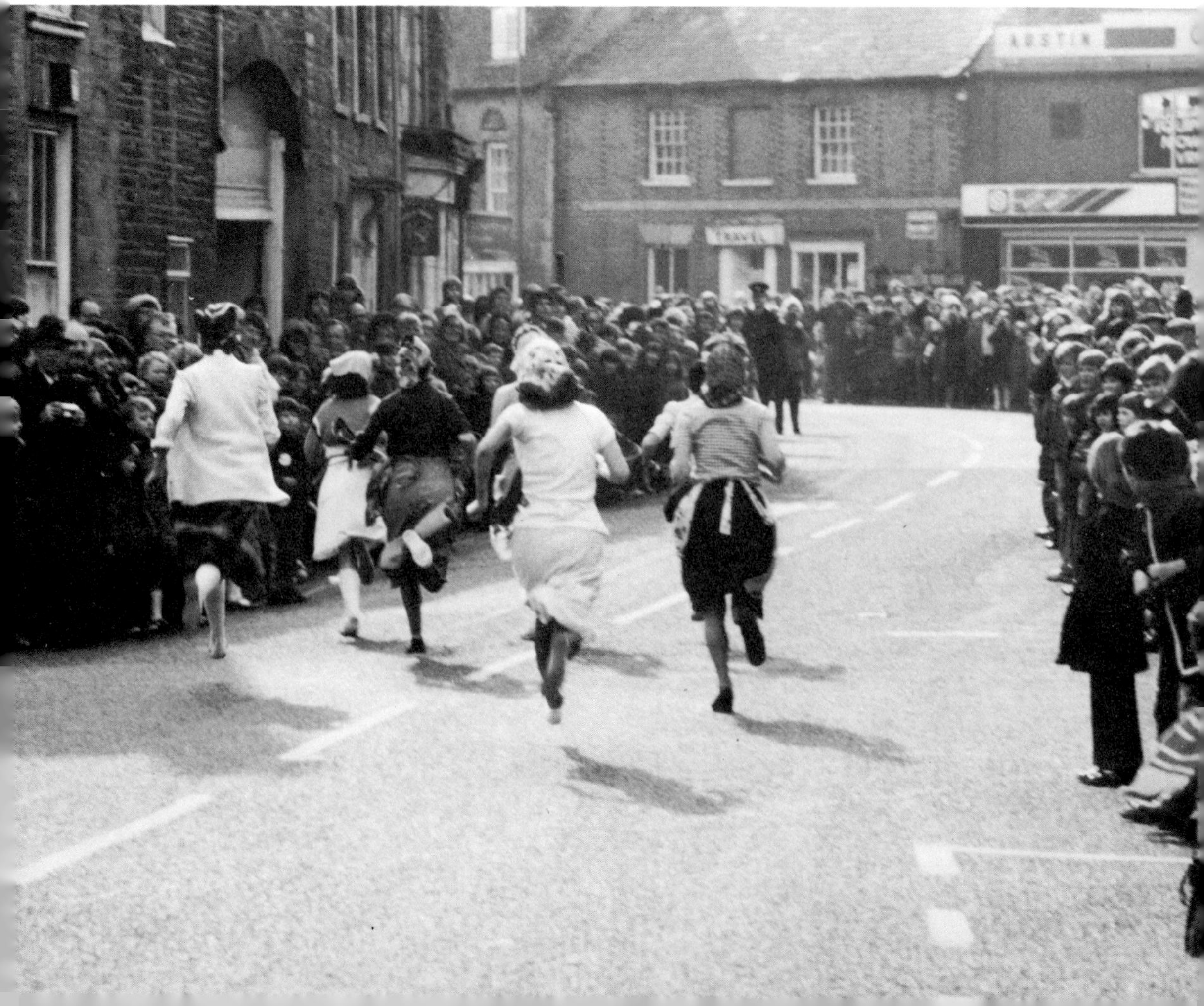

has to be 'thick and horrible' for successful tossing, but since nobody has to eat it after the race any more it doesn't matter too much. Traditionally competitors make their own pancakes, but Sally's Mum made hers. Sally's tactics are simple. 'I try and get an early lead. It's much easier because there are so many bends and you have a job to overtake anybody anyway.'

At the end of the race the winner still kisses the verger, but as well as the traditional gift of a prayer book she also receives a number of prizes from local shops and businesses.

The religious significance of Shrove Tuesday is still celebrated after the race with a service in the church of St Peter and St Paul, with all the competitors' frying pans arranged around the font. 'There's always a crowd in church – they always turn out well for that, and of course they sing all Olney hymns,' Sid Morgan said, then added, with justifiable pride, 'We don't need to go anywhere else for hymns!' The Olney hymns, written by two of the town's most famous sons, the eighteenth-century poet William Cowper and the rector of the time, the Reverend John Newton, include such favourites as, 'God Moves in a Mysterious Way', 'How Sweet the Name of Jesus Sounds', and 'Glorious Things of Thee Are Spoken'.

Since 1950 the race has taken on an international dimension. The town of Liberal in Kansas, which has always celebrated Shrove Tuesday with enthusiasm, decided to take a leaf out of Olney's book and stage their own race over the same distance. The two towns then compare timings over the phone, but unfortunately Liberal is well ahead on numbers of victories. Sid Morgan isn't too down-hearted, though. 'We all think they've got better weather conditions and better running conditions!'

Furmitty at Abbotsbury, Dorset

If Shrove Tuesday marks the beginning of Lent, then in the pretty seaside village of Abbotsbury in Dorset it ends on Good Friday, with the eating – or is it drinking? – of furmitty. Farmer John Wood, who lives at East Farm right in the middle of the village, explained the origins of furmitty. 'I think it must go back to the monks somewhere,' he said with a laugh, 'because it's very alcoholic and, of course, those boys used to like their little bit of wallop! And it is only eaten on Good Friday!'

In the old days, John told us, people used to make it in five-gallon buckets, but these days he's content with a saucepan. 'First of all you get your wheat and you soak it for about forty-eight hours so that it "pims up", as we call it. After two days you get currants, raisins, sultanas and the water – it's the water from the wheat that is so potent, I think – and then you put it all in the saucepan and then you cook it slowly until the wheat breaks, and you can see the white inside.

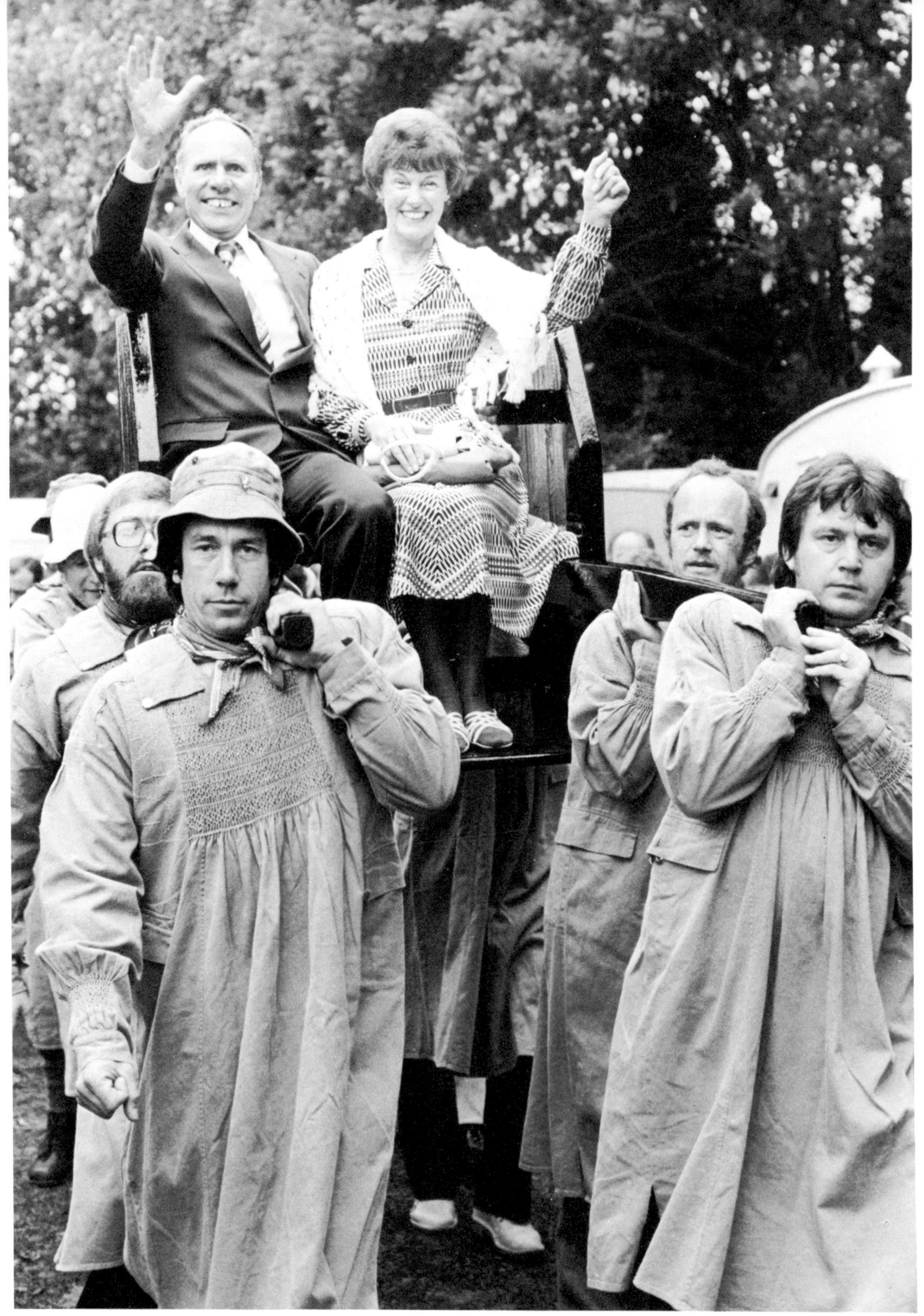

The winning couple at the 1980 Dunmow Flitch Trial.

You've got the husk of the wheat and all in it, and so when it's cooked it all thickens up. I've seen furmitty made which is like brown soup, which isn't right. It should be milk-coloured, and something like rice pudding.'

It is also extremely alcoholic, as anyone who's read Thomas Hardy's classic novel *The Mayor of Casterbridge*, or who saw the marvellous television adaptation a few years ago, starring Alan Bates in the title role, will know. It was while he was drunk on furmitty that he sold his wife to a sailor at a fair, and sowed the seeds of his eventual undoing!

The Dunmow Flitch Trial, Great Dunmow, Essex

Selling your wife to a stranger would certainly disqualify you from winning the side of bacon at the famous Dunmow Flitch ceremony, held every four years on Whit Monday in the Essex town of Great Dunmow! Anyone who lives in the British Isles can enter, provided, as Charlie and Sheila Williams who won it in 1960 told us, '. . . they can claim that they've lived together for a year and a day without having a row and without wishing they were unwed!' It's thought to be an old Breton custom brought to Little Dunmow in the thirteenth century by the Fitzwalter family. In the old days, any man – no mention of women! – who fulfilled the conditions went to Little Dunmow priory and, kneeling on two sharp stones in front of the Prior and a crowd of local people, made a sworn statement – a long and painful business. There is a poem which dates from a slightly later period, which goes:

You shall swear by Custom of Confession
That you ne'er made nuptial Transgression
Nor since you were married Man and Wife,
By Household Brawls or Contentious Strife
Or otherwise at Bed or at Board
Offended each other in deed or word
Or in a Twelve month time and a day
Repented not in Thought anyways
Or since the Church clerk said 'Amen'
Wish'd yourself unmarried again
But continued true and in desire
As when you join'd hands in Holy Choir.

When the ceremony was revived after a long break in 1855 by Harrison Ainsworth, the historical novelist, it was a much more light-hearted affair. These days the couple go 'on trial', with a local dignitary as a judge, a jury made up of six local maidens and six local bachelors, a defence, plus assistant, to speak up

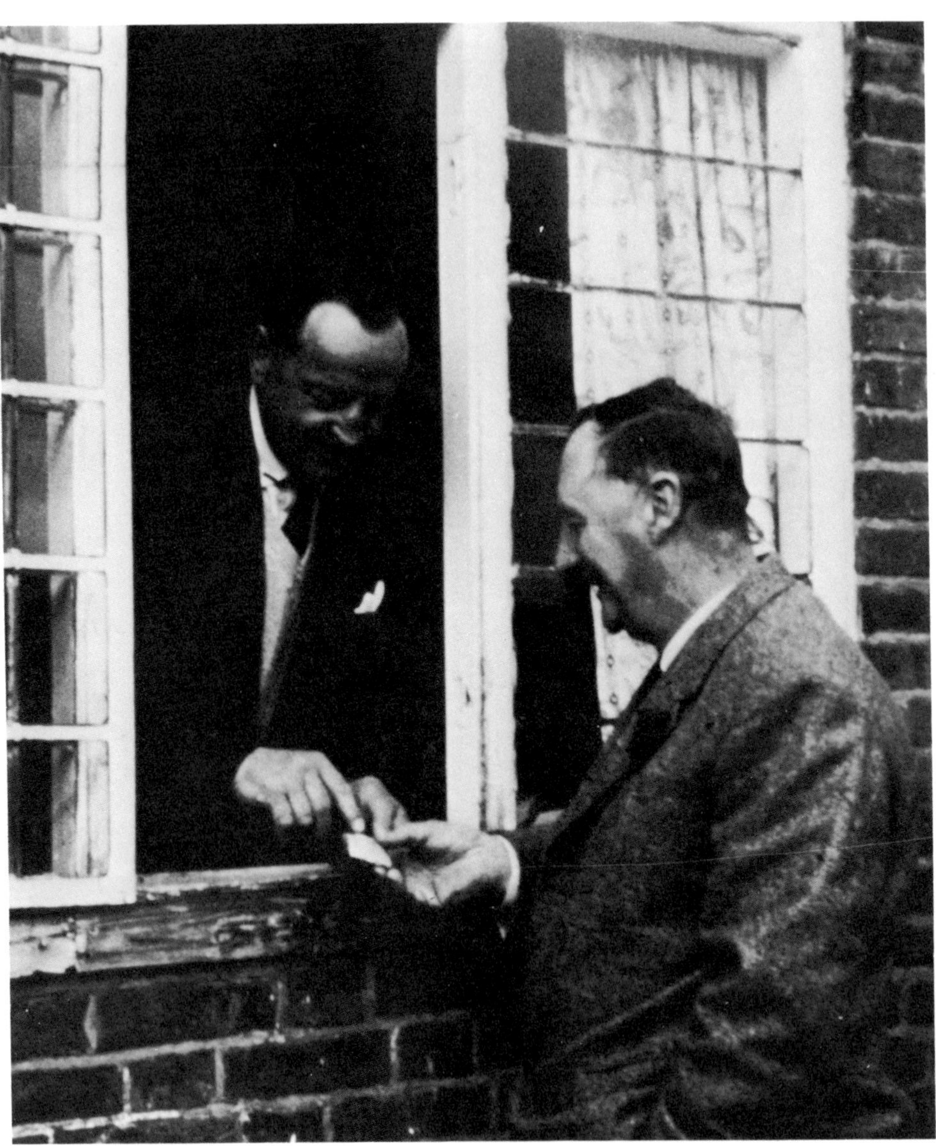

Len Homewood dispensing the Biddenden Dole. Started in the twelfth century by two sisters, this is possibly the oldest charity in England.

for the couple, and a prosecutor, plus assistant, to speak 'for the bacon' and try to trip the couple up.

'He asked me what television programmes we both preferred,' Sheila Williams said, 'or who chose them. He also knew that Charlie has got a terrific temper at work, so he wanted to know how he combatted that temper at home. But he just doesn't lose his temper at home – it's just a work temper!'

'We were able to answer them all,' Charlie said, 'and I still don't think they could trip us up on any of them, because in all the years since we still haven't had a quarrel. We have differences of opinion, but we can talk about them. We don't argue.'

At the end of the 'trial' the jury retires to consider their verdict. In the Williams's case they found for the couple, not for the bacon. 'Then they chaired us through the town to the local Town Hall, where we had to take the sentence kneeling on pointed stones, and we were awarded the bacon. At the time we didn't like bacon,' Sheila said, laughing, 'so we had it all sliced up and gave it all away!'

The Biddenden Dole, Kent

On Easter Monday, at Biddenden in Kent, they give away not bacon but bread, cheese and tea in what's thought to be the oldest charity in England. It is called the Biddenden Dole, or the Maids' Charity after the sisters who are supposed to have founded it over eight hundred years ago. Len Homewood, a retired farmer, and one of the charity's trustees for the last forty years, told us the story.

'They were farmer's daughters, born in 1100, just down below the church on a little farm, about twenty acres. They were joined at the hip and the shoulder – Siamese twins – and their names were Eliza and Mary Chulkhurst. When they died, in 1134, they left the farm to the village for an income to be given to the poorer villagers. And it's been given away ever since, every year, in the way of Bread and Cheese to the poor, until we stopped some of the bread and added some tea.'

The land that provided the income is still known locally as the Bread and Cheese Lands. The ceremony takes place on Easter Monday when a loaf of bread, a pound of cheese and a pound of tea are given away through the old workhouse window to handicapped people and to old age pensioners. 'If they're too old to come and collect it,' said Len, 'they send the children for it, usually their grandchildren. There's now about ninety people who receive it each year. They must be Biddenden people and they must have lived in Biddenden for twelve months.'

The legend also states that the sisters asked for a biscuit, with their picture on it, to be given away to visitors. It is still done today. The hard little biscuits carry the image of two women, either joined together or standing very close together, with their names above their heads, and 'Biddenden' beneath their feet. We asked Len if we could eat the biscuits. 'Well, you can,' he said, 'but I don't think you'd like it. It's just flour and water.'

The Tuttimen Hocktide Ceremony at Hungerford, Berkshire

The great day in Hungerford, Berkshire, is Hocktide Day, the second Monday after Easter. Like many of the town's ancient traditions, its procedures date back to the middle of the fourteenth century. In gratitude for hospitality he had received in the town, John of Gaunt bestowed grazing and shooting rights on the common, and fishing rights in the River Kennet which flows through the town, on the houses which then made up the town of Hungerford. Those rights have been passed down through the ages to every householder living in any house subsequently built on the same site.

'These people are called Commoners,' Hugh Hassell told us. 'There were reputed to be ninety-nine of them, but I think there are a few more than that now.' Hugh Hassell is a Commoner, but a very special one because he is also Constable of the Town and Manor, the two hundred and seventy-seventh holder of the title since records were first kept in 1550.

To help him carry out his now largely ceremonial duties, the Constable has a number of officers, including two 'ale-tasters'. 'I believe their proper title should be "ale-testers", and when certain houses in the town used to brew their own beer, the method of testing was to pour some beer on to an oak seat, and then the ale-testers, in a pair of moleskin breeches, would sit on it for a certain length of time. Then they would get up, and if the trousers stuck to the seat, the beer probably contained too much sugar, and wasn't very good!'

The officers are elected at the annual Hocktide Court. The day starts at eight o'clock with the sounding of a horn to summon the Commoners to court. 'There are two horns – one was reputed to have been given by John of Gaunt in 1350, which resides in the Common Coffer at the moment because it's rather too valuable and too frail to bring out. But we do use another horn, called the Lucas horn, given to the town in 1634 by one Jehosophat Lucas.' The horn bears an inscription:

> JOHN A GAUN DID GIVE AND GRANT THE RIALL OF FISHING TO HUNGERFORD TOUNE FROM ELDRED STUB TO IRISH STILL EXCEPTING SOM SEUEREAL MILL-POND. JEHOSOPHAT LUCAS WAS CUNSTABL. 1634

At nine o'clock the Constable hands their poles of office to two more of his officers, the Tuttimen, and sends them on their way. Mrs Jean Tubb, a trustee of the Town and Manor, and only the second woman to be elected to that office,

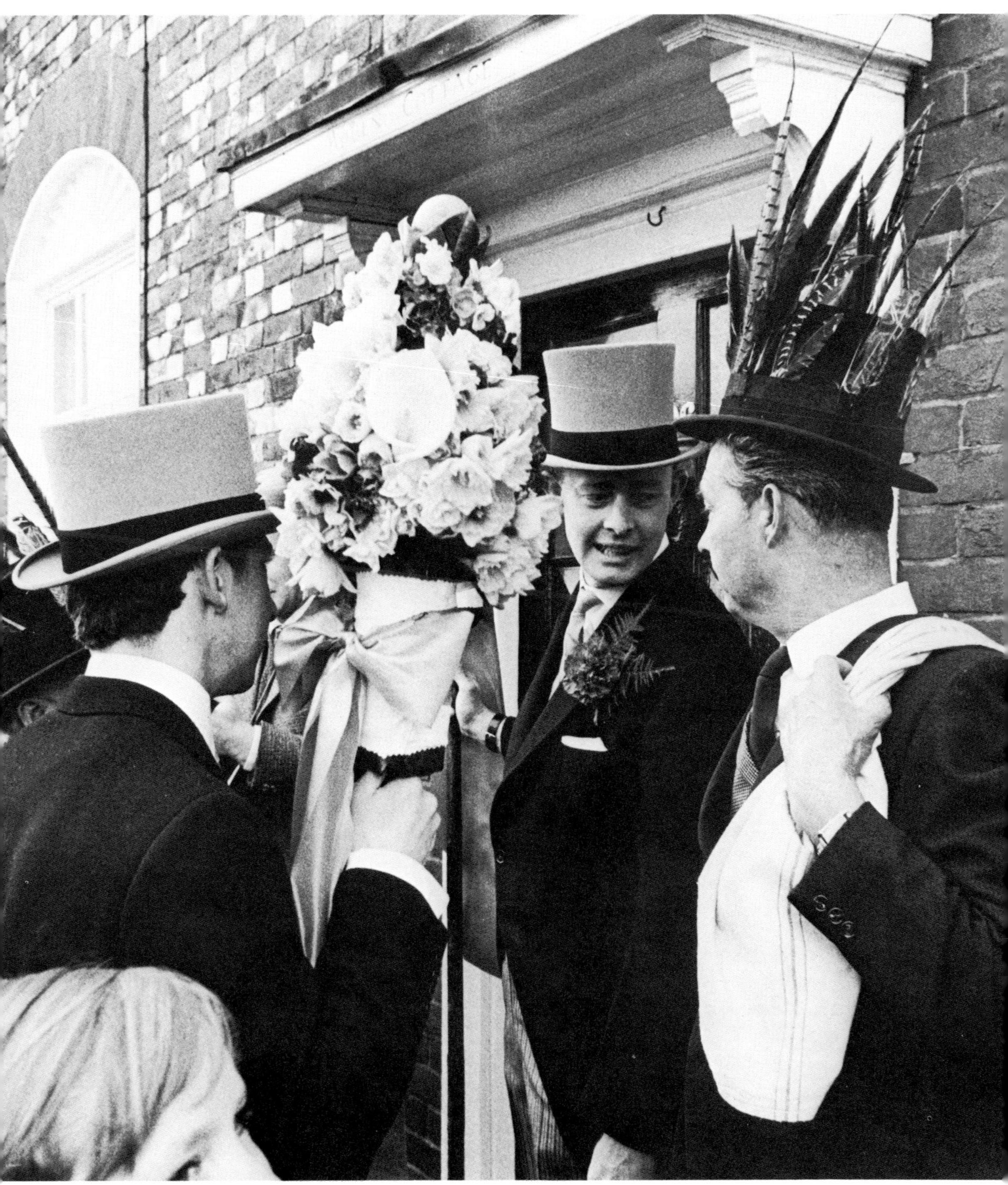

On Hocktide Day in Hungerford the Tuttimen receive a penny or a kiss, in exchange for rights bestowed on the town by John of Gaunt.

explained what Tuttimen are and what they do. 'The Tuttimen, who are usually newcomers to the Common Right houses, go and call on all the ninety-nine houses in the town that have the Common Right. At each house they are usually given money – in the old days, it used to be a penny – and they usually get some sustenance there, which sends them happily on their way. The ladies of the house can either pay the penny or give the Tuttimen a kiss. Sometimes they don't, and there's great sport with the kissing – people run away and make a great thing of it!'

In the old days Hocktide, which was celebrated in many parts of the country, was a two-day holiday, sometimes known as Binding Monday and Binding Tuesday. On the Monday the women went into the streets, captured any man they came across, bound him with ropes and only let him go if he paid a forfeit. On the Tuesday it was the men's turn, and perhaps the Tuttimen's kisses are a vestige of that old custom!

The exact derivation of 'Tutti' isn't known. 'I take it to mean "tithing",' Jean Tubb said, 'because of their collecting a penny or whatever it was from each house. But some people say "tutti" is the name for the posy on the top of the Tuttimen's poles.' The posies are always made according to tradition. At the very end of the pole is a spike with an orange on it. 'Next to that there's a ring of laurel leaves, then next to that you have some polyanthus. I like the red ones best because having red in the posy represents the red rose of Lancaster. [Traditionally, the red rose is presented to any reigning monarch – the Duke of Lancaster – who passes through the town.] And then we have blue, because blue is the town colour, and these are usually anemones, and then perhaps ten or twelve bunches of daffodils in each one. I suppose the original reason for the nosegays was because of the odd smells the Tuttimen encountered when they went into the different houses. It's rather like a judge's nosegay in that respect.'

At each Common Right house where the Tuttimen receive a penny or a kiss, they hand over, in exchange, the orange from the top of the pole, replacing it with another orange before they move on to the next house. While the Tuttimen are doing their rounds, the Hocktide Court is sitting, electing its officers and making any amendments or revisions to the rules governing the Common Rights.

Afterwards there's a celebration lunch, traditionally held at the Three Swans Hotel. 'We like to invite some notable person to be our guest of honour,' said Hugh Hassell. 'One year we had the Duke of Beaufort, who is a direct lineal descendant of John of Gaunt. The first toast after the meal is always "The Queen – Duke of Lancaster", and the next toast we propose is one that has been carried on since time immemorial, and that is "To the immortal memory of John of Gaunt".'

After lunch, according to Jean Tubb, the fun really begins. 'There is what we call the ceremony of Shoeing the Colts, when anyone who hasn't attended the lunch before is literally shod! The Shoeing Smith takes the person's foot between his knees, and literally hammers with a horseshoe nail on the heel!' It sounds very painful, but all the victim has to do to stop the shoeing is call out 'Punch!', and promise to pay for a round of drinks.

In the old days the children of the town had a half-holiday from school on Hocktide Day, but these days they simply come along after school to scramble for pennies from the Town Hall steps. 'They used to scramble at practically every house the Tuttimen had visited. And if you see children with fingers tied up after Tutti-day, that's not in the least unusual. They get fingers trodden on, toes trodden on, they get pushed over! Mums never send their children out in their best clothes to go scrambling for pennies on Tutti-day!'

Man's Best Friends

Those who live and work with animals

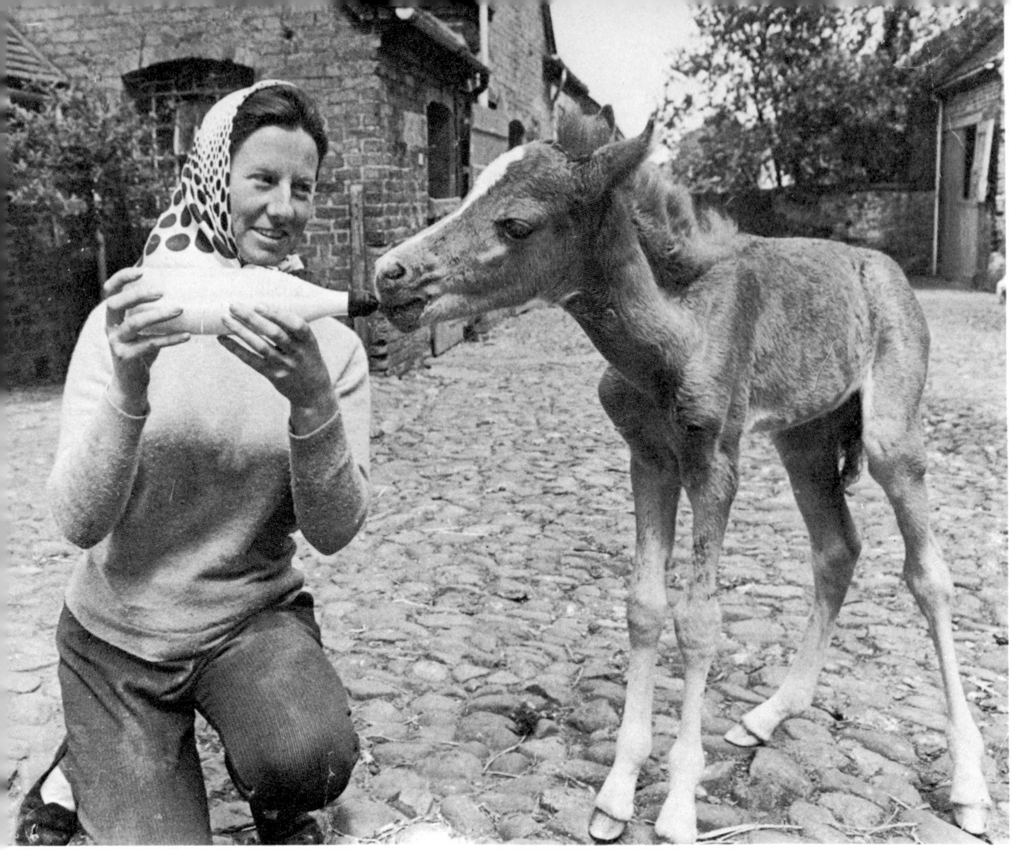

Joanna Varden with a young customer at the National Foaling Bank. Until a suitable foster mare can be found, the orphan has to be hand fed every two hours

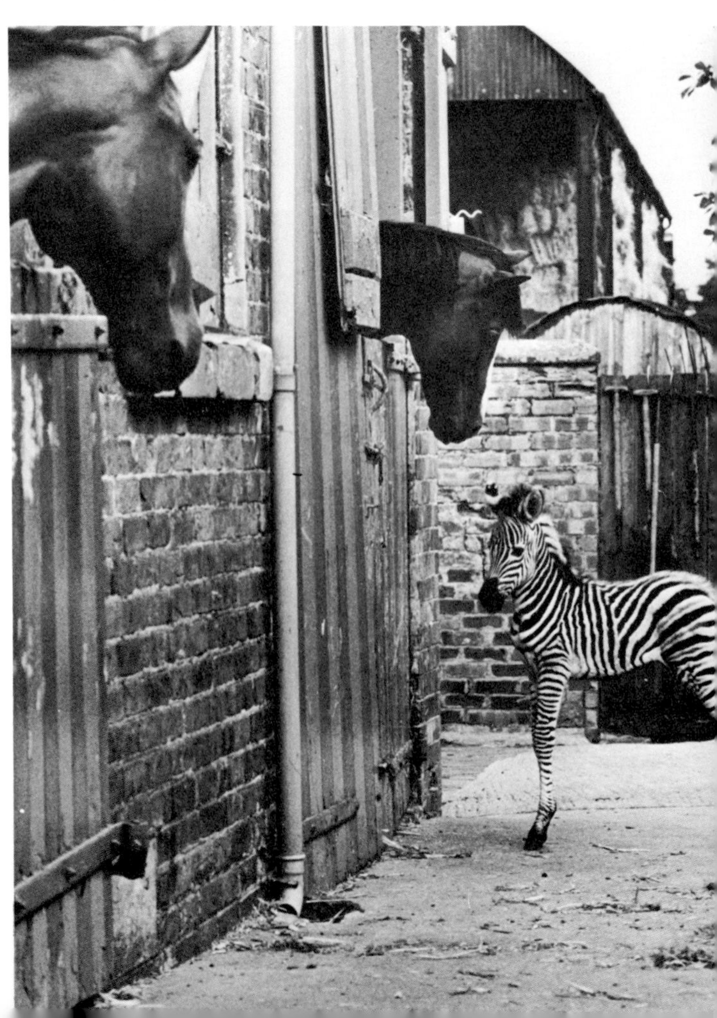

And here's an unusual guest! This orphan zebra foal was quite a surprise for the horses at the stud.

Foal adoption at Newport, Shropshire

It is a truth, universally acknowledged, that we British as a nation are daft about animals. We give millions to animal charities each year, lavish more care and affection on our cats, dogs, budgies, gerbils or horses than we do on each other, and as our European neighbours are quick to point out, our society for the prevention of cruelty to children is merely 'National', while its animal equivalent is 'Royal'! But then, what do Europeans know? They eat horses, don't they?

One of the places we visited which shows the British love for animals at its genuine, practical best is the National Foal Bank at the Meretown Stud near Newport in Shropshire. It was set up fifteen years ago by Joanna Varden who still runs it, and who explained just what it does. 'In brief, it's an equine adoption service – a twenty-four-hour service whereby, should any breeder in the country lose a brood mare or a foal, or they've got any other problem remotely connected with foaling, they ring me up and I either supply them with a foster mare or an orphan foal to help them out of their difficulty.'

That may sound relatively straightforward, but it is anything but. During the foaling season, from February to August, Joanna says she never gets an unbroken night's sleep. 'People either ring up at all hours, or just arrive on the doorstep and say, "Look, we're panic-stricken. Our mare's died, we didn't know what to do, so we've brought the foal here." I mean, foals arrive literally on the back seats of people's cars. It's very amusing to find a Shire foal sitting on the back seat of a Mini, which has happened!'

It all started back in 1965 purely by accident. 'We had one little mare in the stud here, called Crown Emerald, a little pony I found in my kitchen as a Christmas present one year who kept breeding me these marvellous show-winners. When she lost a foal one season, I thought it was so awful to see this dead foal at her feet and her such a marvellous brood mare, so I thought, "Where can I find an orphan foal?" I rang all my friends, but nothing turned up at all. So in desperation I rang the marvellous BBC and said, "Look, I've got a jolly good sob story for you – so put it across!" Five minutes after the appeal went out, I was inundated with telephone calls – people offering me orphan foals to put on my foster mare. I was lucky – I accepted and reared the first one I was offered, but the telephone didn't stop ringing for two days and two nights. You mention it, and I had it offered to me, literally. A foal by a Shetland, another by a Shire. It doesn't make any difference to us – if it's alive it's got to be saved, whether it's worth £5 or £500.' Nor is the work of the Bank confined to horses and ponies. A couple of years ago they were sent an orphan zebra foal from Dudley Zoo!

Joanna arranges about five hundred adoptions a year, with more mares needing foals than vice versa. The mares and foals come from all over the British Isles and even, sometimes, from abroad by air! 'You've got to get a foal to a mare within the first few days of her losing her own. She might still give milk after four days if you're lucky, but that is pushing it a bit!'

During our visit Joanna was trying to get a mare from Yorkshire, whose foal had been born prematurely and died, to accept as her own a beautiful Arab foal that wasn't, strictly speaking, an orphan. 'The mare isn't dead, but she's a savaging mare – wretched little thing! – and wouldn't accept the foal as her own, so to all intents and purposes it is orphaned – it hasn't got a Mum who wants to feed it.' But no mare will accept and feed a strange foal, so she has to be convinced that the newcomer is her own.

'She will only accept a foal on smell, so in order to deceive her, we have to bring in the dead foal, skin it – can you imagine skinning a dead foal in the middle of the night? – and put the skin over the new foal to make the mare believe it is her own.' Mare and foal are then put into adjoining stalls, with a grill in the dividing wall so that the mare can see the foal, but can't get at it to bite it or kick it or smell it. 'The new foal won't take up the smell of the mare until her milk has passed right through its system, which takes a minimum of forty-eight hours. In the meantime we bring the foal in every two hours, with the skin on, to feed. Then, when the milk has passed through, we can take the skin off carefully, and the mare will usually accept the foal as her own.'

Obviously a service like this is expensive to run, and Joanna said it was a struggle to keep going. 'People pay for the livery when we are looking after them here, and then we ask for a nominal fee for the adoption if – and only if – it is successful. It doesn't matter how many mares we might get in for one particular foal, or any amount of foals. We just charge the same nominal fee to each mare or foal owner.'

Shire horses at Higham Ferrers, Northamptonshire

If Eady Robinson ever has a problem with one of his mares or foals, he knows where he can turn for help. For Eady, who lives at Walnut Tree Farm at Higham Ferrers, Northants, which he rents from the Queen's private estate, the Duchy of Lancaster, is a leading breeder of those juggernauts of the horse world, the Shires. 'When I started farming,' Eady told us, 'it was all horse work, and I've always been very fond of a good animal. I was also a very keen enthusiast of agricultural shows in my young days, so I started showing. We worked them for perhaps two or three years, showed and worked them, and then the better ones were sold to the brewers.'

Eady only stopped using horses on the farm in 1972, not because they were too slow, nor because they ate too much, but because the busy A6 road passes right by the farm, and he felt it had become just too dangerous for the horses. He still sells the odd horse to a brewery, though. 'I'm afraid that the price with the export trade has rather outpriced the brewers. But it has been proved by time and motion studies that horses are much more economical to use within a

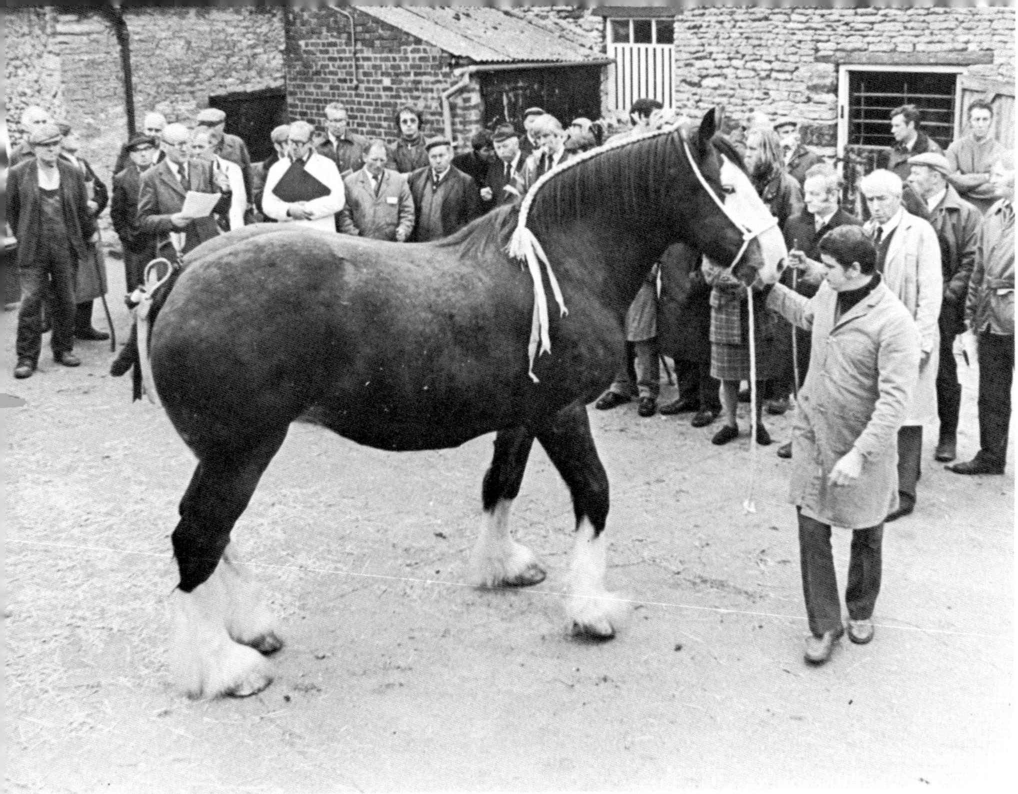

Eady Robinson has bred nearly two hundred and fifty Shire Horses at Higham Ferrers. A full grown Shire like this weighs over a ton.

Ben Nevis, the 1980 Grand National winner, with Charlie Fenwick up, at the Wantage stables of Captain Tim Forster.

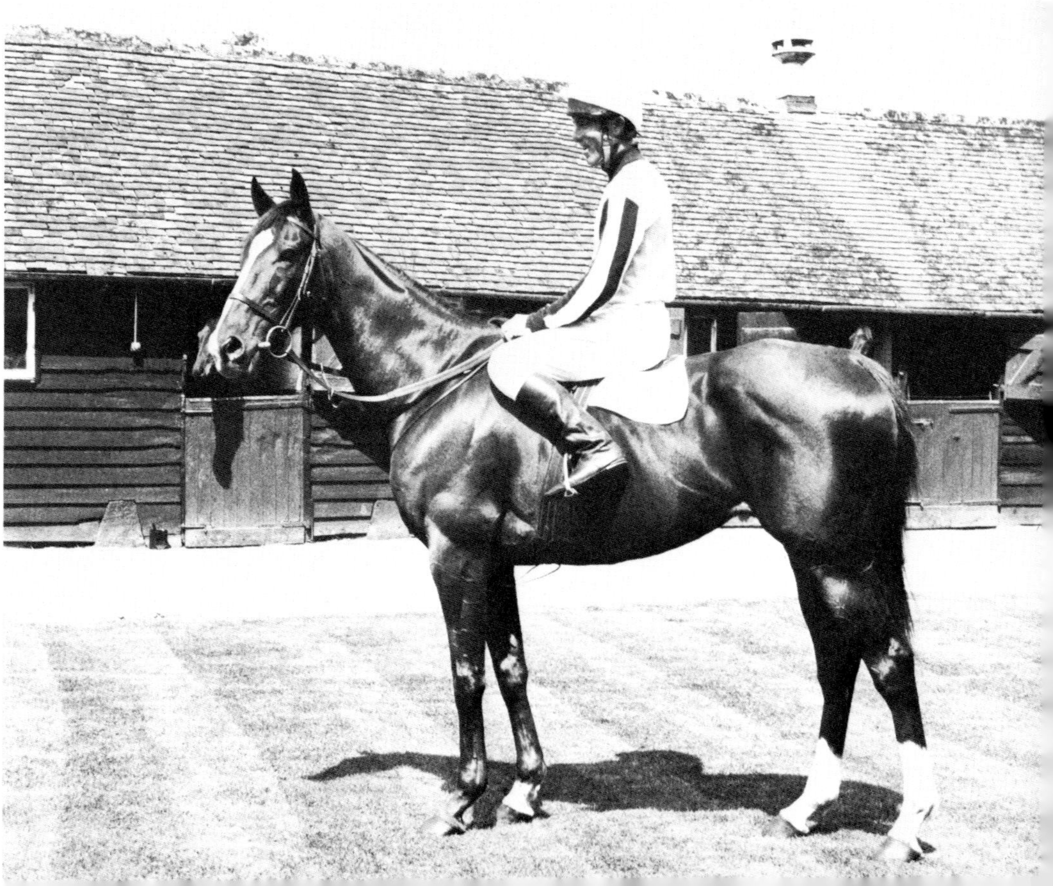

four-mile radius of the brewery than a lorry is. There is no tax on horses, you see!'

In his time, Eady has bred almost two hundred and fifty Shires on his farm and is well aware of the qualities that catch the judges' eye. 'The main thing is to have a big, broad, deep foot which will never wear out, and will stand the jar of the street. The bone in it should be terribly flat and flinty.' A good, grown Shire will weigh anything up to twenty-four hundredweight – well over a ton! 'And they will pull eight times their own weight easily,' Eady told us. 'Or, at least, they can start with that and pull considerably more!'

Not surprisingly, Eady has enormous affection for the gentle giants he breeds. 'They're friendly animals, and they've got more courage, I think, than any other breed of horse. If you ask them to do some work, they just go and do it. They don't stop and look round at it – they just get on with it!' Eady has had a lot of success with his horses at shows, including the Supreme Champion award at the Horse of the Year Show, which he won with a mare bearing the unlikely name of Lillingstone Again.

Racehorse-training at Wantage, Oxfordshire

Although unlucky punters might well believe that the animal on which they have just lost their shirt might be better suited to pulling a brewers' dray, racehorses are built for an entirely different kind of work – and galloping four and a half miles, flat out, over thirty huge obstacles at Aintree certainly qualifies as work. We met one of the more famous contributors to *Down Your Way* at the home of his trainer, Captain Tim Forster, in Wantage, Oxfordshire, which is situated appropriately enough in the Vale of the White Horse which takes its name from the gigantic, ancient carving in the chalk of the Downs. His name is Ben Nevis, winner of the 1980 Grand National. Ridden by an amateur American rider, Charlie Fenwick, he was one of only four horses to survive the mud and finish.

Although another of Captain Forster's horses, Well To Do, which won the National in 1972, loved muddy going, Ben Nevis didn't, and in 1980 the going was so wet that a few days beforehand Captain Forster seriously considered pulling him out of the race. 'Everybody told me that the horse must have it firm, and we had been going out of our way for the last two years never to run him in the soft, and when the morning came, and when Peter O'Sullivan, the BBC commentator, kept saying it was the wettest National there had ever been, we were in despair! I honestly think that if he had been owned by some Englishman, and he'd been a young horse, we would have seriously considered not running him. But when you've got the whole shooting match, as they say, coming over from America, there is no turning back then!' Against all the odds Ben Nevis won, but then he has never been a predictable horse, as Captain Forster told us.

'His owner, Mr Redmond Stewart, bought him unseen up north and took him back to America. When they got him home they found he was well, mad – literally – and they could do very little with him. So as a challenge he said to Charlie Fenwick, who is his son-in-law, "You'd better have him. I bet you're not man enough to tame him!" But Charlie, as anybody who watched him win the National could see, is a fairly determined man and said, " I will show father-in-law who's right, and who's wrong." Over a period of about two years they rebroke him, and got him going quietly again. Then, for a bit of fun, they decided they would run him in a race in America over timber, which he won. So they thought, "Let's run him again, and see what happens," and he won again, and so on, until he'd won everything he could win in America.' As it turned out, the Grand National win was the climax of Ben Nevis's career, because his owners decided to take him back to America and retire him.

Apart from Ben Nevis, though, Captain Forster had another fifty horses in his stables, with approximately sixty-five owners among them. 'Nowadays a lot of people own legs, or a third, or an eighth!' Most of them are jumpers. 'Occasionally, I have flat race horses – you have to be a bit careful with them – but you couldn't have anywhere better to train jumpers. You've got marvellous downland turf which dries out in the winter, you've got wonderful hills to walk and trot them up, and banks to canter them up. It's the ideal place for jumpers, so I can't make any excuses about the facilities!'

Deer at Petworth, West Sussex

The one quality that everyone who loves and works with animals seems to have is a total lack of sentimentality. Take Richard Price, who is the deer warden at Petworth House in Sussex. He loves the herd of deer in his charge, but that doesn't stop him killing a number of them every winter in the annual cull. 'Basically, we have to retain a healthy herd that's in balance with the keep, the food and so on that's available to them. My job is replacing the natural predators of the deer which man has exterminated in the West, so that I cull animals that are past desirable breeding age, or animals which, as we say, have no future – they're obviously not good developing stock, and shouldn't be left to breed. One can assess them quite accurately – antlers and so on are some indication of their condition, but mainly general health and overall appearance of the animal are the best indicators.'

Richard lives with his family in an isolated house in the deer park – some seven hundred acres within the vast Petworth estate, which is open to the public. 'The entire nucleus of the estate is encompassed by a fourteen-mile-long wall, and I suppose there must be three and a half thousand acres inside the wall. I believe that, in fact, it marks the original line of an ancient deer fence. The area here was much hunted in the early 1400s and we have had various kings coming here to hunt at Petworth. The wall was then built around 1750, I believe by prisoners of war.'

There are two main species of deer at Petworth – the small roe deer, which roam the entire estate, and the larger fallow deer, which live within the confines of the deer park. 'The fallow deer herd at Petworth is believed to be the largest herd of fallow deer in the world, numbering something over a thousand head. We have three types, which are all sub-species, really. There's the black sort which are supposed to come from the Scandinavian countries, and some people still call them "Norwegians". Then there's the common type, which are thought to have been introduced by the Normans, and then we have the light spotted type, the Menal deer – which are believed to have originated in the Mediterranean countries.'

They all interbreed freely – and noisily – during October. 'There is a tremendous noise!' Richard said with feeling. 'It sounds like a rather rude sort of belching grunt. It's quite loud and when you get several hundred bucks together, we can hear it over a mile and a half away here on a still night! The bucks compete among themselves for the attention of the does, and a master buck will serve as many does as he can possibly gather round him. Each buck marks out his own small territory – his "stand" or "rutting ring" we call it – and by urinating on the ground and scraping and so on, he makes out a very smelly patch for himself, which for some unknown reason the does seem to find very attractive, and as they come into cycle so he serves them.'

Not surprisingly, in some cultures the buck has become a symbol of great potency and virility, and Petworth has developed a rather unusual export trade with China. 'Various unmentionable organs from the culled male deer are exported to China where, I believe, they are made into aphrodisiacs!' The antlers are sold for ornaments and the carcases for venison. 'This forms a very good cash crop for the estate, and we export several hundred carcases from this estate alone each year.'

Goats at Peebles, Scotland

Like Richard Price, Robert Haslam, who runs a goat farm in Peebles, loves his charges but doesn't hesitate to send off to the slaughterhouse any surplus males that aren't needed for stud purposes. But his goats aren't reared for meat. The seventy-string herd, the biggest in Scotland and one of the biggest in Britain, primarily produces milk.

'Goats yield very highly for their size,' Robert told us. 'I mean, they produce their own weight in milk in ten or eleven days, whereas I think it takes a cow twenty-four days. There is quite a big demand for the milk, mainly from people

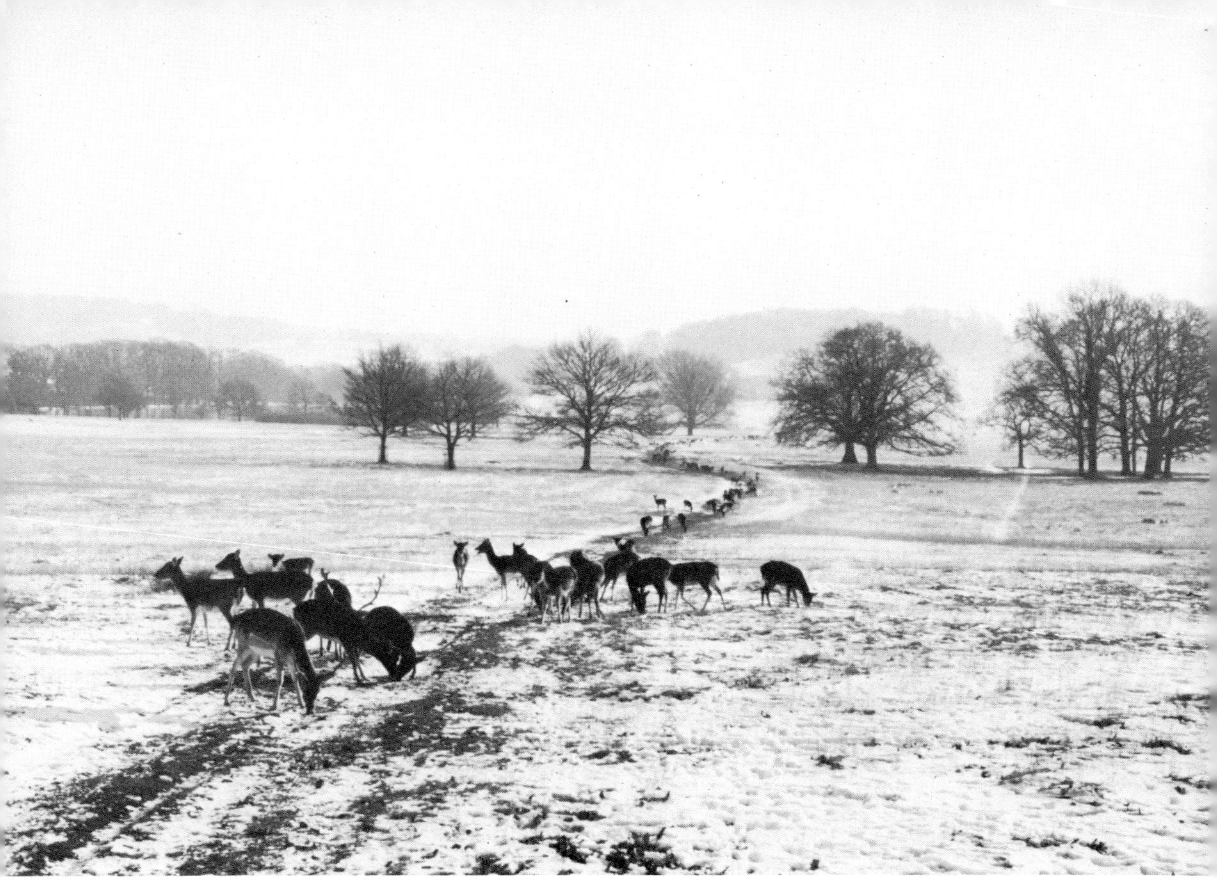

The deer at Petworth consist mainly of roe and the larger fallow. The fallow deer herd is believed to be the biggest in the world.

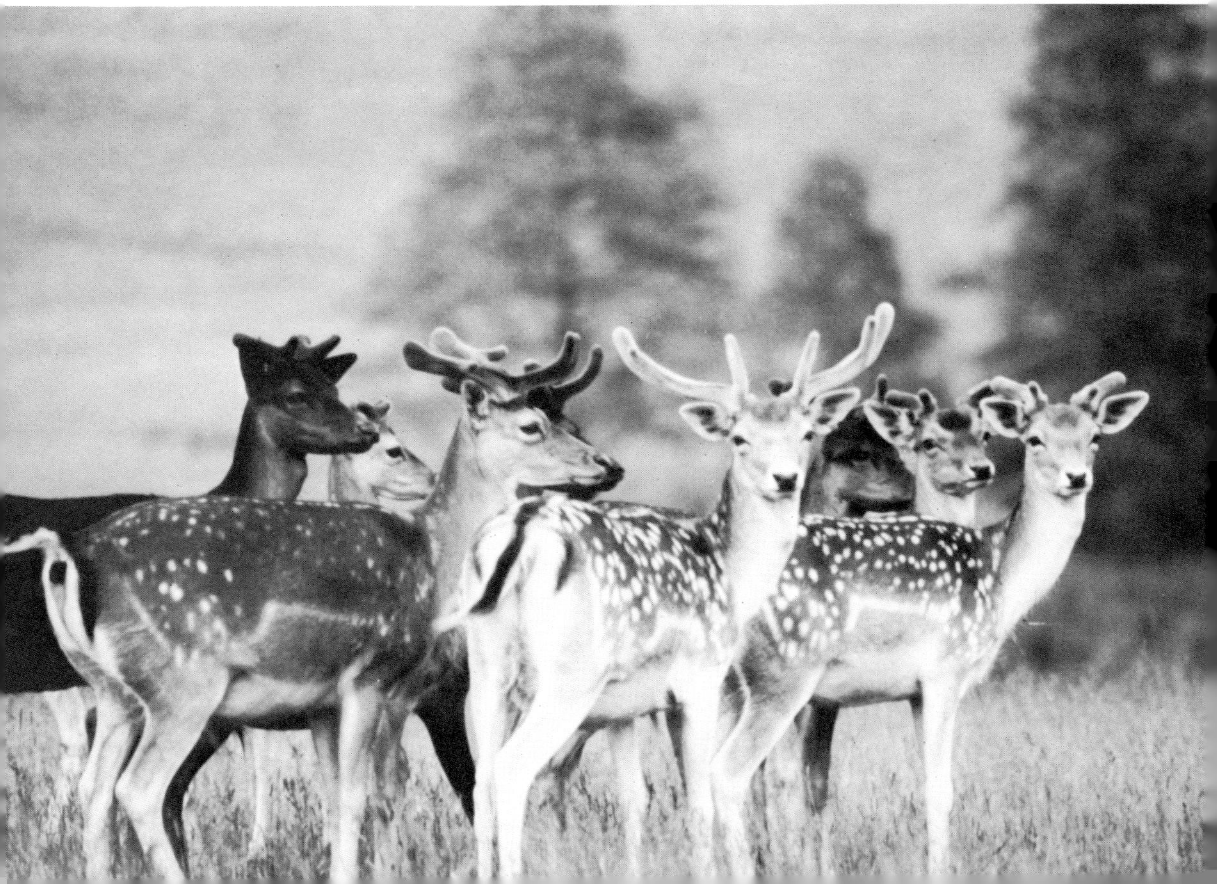

who need it for medicinal reasons, because it is more digestible than cow's milk, and some people have an allergy to cow's milk which they don't have to goat's. One very important thing, becoming more and more widely recognized by the medical profession, is that in a lot of babies eczema is caused by cow's milk. Goat's milk won't cure it, but if a baby is taken off cow's milk and put on to goat's instead, just the removal of the cow's milk will be enough to cure it.' Robert Haslam isn't just a goat farmer, though. Wearing his other hat – or perhaps 'other collar' might be more appropriate – he is also the rector of the Scottish Episcopal church in Eastgate, Peebles.

'Basically I was an ordained clergyman, but I happened to be here, running the goat farm, when a vacancy arose for a part-time minister at the Episcopal church. The bishop suddenly discovered me, and asked if I would take the job on. I work in Peebles on Sundays and three days during the week, and the rest of the time I'm here. In addition, I find that the mornings are not a good time for parish work, whereas they are the busiest time on the farm, so it works quite well. The two jobs go very pleasantly together, and because they are so different they are a relaxation from each other.'

The goats were certainly a friendly crowd, and the one who nibbled Brian Johnston's trousers, Robert assured us, was definitely curious rather than hostile! 'I think they are very friendly,' Robert said. 'Of course, they have all been bottle-reared, so this accounts for a lot of it. But they are full of character, and I think people enjoy meeting them for that reason.' Robert – and the herd – also scotched the popular misconception that goats smell. 'It's only the billies that smell, and then only during the mating season!'

Sheep-shearing at Wigtown, Scotland

Obviously, with his qualifications, Robert Haslam has no difficulty in separating the sheep from the goats. Nor would Willie Lawson, from Wigtown in Scotland, who has sheared more sheep in his time than most of us have had hot roast lamb dinners. Willie has been both British and European record-holder – thirty-five seconds for a single sheep, and three hundred and thirty-eight sheep in a day! He was also the joint holder of the two-man record when we met him, six hundred and fifty-four sheep in nine hours, and at two kilos of wool on average from each sheep, that's enough to keep Marks and Spencer's in jumpers for an hour or two!

In his lovely lilting Scottish accent, Willie described a shearing competition for us, after the competitor has gone into the ring and caught his sheep, though that isn't as simple as it sounds. 'Most beginners always look at the one facing them, but you must always catch a sheep that's facing away from you. You put your hand under its jaw, ease its head up, and walk it backwards – there's no real strength in it then!'

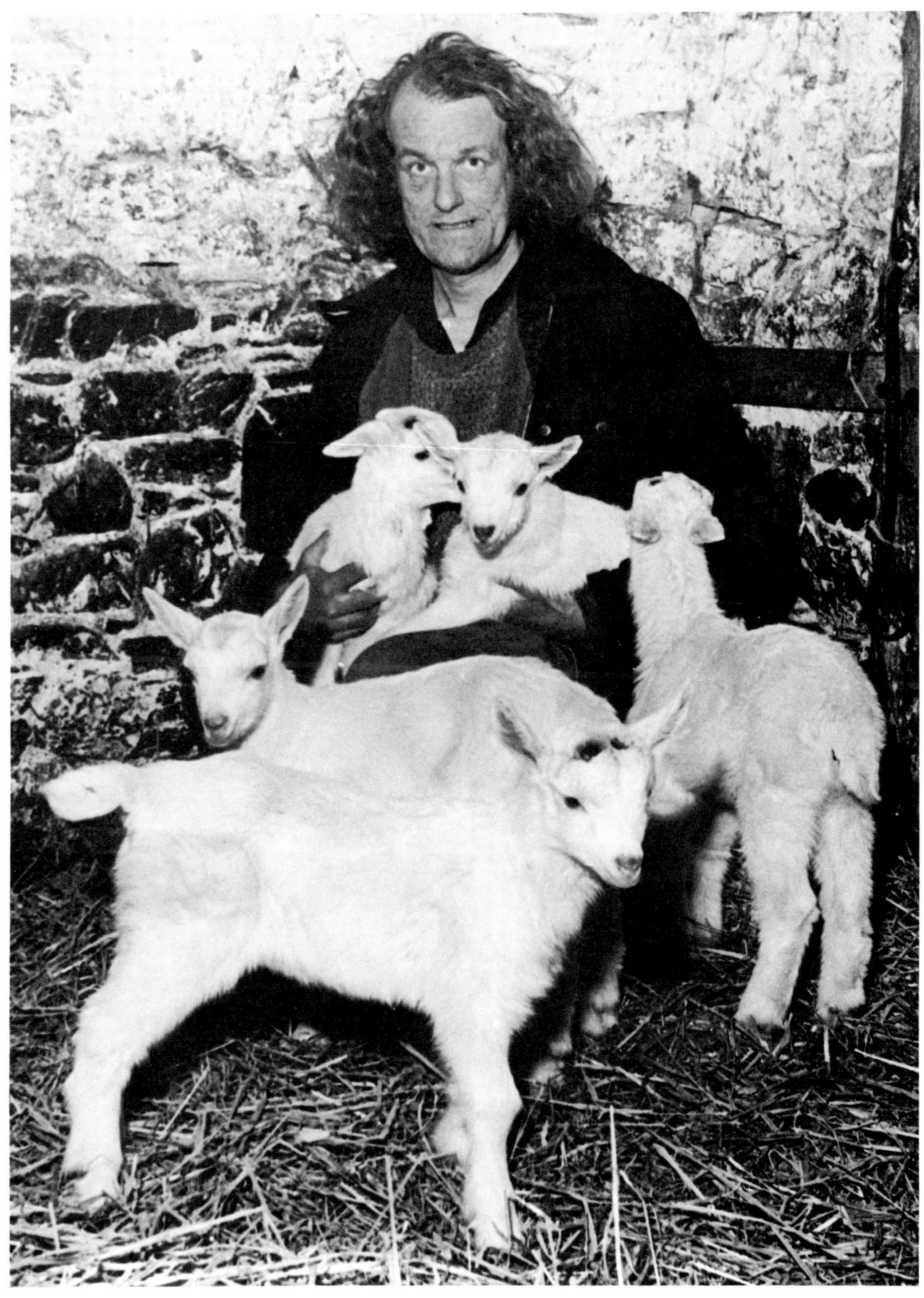

As well as a herd, this goat farmer also has a flock – he is the Reverend Robert Haslam.

Then, gripping it between your knees, you start to shear. 'You start down the belly, and take the wool off the belly, then through the crutch. Then you go on to the left back leg, and work forward up to the neck and front shoulder. Then, as you turn the machine round, you put the sheep down, and take long "blows" from the tail up towards the head, and for the last side you roll the sheep over and go down it, finishing out on the back leg.

'If a competitor rough-handles the sheep, he loses points. If he chops up the wool he also loses points, because you must get the fleece off whole, and when the sheep goes down the shute at the end there's a judge who looks at the sheep, and if there's any skin cuts or any wool left on, he loses more points. And time comes into it – the fastest man gets the best marks.' Like the bulls pitted against matadors in the bull-ring, the sheep used for shearing competitions have never been sheared before – called 'ewe hoggits' in Scotland, and 'tegs' in England – so they don't know what's about to hit them!

'The sheep doesn't struggle much as a rule,' Willie told us. 'It may be a bit frightened, but it doesn't struggle. It can kick you sometimes, and the odd one will bite you, but it doesn't hurt much.' For shearing competitions, Willie told us, the shearers wear special clothing – much of it made, appropriately, from wool. 'We wear woollen socks and woollen trousers to keep the lanolin from going through to the skin, because lanolin becomes poisonous in the large doses we get it in. We also wear a woollen singlet to keep the sweat from sticking to you, as it evaporates clean through and keeps you from getting cold when you stop.'

Although Willie has been both British and European champion, he is the first to admit that he wouldn't compete with a New Zealand shearer. 'They are professionals! Although I'm a professional too, they shear ten months of each year while we shear only two, two and a half months. I actually shear more than the average in this country because I go over to Norway for three months of the year, shearing.' Willie doesn't compete much these days. 'I usually only do one competition, in Northern Ireland. I feel it would be unfair to compete on this side of the water because they would be mostly my own pupils! Besides, I'm too old for that caper now!'

Sheepdog-training at Ruthin, Clwyd

If Willie Lawson can tell you everything there is to know about shearing sheep, then Gwyn Jones, who lives on a farm just outside Ruthin, a small market town in the fertile Clwyd valley, is the man to ask if you want to know anything about rounding them up. For Gwyn breeds and trains sheepdogs, prize-winning sheepdogs at that. Anyone who has watched those fascinating BBC TV programmes *One Man and His Dog* will have seen Gwyn with his dog Gell and his bitch

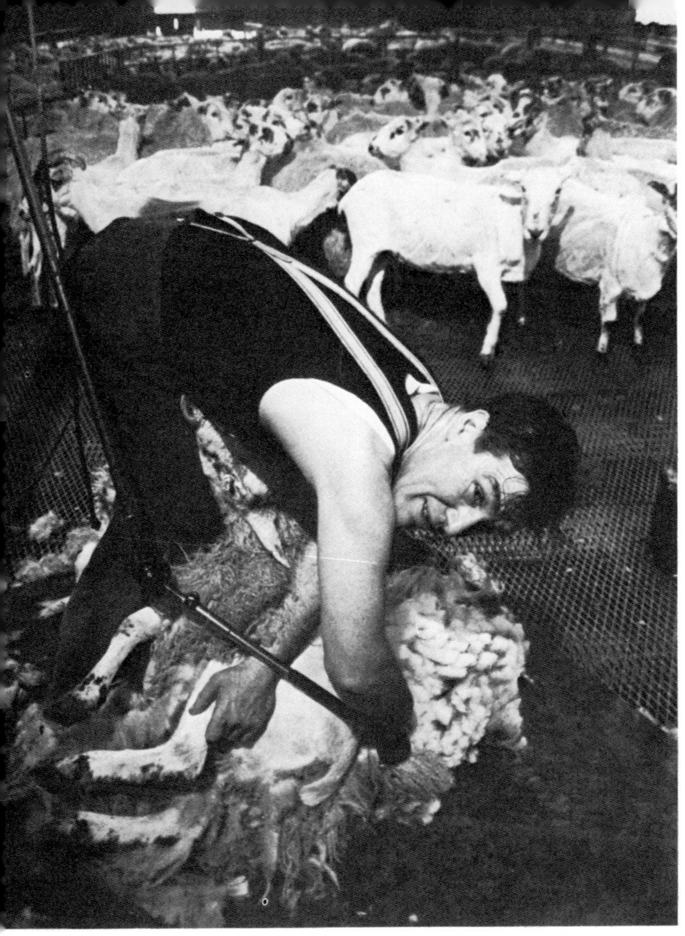

Willie Lawson demonstrates the art of sheep-shearing.

'One Man and his Dog.' The remarkable teamwork shown by the sheepdog and handler almost amounts to telepathy.

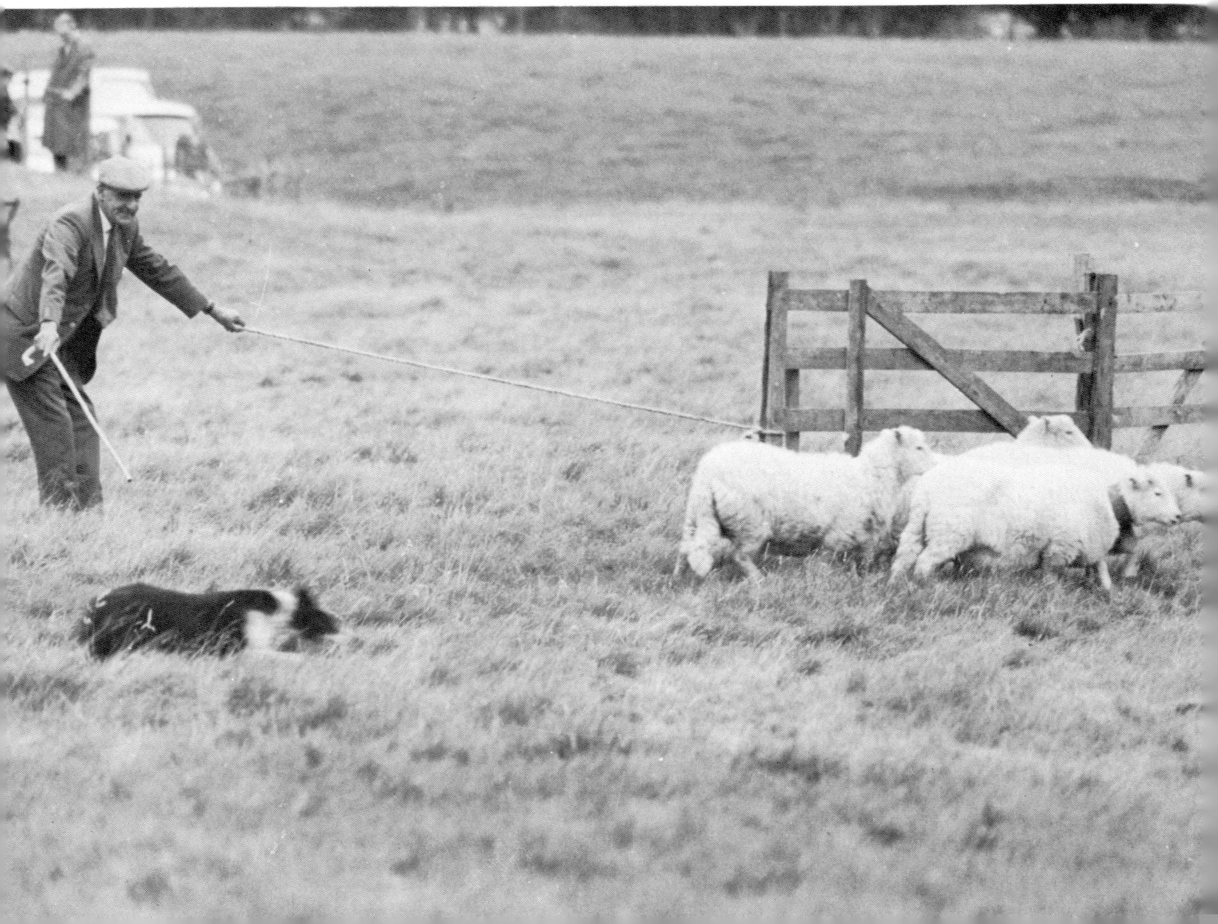

Bracken bringing home a flock of sheep like clockwork! The dogs are a special breed of collie. 'They are registered with the International Sheepdog Association. It's a distinct, working collie, and quite different from the showbench pets, as we call them. All my pups are sort of reared as pets in the house by my wife and children, and then, at about seven or eight months old, I take over. They're not really allowed to be pets any longer, and gradually I get them to the stage – at about twelve or fourteen months – when I really start training in earnest, and from then on it's all work.'

The basic training takes anything between four and six months according to the temperament of the dog. 'They're born with the instinct to herd sheep – the good ones are, anyway – and then it's my job to get the best out of them by putting a command to that instinct.' Gwyn demonstrated for us the signals he uses with Gell – a series of whistles which tell him to go forward, go back, go left, go right, or speed up. These are the long-distance signals that Gwyn uses when Gell is working up to half a mile away – the distance from which he has to fetch sheep in competitions. Close to, for the final penning of the sheep for instance, Gwyn uses verbal commands. 'They're quite simple – I usually say "Away", or "Away to me" when I want him to go to the left, and "Come by" when I want him to go to the right. Bracken has her own set of signals, and when you issue commands to one dog, the other one should take no notice whatsoever.'

What happens, though, when Gwyn sells a dog to someone else? Does he have to teach the new owner the signals he has been using, or does the man invent his own, and hope that the dog will pick them up? 'The majority of people invent their own – and if the man knows anything about the job, the dog should be able to relearn pretty easily.'

Apart from winning the *One Man and His Dog* trophy for the brace – the competition for two dogs working together – Gwyn's pride and joy is the trophy he won with Gell at the International Centenary Competition at Bala. 'It's the ambition of every sheepdog handler to win the International, and winning it in your own country is a fantastic feeling!'

Pigeons at Marple, Cheshire

It's remarkable to see what amounts almost to telepathy between sheepdog and handler, but even more remarkable is the instinct that enables a bird released hundreds of miles away to find its way unerringly home. One of the most famous and successful pigeon-fanciers and -breeders in this country is Jack Roberts, known to his colleagues and friends as 'JL' and to many of the locals in his home town of Marple, Cheshire as the 'Bird man'.

Nobody knows for certain exactly what it is that enables a pigeon to find its way home from vast distances, but JL has a theory. He likens it to tuning a transistor radio. A pigeon that isn't very fit is on a crackly wavelength. 'But a pigeon that's very fit seems to get it crystal-clear and flies in a straight line and gets home very quickly.'

When we went to see him, one of JL's birds had won a race in Manchester area recently, and topped an astonishing eighty-two miles an hour in the process. 'I think the thing all great racing pigeons have in common would be that something extra – that is, wanting to be very great friends. From the moment they are weaned from their parents they seem to have a very great love for home.'

The success that JL has had in breeding champions over the years is not simply a matter of chance. He has studied the birds closely, and put his findings into practice. 'The heaviest part of a pigeon is its skull, and so over the years I have been breeding less weight in the skull and going for a more streamlined shape in bone structure. This gives them more buoyancy of feather and less heavy bone to carry in flight, and they can fly for fifteen hours and think nothing of it. They can fly the clock round.'

JL keeps his fifty birds in a special pigeon loft in his garden, and knows every single one by name. 'I can tell each bird even when it's flying, before it drops. I know each one from the way it flies.' Every bird has its own nesting box within the pigeon house. 'The males are all given a female at the beginning of spring – around 15 March every year – and they rear a couple of youngsters in the first nest and go on breeding throughout the season. And of course we start racing them when the better weather comes.'

Rare chickens at Hailsham, East Sussex

Burt Burton has farmed in Hailsham, East Sussex all his adult life, starting in September 1920 with just one cow. Although he was officially semi-retired when we met him he still had a small herd of beef heifers, though most of his energies were going into his chickens – not just common or garden farmyard chickens, though, because Burt specializes in rare breeds, like the Brahmas.

'They came from India originally,' Burt said, 'but they were imported into America, and an American breeder, after he was successful in getting them near to perfection, thought it would be a good idea to present Queen Victoria with a trio, so he sent them to her in 1854.' They are rather strange-looking, ungainly birds, or so Brian Johnston thought, with their feathers going right down their legs like plus fours. 'They are pretty heavy-feathered,' Burt said, 'and I think it's the feathers that give them that awkward sort of gait. . . .'

Burt, who was made a life member of the Poultry Society in its centenary year, in recognition of his work with chickens, has won any number of prizes with his birds at shows, which involves him in quite a lot of effort. Indeed, he's got a special pen where he prepares the birds for showing. 'Naturally, some of them are a little bit on the wild side and you don't want to send them to a show like that because the judges just wouldn't waste any time on them, so you need to tame them a bit. It might take a bit of time – you can't do it in a day – but I just talk to them, tickle them under the chin a bit and so on, and get them to face the front of the pen. After a bit, you achieve your object. It's surprising how steady they are, and they very soon adapt themselves. On the day, we like to get them to the show a few hours before the judging starts, so they have time to settle themselves down, and they're not there long, the male birds, before they're crowing to the ones in the opposite pens!'

It could be that they know they look their best, because Burt will have spent hours sprucing them up – feathers all washed, the deep yellow pigment on the inside of their legs clean and bright, their beaks polished. 'A friend of mine over at Uckfield, when he used to show his game, always gave them a spot of gin on a sponge – not to drink but to bring their combs and lobes up a nice bright red!'

Pets' cemetery at Rawtenstall, Lancashire

If you want to see British animal-lovers at their most sentimental, you need look no further than the small Lancashire town of Rawtenstall. There you'll find the Pets' Cemetery, with its rows of neat headstones with inscriptions like 'Timmy Our faithful big fellow. Sadly, missed', 'Wee Mandy. Mum's little treasure', and 'Danny. God bless our little Yorkie. Aged 13 years'. It's run by Ernie Holt, who with his wife Jan also runs the Sunnybank Boarding Kennels and Cattery. Apart from dogs, Ernie told us, almost every kind of domestic pet is buried there, 'Cats, dogs, rabbits, ponies, two monkeys. . . . There is a special plot for budgies, where I think there are five budgies buried all together with little headstones.' The Holts decided to start the Pets' Cemetery some years ago because they felt that there was a real need among pet-owners. 'Some animals which are left with the vet after they've been put down', Ernie said, 'are collected from the practice by skin merchants, and the skins exported.' Some vets have their own facilities for disposing of dead animals, and in some areas the local authority will take responsibility for them, but for those owners who want to give their pet a send-off with the personal touch, the Holts offer the full works – a Chapel of Rest, coffins of polished oak lined with silk, and a funeral service conducted by one of three ministers happy to oblige.

Naturally all this does not come cheap. 'Unfortunately, the cost is rather high,' Ernie admitted, 'because of the cost of labour involved. The only thing that varies is the cost of the casket, which could be anything from £100 to £150,

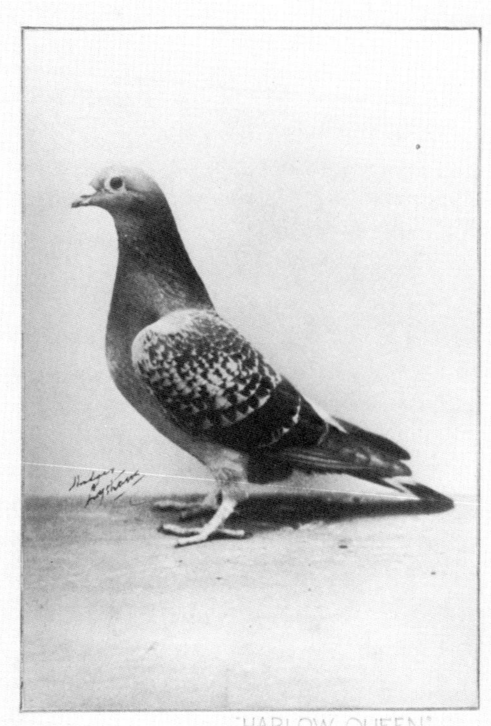

A champion pigeon.

It looks like an ordinary cemetery, but the names read Pippa, Sabra, Lady, Sherry. . . .

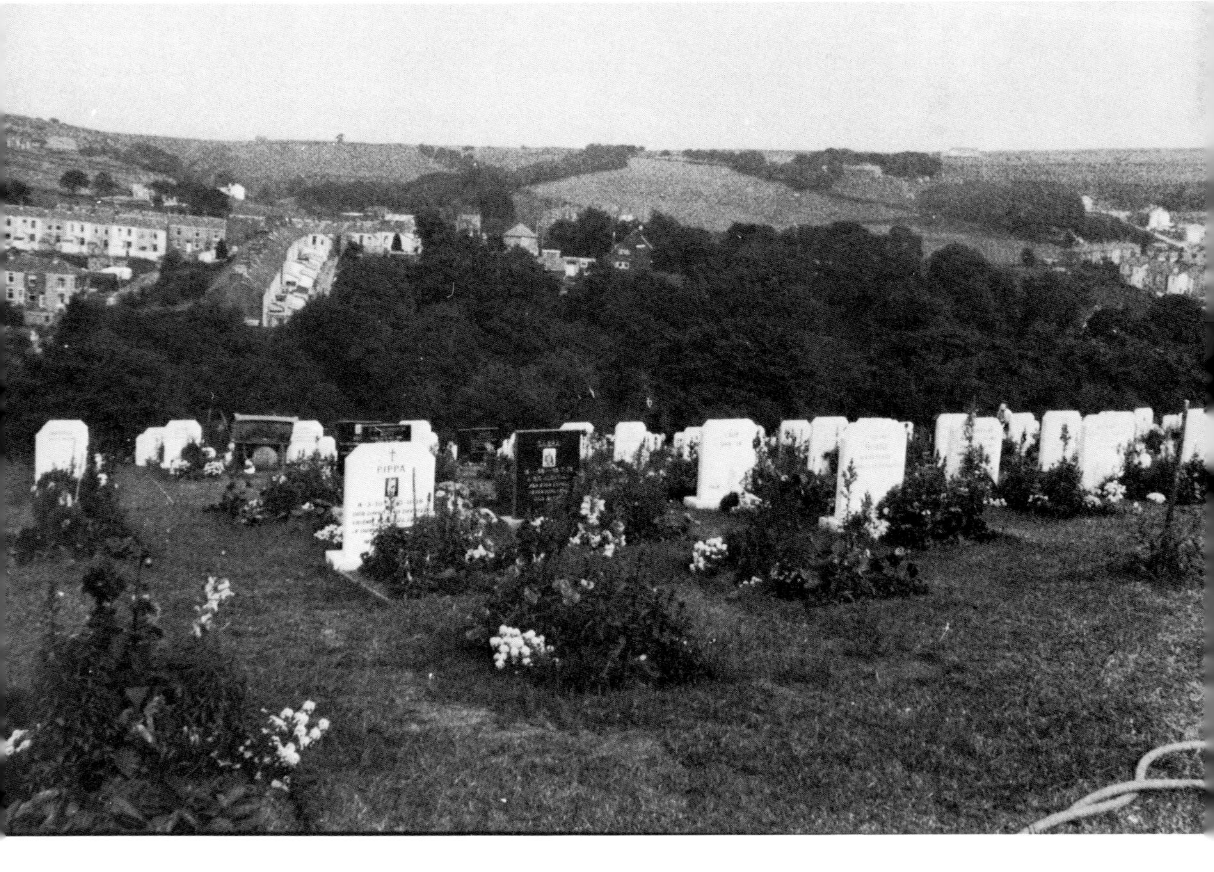

depending on its size. That also includes the maintenance charge for the first twelve months and, of course, all the plants and bulbs for the grave.'

But most people who have a pet buried in the cemetery prefer to look after the grave themselves. 'They come on a very regular basis – on Saturdays and Sundays we're packed out. We've had to extend the car park!'

To meet public demand, the Holts have also built a pets' crematorium at a cost of £30,000, having mortgaged their house and invested all their savings to do it. 'For a start, we laid on a service specifically for the veterinary profession at a cost of £4.60, and we can just break even at that cost. For that particular price, people will understand, more than one animal is cremated at one time – possibly three or four – and while the remains are mingled, they are spread in the garden of remembrance.

'I'm sure that there are an awful lot of animal-lovers in this country that get some sort of satisfaction and peace of mind out of knowing that the body of their pet is handled with some dignity.' The crematorium does individual cremations, too. 'The cost of that, unfortunately, is about £35, and that includes the preservation of the remains in a solid oak casket with an inscribed plate, which can either be taken away or returned via the vet, sent direct by post to the owner, or buried in a private plot in the cemetery.'

In Very Good Taste

Fine food and drink –
and those who make it

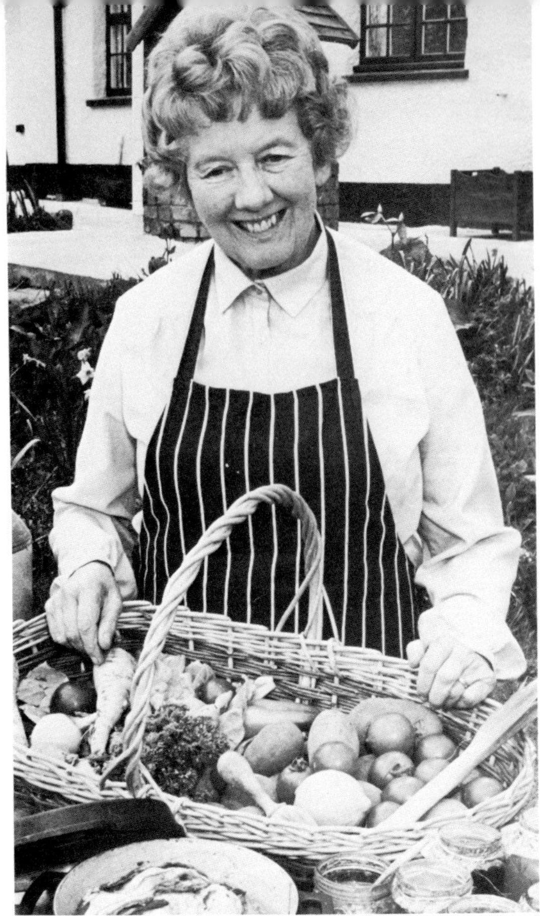

Queenie Newcombe, an expert cook and cookery writer herself, still comes across new local recipes all the time.

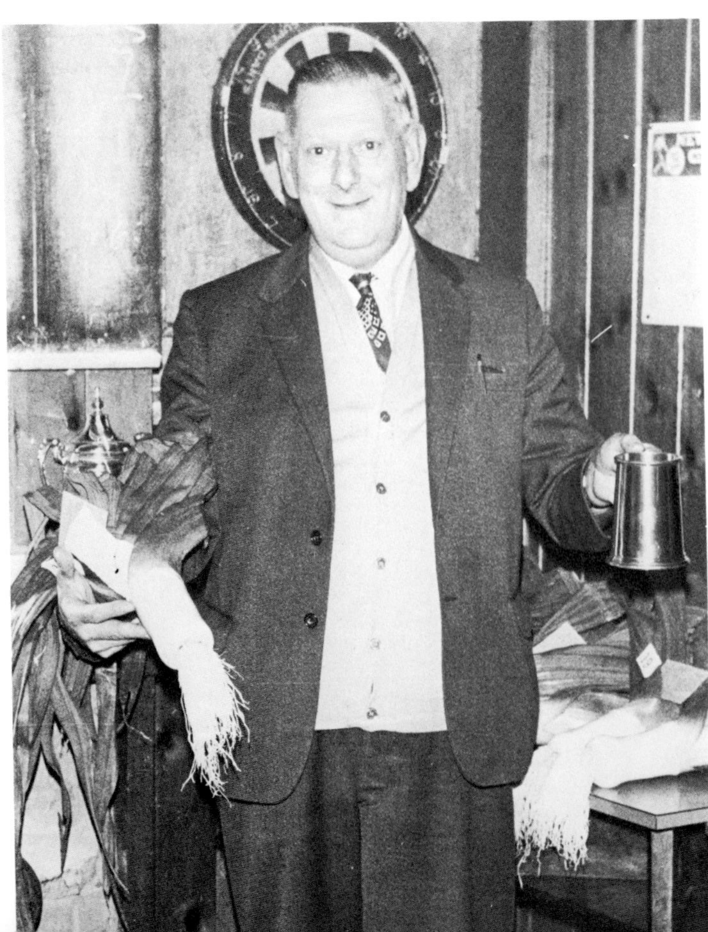

Syd Beadle of Alston with his prize-winning leek and the tankard it won him.

A honey farm at South Molton, Devon

You can eat and drink as well in Britain as you can anywhere in the world. That may sound like a rash statement, since the people who praise French and Italian food to the skies would dismiss our own native fare as 'plain' by comparison. What they are forgetting, though, is the reason for its plainness – our basic raw ingredients are so good that they don't need heavy seasoning or rich, elaborate sauces to make them palatable. Naturally if you want the best of British you have to know where to look, and it isn't in motorway cafés, fast food chains, or pretentious, overpriced restaurants run by licensed bandits in chefs' hats! It is in precisely those small towns and villages which the *Down Your Way* team visits all the time that you will find delicious regional dishes and people dedicated to producing the finest food and drink.

Take the Wallace family – father, mother and two sons – who run Quince Honey Farm from what used to be the old workhouse in South Molton, a pretty North Devon village on the edge of Exmoor. With fifteen hundred hives, each containing up to eighty thousand bees and producing, in a good year, an astonishing seventy tons of honey, it is the biggest bee farm in Britain. On the day of our visit, though, there wasn't a bee in sight. Paddy Wallace, the elder son of the family, explained why. 'The hives are all out on pieces of ground that we rent from farmers in sites we call apiaries – sixty to sixty-five sites with twenty to twenty-five hives on each.'

Everyone knows that bees make honey, but we, at least, didn't really know how, so Paddy explained. 'Flowers attract bees to themselves by secreting nectar, a sweet substance which the bees then eat, and produce honey by disgorging the nectar into the cells of the comb back at the hive. It's then ripened by bees lining up underneath the comb and fanning their wings, causing a draught to flow over the comb, which draws the water off the nectar. The bees also collect pollen for themselves. They clean it off their bodies and put it in sacs on their back legs – the pollen sacs. They then take it back to the hive and feed the larvae with it. It's the sole source of protein for a bee!'

Quince Honey Farm is now open to the public all year round. There aren't any guided tours, but there's plenty of information about bees and honey provided and you are free to wander round at will. You are also free to buy honey, and the Wallaces' bees produce two kinds – clover honey in June and July, and heather honey in August and September. Producing the different kinds isn't left to chance, though.

'We take the bees up to the moors in August. We move anything between seven hundred and a thousand hives to the heather – depending on how well the clover crop is going – especially for the heather crop.' It's planned like a military operation. Paddy and his helpers wait until all the bees have returned to the hives in the evening, then load the hives on to a Land Rover, drive them up to the moors and unload them. Then they come back for the next batch, and so on. It takes pretty well all night.

Before the loading begins Paddy puffs smoke from burning sacking or hemp binder twine into the entrance of each hive to keep the bees quiet during the move. Quite why smoke has that effect on bees he isn't sure. 'It could go back to when bees lived in the wild state in the forest. The theory is that when there was a forest fire the bees smelt smoke, and because of the danger to the colony rushed back to the nest, gorged themselves with honey in case the fire threatened them and they'd have to leave, so that they felt very contented and too full to move! Mind you, if I puffed smoke in your face, you'd be choking, your eyes would be watering and you'd be pretty disorientated, so I dare say it's the same for bees!' Perhaps the fact that it is hemp smoke means that it has the same effect on bees as the smoke from other related and illegal substances has on people? Paddy laughed. 'I don't think so – we inhale it all the time, and it doesn't do anything for us!'

But smoke or no smoke, if you are working with something like twelve million bees every day, chances are that you'll get stung – not because bees are by nature bad-tempered and hostile, but because, as Paddy said, bees will defend their homes against intruders, like all creatures, and from their point of view that's just what a honey farmer is. 'We get stung up to fifty times a day, every day, throughout the summer. We wear ordinary clothing, with overalls over the top, wellington boots, gauntlets and a veil, so this shows that bees really do mean business when they are being interfered with! We are immune to the venom, but you never become immune to the initial pain of the sting!'

As something of an expert on bee stings – albeit a reluctant one – Paddy offered this advice to anyone unlucky enough to be stung. 'There's a little venom sac on the end of the sting which you can see on the surface of your skin. This will go on pumping venom into your body for up to twenty minutes after you've been stung, unless you break it off. And you must break it off *away* from your skin and not squeeze it, because if you do squeeze it as you pull the sting out, you pump all the venom in in one go, and it is exceedingly painful!'

Squab, Parsley and Licky Pies at South Molton, Devon

If we needed any reminding about the positive side of bees, we certainly got it when we called on Queenie Newcombe, the well-known West Country television cook and cookery writer, who lives just down the road from Quince Honey Farm. She had baked a special honey cake for us, which was deliciously moist without being in the least bit sticky. Queenie was born in Barnstaple and has lived in South Molton for the last twenty-five years. Not surprisingly she has become something of an expert on local dishes with marvellous names like Squab Pie.

'That's made with lamb, tender lamb,' said Queenie, who sounds a little like Mrs Thatcher, 'and apple and onions, and it really goes back in history. Once I made it for some people and they said, "There's no pigeon in this!" I said, "No, of course not. It's made with lamb, apples and onions! If you look up 'squab' in the dictionary, though, you'll see that it means 'a young pigeon'. Never mind – we can't help that!" ' She laughed, 'It really is traditional here that it's made with lamb.'

Even though Queenie is acknowledged as a local expert, she still comes across new local dishes all the time. 'I met a farmer the other day, and he said, "Y'ere, my dear, how do you make parsley pie? My missus can't make it – 'er bin and gone and lost the recipe, or somethin'." But I have to admit that I didn't know how to make it, so I asked around because I know lots of farmers' wives, and they all said, "All parsley, my dear! a couple of fistfuls of chopped-up parsley, put it on some pastry, put some egg on it and some cream." So I did it, and it was absolutely marvellous – something you can cut in wedges and take for a packed lunch!'

Another great local favourite of Queenie's which is also ideal for a packed lunch is Licky Pie. 'Boil some leeks for about ten minutes, chop them up in inch-sized pieces, put them on some pastry, put on a bit of bacon, and some egg, cream, salt and pepper, then cover it with pastry and bake it. It's absolutely lovely!' (Queenie's recipe for honey cake can be found at the back of the book.)

The Leek Club at Alston, Cumbria

No doubt Percy Renwick, who used to be a lorry driver in the market town of Alston in Cumbria, would have enjoyed Licky Pie if he'd ever had the chance to try it! Percy is an expert on leeks – growing them rather than cooking them, though unlike many passionate growers of things edible, he isn't at all averse to eating them!

Percy was a founder member of the Alston Leek Club. Started back in 1968 as the result of a chat over a glass of beer one night, the club now has twenty-seven members, each paying a subscription of £5 a year. Alston's mountain climate – the town is often cut off by snow in winter – means that the vegetable crops are about six weeks later than average, so the Leek Club doesn't even try to produce the giants they produce in the north-east. 'Our maximum standard', Percy said, 'is six inches from the root bed to the fast button – the part of the leek that's been in the ground and has got blanched.'

At the annual show, on the first Saturday in October, each member has to show two leeks. 'The two together are measured and added up, and that gives you the cubic inches. Weight doesn't come into it at all. The winner this year was eight cubic inches, and it was quite a good show, I may say!'

Growing prize leeks is such a matter of pride and the competition so fierce that the club has to ensure that there is no skulduggery. 'Each member has a number, and the Secretary, accompanied by another committee member, goes round the members' gardens and stamps this number on his leeks.' To counteract any possible accusations of bias in the judging, the club always invites an outsider to judge the competition, and only he, two stewards and the Secretary are allowed inside the room while the judging is going on. First prize is £50 – well worth winning – but nobody goes away empty-handed because there are twenty-seven prizes in all, one for every competitor.

Orange-growing at Sawbridgeworth, Hertfordshire

You expect to find people growing leeks in Britain, particularly in the north, but you really don't expect to find someone growing oranges in Hertfordshire. But that is exactly what we found when we visited Rivers Nurseries in Sawbridgeworth, which lays claim to being the oldest nursery in England. According to Tim Nattrass, one of the firm's directors, it was founded in 1725 by his ancestor John Rivers, and while the family's interest in oranges doesn't go back quite that far, it certainly goes back a long way.

'I think it must have been in the middle of the last century,' Tim Nattrass said, 'because my great-great-grandfather, Thomas Rivers, was responsible for the introduction of oranges to California in 1876, one variety in particular, called Valencia Late.' When you consider the millions of acres of orange groves in the United States that sounds a little like taking coals to Newcastle, but, as Tim Nattrass pointed out, the local variety grown in Florida just wasn't suitable for the conditions in California.

These days, Rivers Nurseries concentrates on producing not citrus fruit, but citrus fruit trees – orange, lemon, satsuma, and even grapefruit. They're grown in a huge greenhouse which could easily double as a sauna, since the young trees need a temperature of between 75 and 80 degrees Fahrenheit, and high humidity, produced by overhead spraying. Producing the trees for sale is a complicated business, as Tim Nattrass explained. 'A lemon pip – an ordinary lemon pip – is allowed to grow to produce a tree which is getting on for four feet high. We then insert a bud from the variety we want to grow – let's say a satsuma – on the base of the stock. It is then covered in polythene, and kept in that state for about a year. Then once you see the bud starting to grow, you cut the top of the lemon tree off, and then you have a satsuma tree which carries on growing from the bud.'

Because it is such a long business you can't simply walk into the nursery and buy your grapefruit or satsuma tree 'off the peg' as it were. 'What we do is take orders throughout the year, and when they are ready to collect, we notify

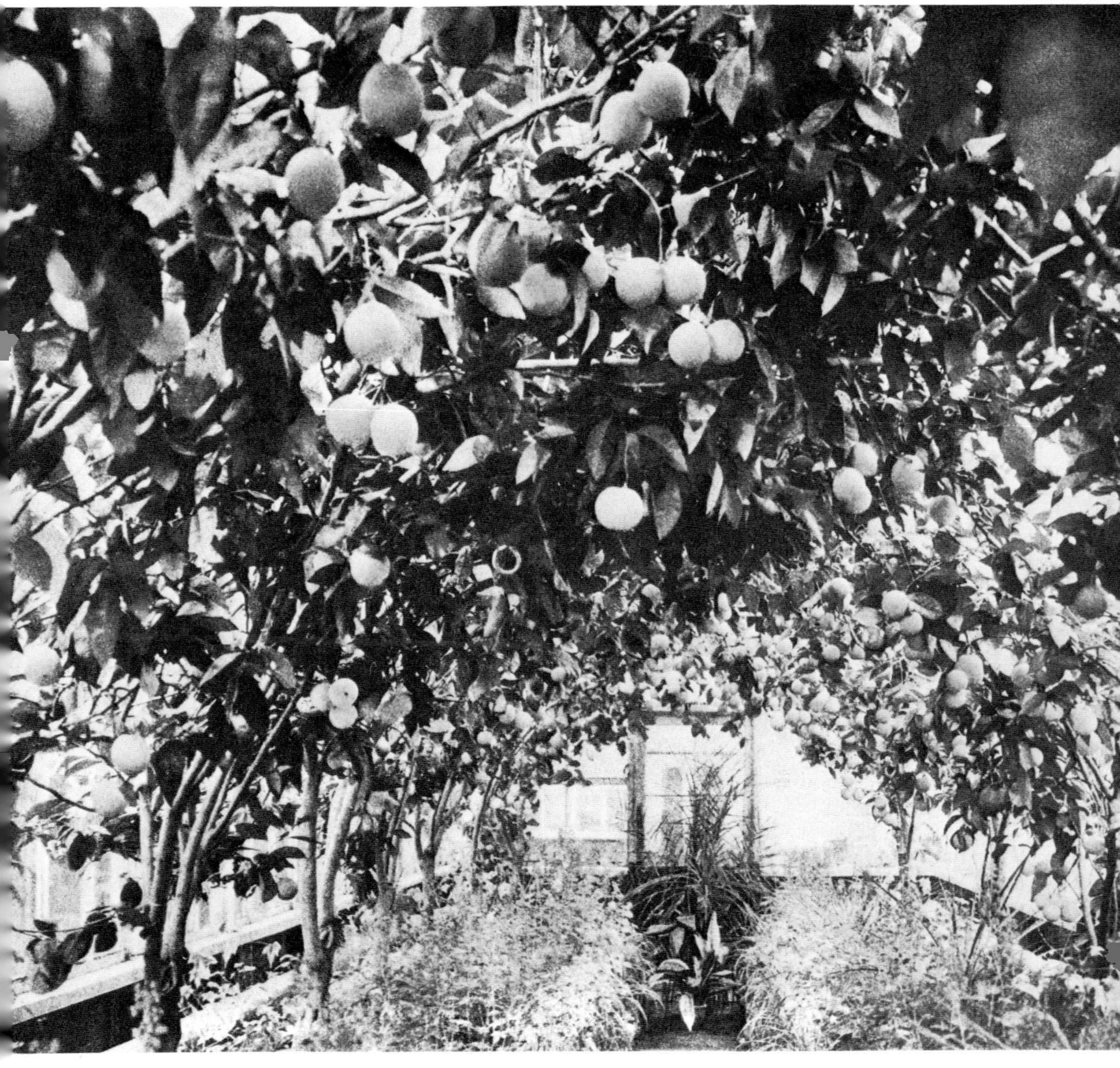

The orange house at Rivers Nurseries – an unexpected sight in the Home Counties.

the customers.' A two- to three-foot-high orange tree will cost about £13, and provided you give it the warmth, light and humidity it needs you can expect to pick your first fruit in about two years, and after about ten years the tree could bear up to a hundred fruit.

Jam-making at Tiptree, Essex

Most people would be thrilled with a crop of a hundred oranges, but to Peter Cook, sales director of Wilkin and Sons of Tiptree in Essex, it wouldn't – if you'll pardon the mixture of metaphors – add up to a row of beans. From January to March oranges from Seville arrive at the factory by the lorryload, to be turned into one of the ten varieties of marmalade which, along with the thirty-six different kinds of jam, have made the name 'Tiptree' synonymous all over the world with the finest preserves.

'It's always been my belief', Peter Cook told us, 'that our main competitor is the housewife who produces her own preserves. We make jam from sugar and fruit, too, but we do have advantages over her in that, with our steam-cooking facilities, we can cook the fruit much more quickly, and thus retain a greater degree of flavour!'

Wilkin and Sons began making jam at Tiptree nearly a hundred years ago, almost as a by-product. The family was primarily involved in fruit-growing and was looking for an outlet for the fruit they couldn't sell anywhere else. In the early days most of the jam was sold direct to customers, and very little was sold through the shops. In the office files you can still see letters from the crowned heads of Europe, the Empress of Russia for example, and the Queen of Spain who in 1912 ordered 'three dozen raspberry, three dozen strawberry (large strawberry), two dozen marmalade, two dozen blackberry with apple slices, one dozen apple jelly and one dozen golden gage'. In 1914 the company received a letter from the housekeeper to the Queen of Greece placing an order for several dozen pots of jam and conserve. She ends her letter plaintively, conjuring up a marvellous picture of monarchs growing faint for lack of Wilkin and Sons' delicious products. 'Could you please send two parcels of Strawberry Conserve by post, and the rest by rail, but please post everything immediately. It is such a long time till the boxes arrive here.' 'In those days,' Peter Cook said, 'the typical customer could be found in *Debrett's* or *Crockford's Clerical Directory*. But nowadays we sell totally through the trade, with no direct supplies at all.'

They still grow as much of their own fruit as possible, on the eleven hundred acres they farm – strawberries, raspberries, damsons, cherries – but the pride of the factory is the 'Little Scarlet Strawberry' made from specially grown, tiny strawberries the size of an old sixpence. 'That's the top of the tree, undoubtedly!'

Picking the fruit presents Peter Cook and his colleagues with a major problem.

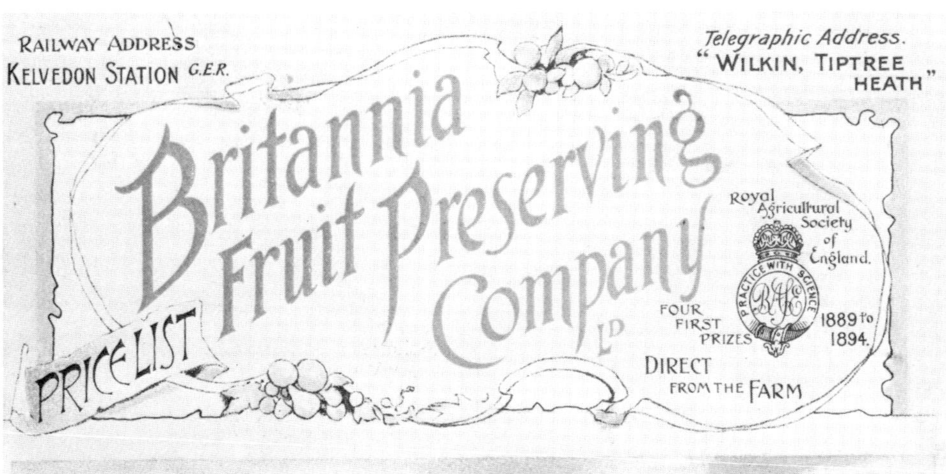

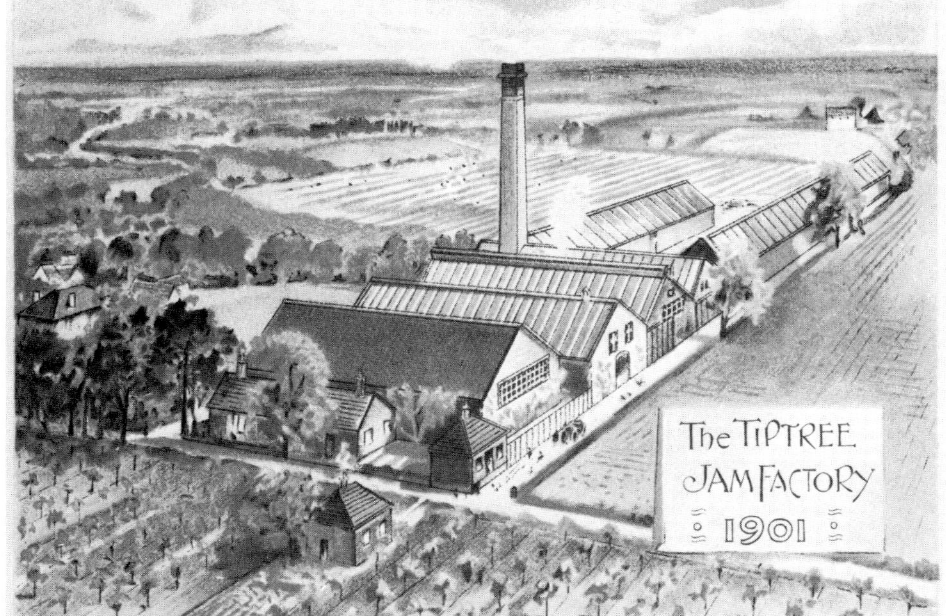

TIPTREE FRUIT FARM Nr KELVEDON, ESSEX.

"No foreign gums, nor essence fetched from far,
No volatile spirits, nor compounds that are
Adulterate; but at Nature's cheap expense,
With far more genuine sweets refresh the sense."
—*Carew.*

This Price List is issued annually and is intended as a general guide to the Standard Preserves prepared by the Company. The Stock may in some cases be exhausted as the season advances. For the latest information reference should be made to the Monthly "Order Form."

Sir Joseph Causton & Sons Limited. Printers London

Wilkin and Sons have been making jam at Tiptree for almost a hundred years. This is an illustration from a price-list printed at the turn of the century.

'To overcome this partially, we have opened a student camp to which we draw students from all over the world, who stay for a period of weeks. In addition we have a caravan site, which is approved by the Caravan Club of Great Britain. People can bring their caravans along, and provided they are prepared to give an undertaking to work at least thirty hours (a total of thirty hours from the occupants of each van, so if there are three of you, that means you only have to do ten hours each) they have all the facilities of the site free. And of course, they are paid on a piece-work basis for the amount of fruit they pick!'

Canning at Wisbech, Cambridgeshire

Moving north from Tiptree into East Anglia proper, you find yourself in the heart of strawberry country – not so much the strawberries we buy in punnets for eating as those that wind up in jam, or in supermarket frozen food cabinets, or in tins. Of course it's not just strawberries that they grow around Wisbech, in the north of Cambridgeshire. They grow all kinds of fruit and vegetables too, so it's not surprising to find one of the largest canning firms in the country, Smedley's, on the outskirts of the town.

One of their best-known products are tinned peas, and as we learnt from David Hipwood, Smedley's deputy general manager, the time they are harvested is absolutely crucial. 'We have very close co-operation between the grower and our staff who go out and inspect the field prior to harvesting, because we have to harvest them at exactly the right "tendrometer" reading.' Although it sounds like something Ken Dodd might have invented, the 'tendrometer' measures the tenderness of the peas, and when it's exactly right the huge mobile harvesters swing into action, picking and de-podding the peas all in one go. 'Then they're rushed here,' David Hipwood said, 'and in fact our aim is to have them canned within two or three hours.' As fresh as the moment when the pod went pop, you could say – if only someone else in the pea business hadn't got there first!

The fruit canning business has a language all its own, and we had to ask David Hipwood to translate words like 'seaming', 'plugging', 'snibbing' and 'strigging' for our benefit! ' "Seaming",' David said, 'is what happens to the can after the fruit and syrup have been poured in. The top is then put on to the open can and sealed – that's seaming. It then goes to be processed – put into a retort and cooked for about twelve or fourteen minutes. From there the can goes into a case and then out to be sold to the public.' Although 'plugging' sounds like something out of a James Cagney gangster movie, it is, in fact, what happens to strawberries after they've been picked – the calyx, the white part attached to the stalk inside the berry, is removed. Gooseberries aren't 'plugged' – they're 'snibbed', what we'd called 'topped and tailed'. A very tedious chore it is too, but naturally they don't do it by hand at Smedley's. They have a machine that does it for them, David Hipwood told us, which also pricks the skin so that the fruit doesn't collapse during cooking. And yes – any especially hairy gooseberries are also shaved first! Probably the most difficult fruit to handle is the black currant, so the fruit is frozen before it is 'strigged' – stripped from the stalk. 'If you try and strig the fruit in its natural state it gets very badly damaged, so we have to freeze it first.'

Beanjar on Guernsey

The Channel Island of Guernsey has more than its fair share of indigenous words, but then that is only to be expected. Although it's only thirty miles from the French coast in the bay of St Malo, it is part of the British Isles, having chosen loyalty to the English crown in the time of William the Conqueror. Its Norman ancestry is still very much in evidence today though, in its culture, in the Guernsey-French *patois* many of the older islanders still speak, and in its cuisine. Who better to talk about native Guernsey dishes than Mrs Marie De Garis, a member of a very old island family who has compiled an English-Guernsey-French dictionary.

Although 'gosh' may sound like something from an old girls' reunion than a dish, it is in fact one of the island's specialities. '"Gosh" is a kind of cake made with plain flour, and half its weight in butter, and either sultanas or currants, yeast – one ounce to a pound and a half of flour – plus some nutmeg and salt. And also, any kind of pastry is called "gosh". Apple tarts or rhubarb tarts are "*gosh à pommes*" or "*gosh à rhubarb*". For those with a more savoury tooth there's a marvellous traditional dish – a sort of *cassoulet* – called "Beanjar".

'It's made with haricot beans, and a pig's trotter or a piece of beef, with dried herbs and onions, and some people put in carrots. The beans are soaked overnight, and then placed in a stone or earthenware jar, covered with water, brought to the boil, and then cooked in a slow oven for five to eight hours. It you forget it for an hour or two it doesn't matter! In the old days it used to be made on a Saturday evening, and taken to the baker's to put in their oven and fetched on a Sunday morning for breakfast. Nowadays people eat it at any time!' (This recipe can be found at the back of the book.)

Groaty Dick and Fillbelly at Dudley, West Midlands

Although the words 'Groaty Dick' wouldn't mean much to Marie De Garis, she would certainly recognize the dish they describe. We tasted it in, of all places, a museum – the Black Country Museum at Dudley in the West Midlands, which is devoted to the life and industrial history of the region. Majorie Cashmore, the museum's secretary, demonstrates for visitors how they used to cook in the old days, wearing the long black dress and big white apron that most women wore, and using an old black range.

'Groaty Dick or Groaty Pudding is a very substantial casserole meal, made from shin of beef, onions, leeks and, of course, groats, which are a cereal – oats before the husk has been hulled off. In poor families any cheaper cut of meat or even bacon pieces would have gone into a dish of this kind, and it's the sort of food that can be left simmering in the oven or on the hob all day while the members of the family went out to make chain or nails or whatever.'

After you'd eaten your Groaty Dick, you could round your meal off with a hunk of Fillbelly, the local name for bread pudding. 'Most people found it hard to make a living, and they couldn't afford to waste anything at all, so if there was any bread left at the end of the week this would be made into a bread pudding, which consists of soaked stale bread, to which is added sugar, suet, dried fruit and eggs and, of course, mixed spice. This makes a very nutritious meal!' (Marjorie's recipes can be found at the back of the book.)

Cheese-making at Malpas, Cheshire

To round off a meal, many people would happily trade the pudding for a first-rate piece of cheese – some Cheshire, perhaps, that Mrs Helen Barnett makes at Overton Hall, just outside the attractive and historic town of Malpas in Cheshire. Overton Hall itself is a beautiful old black and white, timbered farmhouse, part of which dates back to pre-Tudor times. During the Civil War it was plundered by Cromwell's supporters, but the house took its revenge. 'In 1656,' Mrs Barnett told us, 'after Cromwell had taken over the whole of Cheshire, he appointed a Major General to rig the county election. The High Sherriff and the Justice came to Overton Hall to plan their opposition, and stayed three days. And their opposition was successful.'

The present-day Overton Hall is a busy, working mixed farm, and Helen Barnett's domain is the dairy where along with two helpers, she produces a hundred cheeses a week. 'There are three types of Cheshire cheese – white, red and the blue, which is only made at one farm, so it's unique. We make the traditional, red Cheshire. The red is added to the cheese in the form of anatto, which is a vegetable dye. This is the only difference. We think it's a better flavour, but that's only an illusion!'

There are twenty other farms making genuine Cheshire cheese, either in Cheshire itself or in neighbouring Shropshire, which has the same lush grazing. Not surprisingly, Helen Barnett thinks that Cheshire is one of the finest English cheeses there is. 'It's got a nutty flavour and an open texture. It's quick-maturing, too, compared with Cheddar. You can eat it in a month to eight weeks, when

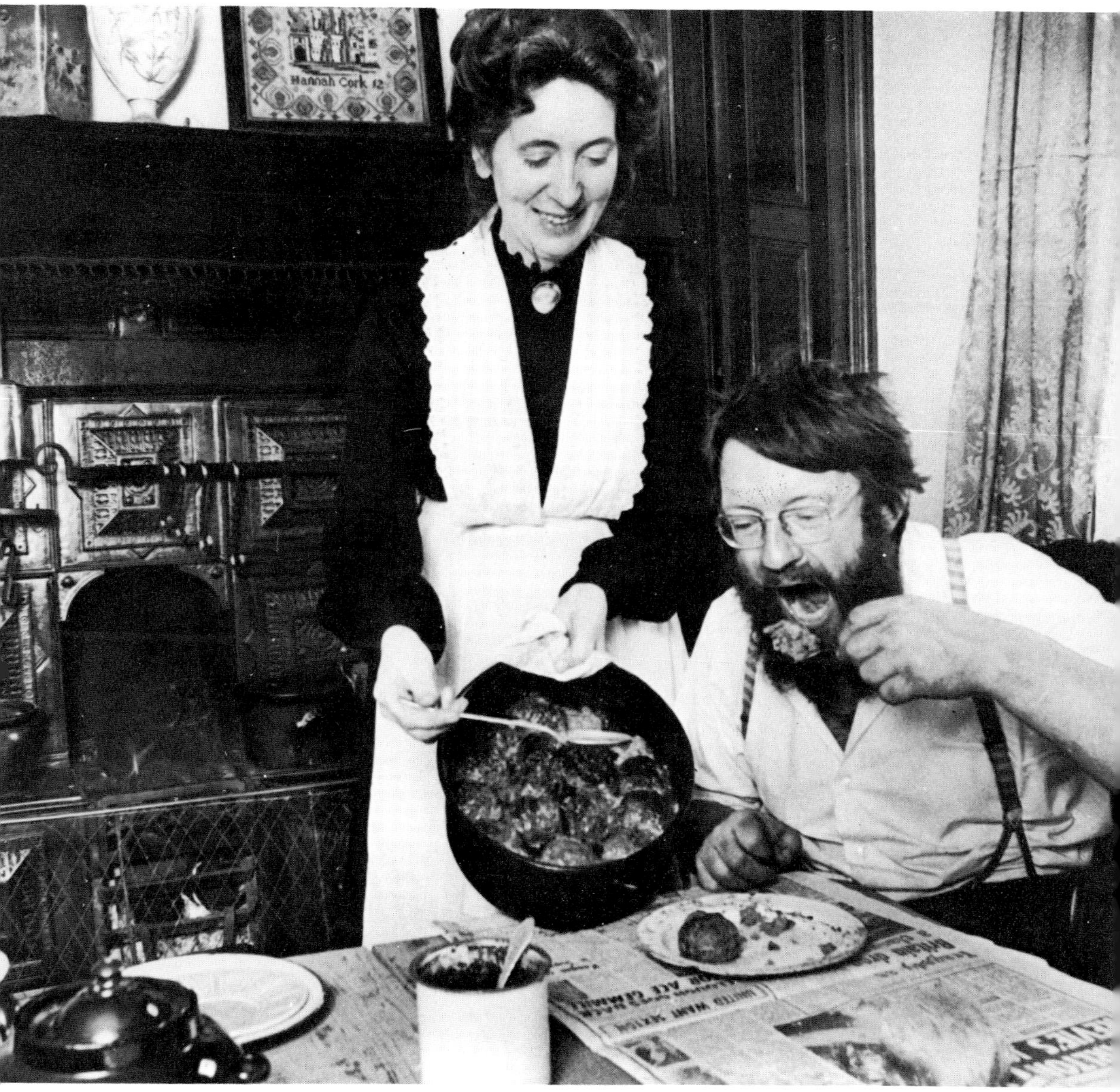

A traditional scene in the Black Country Museum at Dudley. Marjorie Cashmore has an eager customer for her faggots.

it is supposed to be at its best, but if you have truly good taste you can eat it at eight or nine months, when it is mellow and mature.'

The milk from which the cheese is made comes from the farm's herd of champion Friesians. It's put into a large vat, and then lactic acid cultures are added to it. 'It then coagulates and is cut up with automatic cutters. It is then stirred, cooked, and run off into a drainer, where the whey separates and goes to the pigs and the curds remain. They are ground up and put into a vat which is pressed to mould the cheese. It then goes through, and as soon as it is dry it is waxed and taken down to the store-room which is kept at a temperature of 48–50 degrees.'

Toffee-making at Moffat, Dumfriesshire

Moffat, Dumfriesshire, in border country, is a popular holiday centre, what with one of Scotland's highest waterfalls, the Grey Mare's Tail, and the spectacular Devil's Beef Tub – a natural hiding-place in days gone by for cattle stolen on cross-border raids – within easy reach. The heroes of the town, all buried in the kirkyard, were John Loudon McAdam, inventor of Macadamized roads, and McGeorge and Goodfellow, the two Post Office men who perished in the great snowstorm of 1831 while trying to get the mail through from Moffat to Edinburgh.

The town's heroine – to the local children and any visitors with a sweet tooth at least – is Elizabeth Blacklock, who began making the now-famous Moffat toffee in a tiny factory just off the High Street over a hundred years ago. You can't miss the factory – all you have to do is follow your nose, although Blair Blacklock, the great-grandson of the founder, who runs the factory today, claims to be immune to the sweet, sticky smell! 'Except when it's burning – which it shouldn't be!'

Blair came into the business twenty years ago as a boy, and knows all the tricks of the trade. 'The toffee is made from brown sugar, white sugar and glucose – a bucket of each. You just throw it in. It's been done so often now that we just throw it in!' There is a secret ingredient, but not even wild horses or Brian Johnston's charm could make him reveal what it was! The whole gooey mass is then boiled up to a temperature of 300 degrees Fahrenheit, then turned out on to a special table and left to cool until it becomes more workable. It then goes into the pulling machine which stretches it out, like plasticine, to improve its texture and to make it crunchy. The machine is a relatively new acquisition. 'I used to do it by hand when I was young and fit,' Blair said with a smile, 'rather like chest expanders!'

After it's been pulled, the toffee goes into another machine and comes out the other end in a thin rope which is then chopped up into small pieces. The still

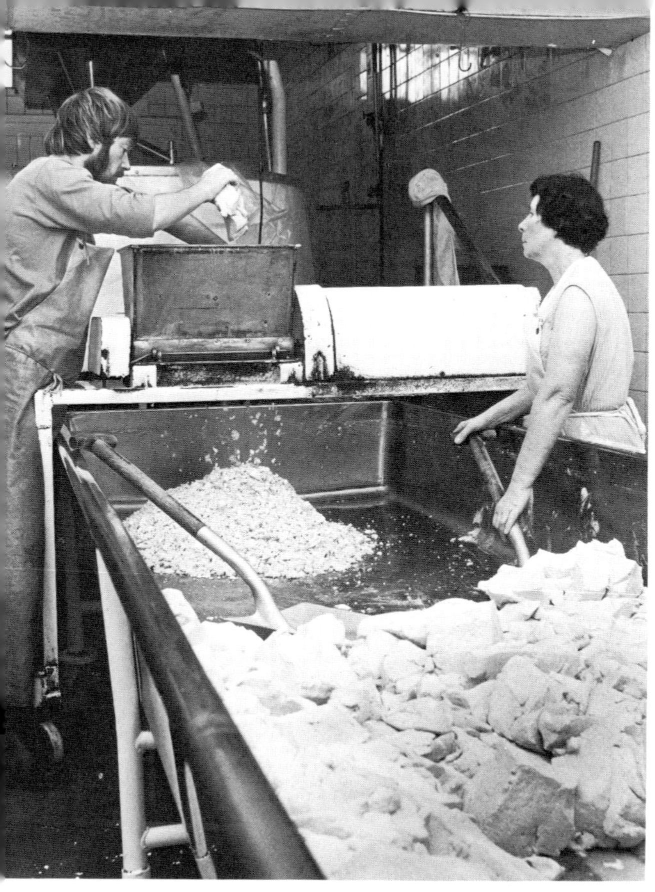

At Overton Hall the traditional red Cheshire cheese is made.
Above: The curds are ground up.
Below: The finished product.

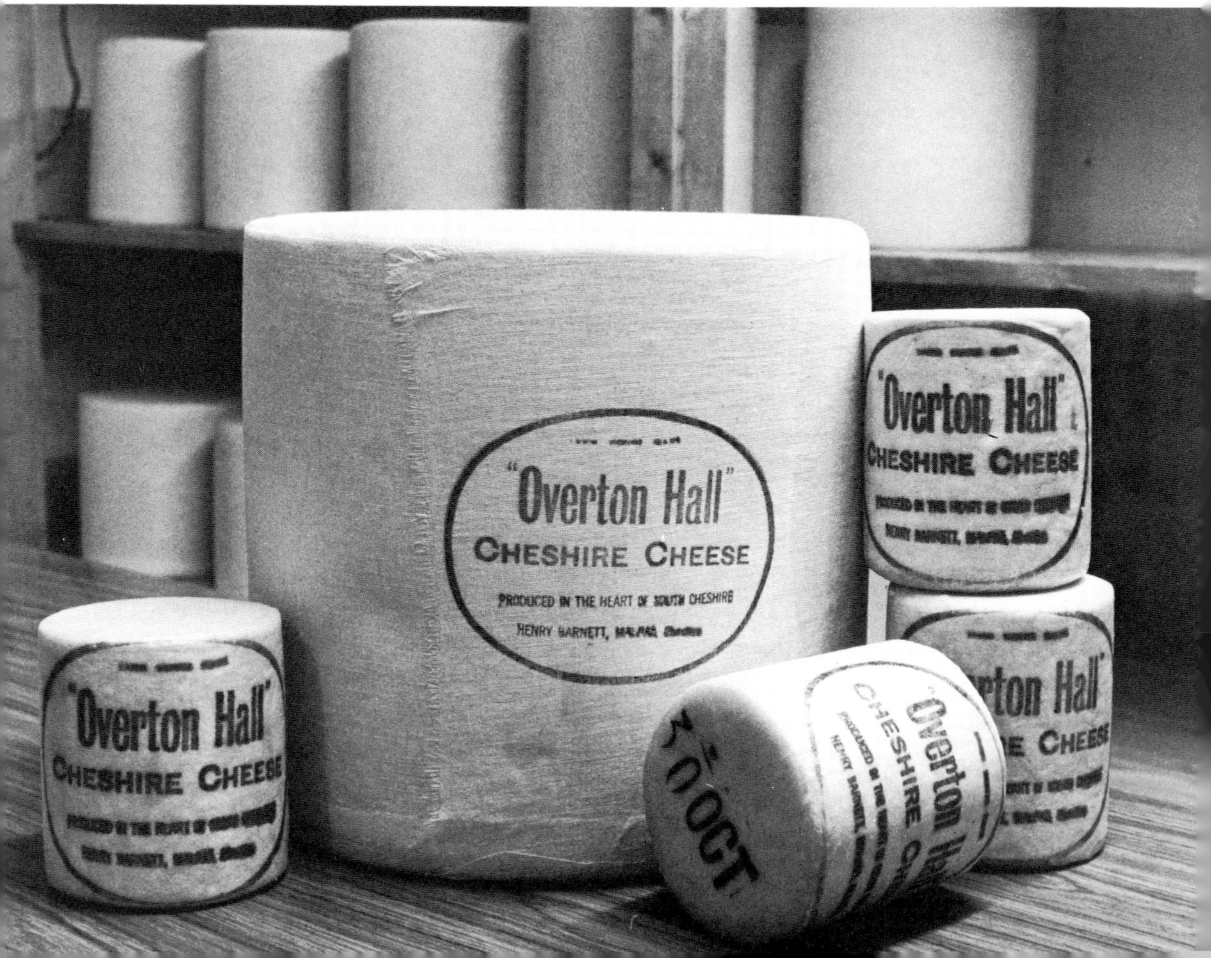

soft pieces are then flattened a little before going into the air tunnel to cool and harden. The factory, with its staff of six, turns out about four hundred pounds of toffee a day, most of which is sold from their own shop in the High Street. 'But then we also send it abroad to all the exiled Scots who long for it during their Christmas break!'

Having exercised our jaws on a piece of Moffat toffee, we asked Blair Blacklock how many he thought people could eat in a day. Like the good salesman he is, he replied cheerfully, 'Oh, pounds!'

Shortbread and whisky at Campbeltown, Argyllshire

Think of good, wholesome Scottish food, and bannocks, oatcakes and shortbread must come pretty close to the top of your list. They are exactly what Campbell McIlchere makes in his bakery in Campbeltown, the main town on the beautiful Kintyre peninsula on the west coast of Scotland, and exports in quantity all over the world. It's a family business, founded in 1906 when Campbell's grandfather set up a small grocery business in Campbeltown.

'My father carried on in his footsteps, and then I came into the grocery side of the business in 1959. My side of the business had obvious limitations, and we branched out into the bakery side – "we" being my brother and myself. We started off by buying in cake bases, and filling them with local produce, like the cream produced on the farms in the peninsula of Kintyre.'

But after a couple of years Campbell McIlchere decided to expand, still keeping it in the family. 'I had a chat with an aunt of mine, and asked her for a loan of £400 to buy my first oven. That was back in 1965. The small bakery partnership grew, and in 1970 we approached the Highlands and Islands Development Board and presented them with a proposition to build premises in Campbeltown and develop a bakery business there. When we set out we were employing two girls, and our first order to our flour supplier was for one seventy-pound bag. Now we are employing eighty people and the flour comes in in ten-ton loads!'

The bakery's best-known lines are oatcakes, bannocks – a sweet oatcake – and shortbread – not to be confused with shortcake. 'Shortcake is more of a biscuit,' Campbell said, 'and shortbread.... Well, let's say that shortbread is made in Scotland, and shortcake is made in England! The basic recipe for shortbread is simply three ingredients – butter, flour and sugar. Without giving away any trade secrets, if you take four parts flour, two parts butter and one part sugar, put them all together, mould them and bake them in a moderate oven for approximately twenty minutes, you should produce a very attractive and tasty piece of shortbread!'

You can, of course, eat your shortbread with a nice cup of tea, but Campbell

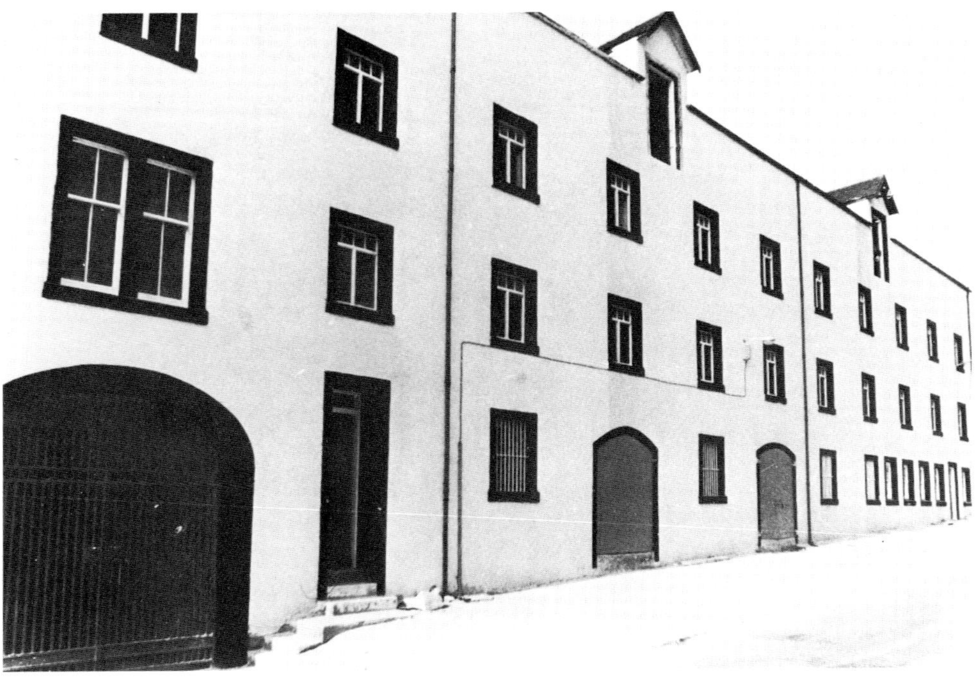

The Glen Scotia distillery in Campbeltown. The water they use to make the whisky comes from a local loch.

There are few sights more English than a Kentish oast-house.

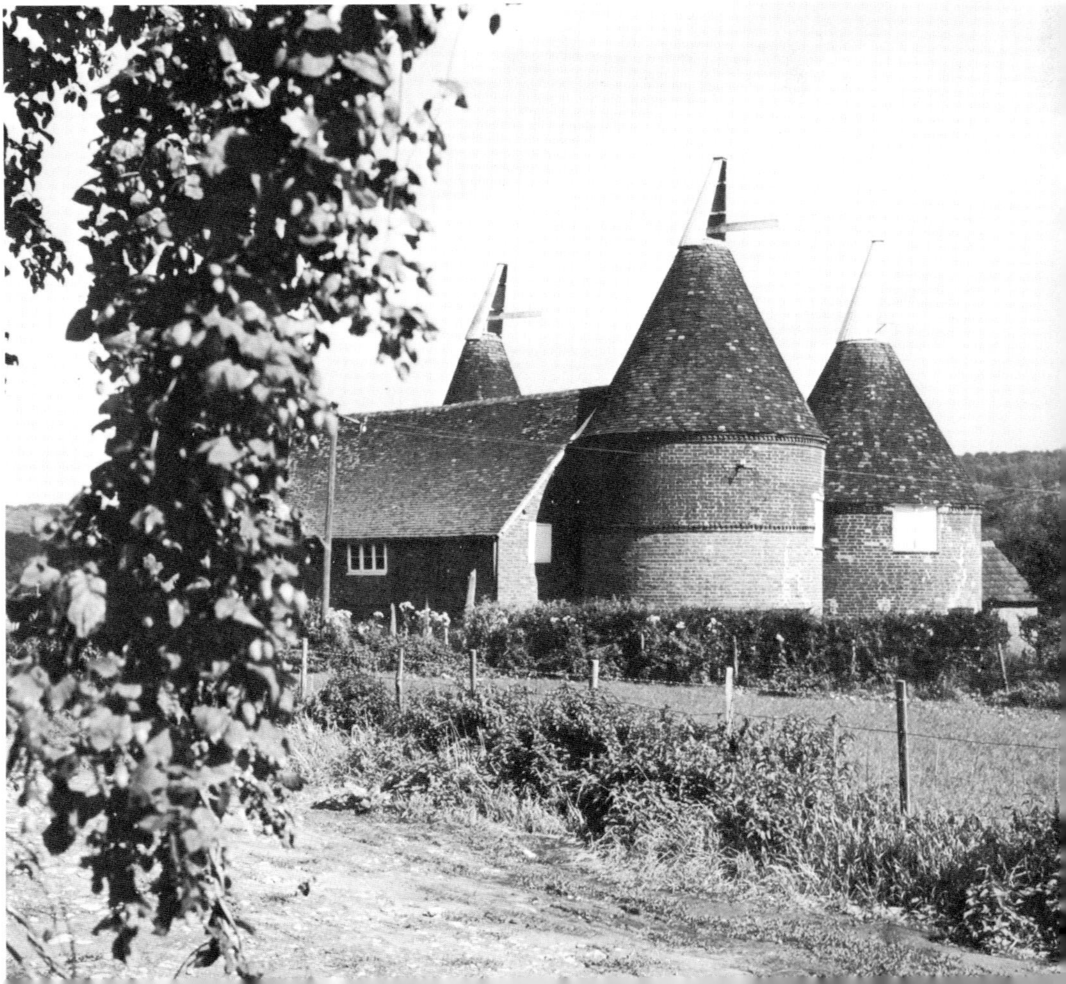

McIlchere has a more interesting suggestion. 'Whisky complements shortbread. I suppose it goes back to the old days when whisky and shortbread were – and maybe still are – the staple diet of the Scotsman!'

As luck would have it, we didn't have to travel far to find the whisky, since there are two distilleries in Campbeltown. We visited the Glen Scotia distillery, whose precise origins are somewhat shrouded in the mists of time. 'Officially, we were founded in 1835,' said the manager, Mike Smith, who is one hundred per cent Scots, despite his name, 'but who knows how old before that? It took a wee while for the customs people to find us! We are rather detached!'

Making whisky is a complicated business, but Mike Smith tried to explain the process as simply as he could. 'We take barley, and we let it soak up a certain amount of water, and spread it out on the floors – the traditional method! We let it germinate, and after a certain period of time we then kiln-dry it, using peat and other fuels. This makes it possible to extract the sugar at a later stage in the process. We then extract these sugars, and put them into fermenting tanks. We convert the sugar to alcohol with the use of yeast, and then we start the distillation. The first distillation is purely a run-through to reduce the amount of water, and increase the amount of alcohol present in the liquid. We then boil this liquid up and take a "choice cut" – just like a sirloin steak – out of the middle. We call this "plain British spirits". We then mature it in wooden barrels – oak, in fact – and during the maturation it slowly assumes this beautiful, golden corn colour.'

The whisky has to stay in the barrels for a minimum of three years, though in many cases it stays much longer than that. 'It's not so long that we put out a whisky that was 1937 – that was obviously for a very de luxe blend, and it tasted superb! But it's impossible to say how long whisky should mature because some mature more quickly than others, and quite honestly if I tried to say "Ten years" or "Fifteen years" other people in my position would equally quickly say, "Well, mine takes eighteen years, or nine years." But I don't know too many whiskies which mature before twelve years – to perfection, that is!'

The water they use at Glen Scotia comes from a local loch, Loch Crosshill, and it's completely untreated. But Mike Smith doesn't think that it's the water which gives each whisky its individual flavour. 'The shape of your stills does contribute a tremendous amount to the actual character of the end product. Malt whisky is made in pot stills, and they all have different types of construction. We have our own, and should we have to replace it, then it'll be identical – or as near as possible to identical!'

Hop-growing at Tenbury Wells, Hereford and Worcester

Many beer-drinkers would argue that the brewing of their favourite tipple is an equally delicate and subtle process, though not such a lengthy one. We started our look at brewing in the market town of Tenbury Wells, close to the border of the counties of Hereford and Worcester, and of Shropshire. This little town was described by Queen Victoria as 'my lovely town in the orchard', and the 'Wells' part of its name refers to the saline spring discovered in 1859, but though a pump room was built, spas were already going out of fashion and today the town is known for its fruit-growing, its mistletoe and holly sales each Christmas, and, of course, its hops.

About a mile outside the town, in the village of Carwood, above the Teme valley, we met Humphrey Nott, who is a hop farmer, and asked him why Kent and Hereford and Worcester are such good hop-growing areas. The answer, he said, in so many words, lies in the soil!

Though Humphrey is a hop farmer, he only devotes to hops forty-two acres from a total of three hundred and fifty. 'It *is* a small percentage, but hop-growing is very intensive and very time- and labour-consuming, and if we are going to go any bigger we have got to more or less double the size because we need twice the amount of equipment to cope with it.'

It is crucial, as it is with peas in Wisbech, to harvest the hops at exactly the right moment. 'The date of picking is very tricky to estimate – it all depends on the weather, the way they feel, what the climate is doing. It's a thing you learn – something you are brought up with rather than something you're told.' Today all the hop-picking is done mechanically on Humphrey Nott's farm. 'I don't think there's a farm in the UK that picks by hand these days.'

Hop-picking at Goudhurst, Kent

Ninety-nine-year-old Mrs Kate Jones, or 'Aunt Kate' as she's known to everybody in the Kent village of Goudhurst, remembers very vividly the days when all the hops were picked by hand, and nobody even imagined that one day a machine would take over. 'You'd go out to start picking at seven in the morning. You'd carry on picking till they called out "Get your hops ready!" and then the man would come round and measure them up. We made up a song about it:

> When the measurer he comes around
> And bangs the basket on the ground,
> When he starts a-measuring, he don't know when to stop,
> Why don't he dump it in the bin and take the bloomin' lot!'

The name of Aunt Kate is so inextricably tied up with hops and Goudhurst that it seems only fitting somehow that the connection is now immortalized in the hop field next to the cottage at Three Chimneys Farm, where she lived until recently. 'It was empty for years, that field, and I helped clear it before the hops went in. When it was done, Mr Benton who had the hops growing there, said to me, "Aunt Kate, what did they call this field?" I said, "Oh Mr Benton, don't ask me now! I've forgotten." "I know," he said, "we'll call it 'Aunt Kate's field'!" I said "Oh no! They'll think somebody's died and left me a lot of money and I'm buying up all the hops!" But it's now christened "Aunt Kate's Field".'

Brewing at Donnington, Gloucestershire

It's not often that you hear people singing the praises of a brewery itself, rather than its product, but the Donnington Brewery near Stow-on-the-Wold, Gloucestershire, is an exception. Built from mellow Cotswold stone, it stands among trees beside a large, ornamental lake – the old mill pond – where you can see up to thirty different species of wildfowl. Like so many of the places we visit, it, too, is an old family business, founded in 1865 by Richard Arkell.

'In those days,' Claude Arkell, the current proprietor and grandson of the founder, told us, 'we actually grew the barley on the farm and malted it ourselves and converted it into beer. We ceased doing that about twenty years ago, but we still buy the malt locally from Cirencester.'

Although in the early days the brewery had no inns of its own, it now has seventeen, each one in a pretty Cotswold village within a fifteen-mile radius of the brewery, so that anyone with a taste for good beer who doesn't want to be accused of merely pub-crawling can always claim he's on a sight-seeing tour of the area!

Recently, as a result of the Campaign for Real Ale, there's been a growing demand for Donnington beer from free houses in the district, and so the brewery now exports as far afield as Stratford-on-Avon and Malvern. '"Real Ale" is, in fact, a misnomer,' Claude Arkell said. 'All ale is real ale if you like, but ours is brewed in the traditional manner, and is not processed at all. Every brewer uses malt, hops, and sugar and what have you, but we just use malted barley now, and hops, and at the moment we don't use any sugar at all. It all goes out in casks in a "live" condition. Then it's got to be nursed – the whole secret of the ultimate drink rests in the hands of the publicans. We like to think they can keep it a week to get the secondary fermentation going, and once they've tapped it, and started using it, it wants using probably within a week to ten days, and the conditions should be very good throughout that period.'

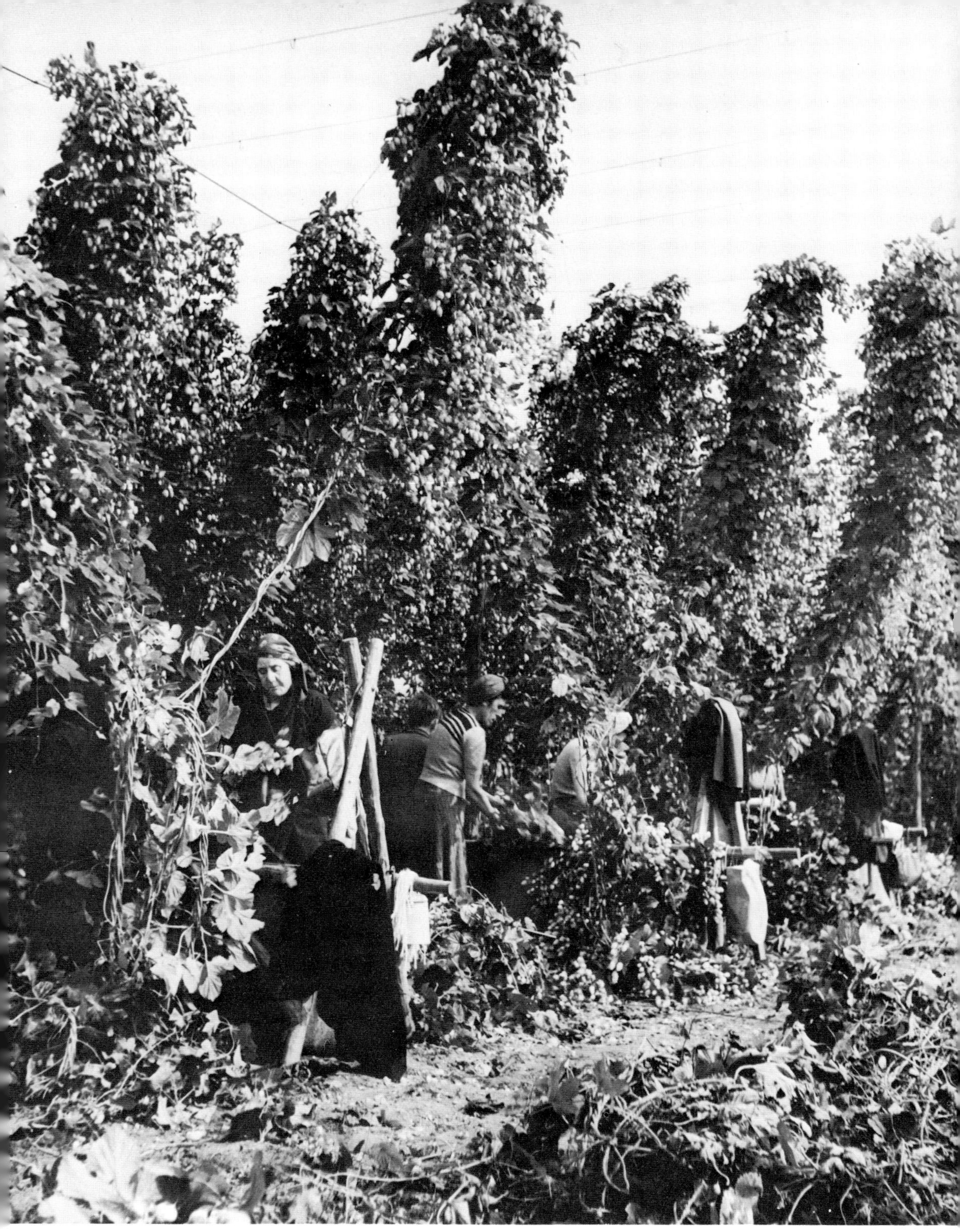

Hop-picking the old-fashioned way. Many people from London used to go to Kent every autumn to do this work.

Donnington is a very small operation, with a staff of ten producing no more than a hundred barrels a week. Ask Claude Arkell how Donnington beer differs from other brewers', and he says, 'Ours probably isn't as sweet as some, but it's a matter of opinion, really. We don't have to use any additives from the point of view of preserving it, and we don't trundle it very far around the country. And it's about as natural as you can get!'

Cider-making at Bromyard, Hereford and Worcester

We could hardly look at brewing without also looking at another of our great national drinks – cider – and we called on Bill Symonds at Ye Olde Cider Mill at Stoke Lacey, just outside the ancient Herefordshire town of Bromyard. Bill's ancestor William Symonds started the business in 1727.

Though it would be a brave man who'd say so in Somerset or Devon, many people – Bill Symonds among them – think that the finest cider comes from Herefordshire. 'Hereford has got the finest soil in the world for producing cider. It produces a nice, deep red drink, where the soils in Devon produce a drink that's more of a whey colour, and they have to add artificial colouring to bring it up to the standard of Herefordshire!'

Bill gets his specially grown cider apples locally, from the Loden valley which runs through Stoke Lacey down to Hereford, and which, Bill says, produces beautiful vintage cider apples. The busy time at Ye Olde Cider Mill starts around the first week in October when the first apples – sweet apples for the sweet cider – arrive and are crushed in the hydraulic presses (Bill does have an old horse-drawn stone-crusher, but that now stands outside the mill as a sign!), before going into the vat to ferment. 'As you go on in the season, you get the later varieties coming in. They're a little bit sharper and have got a little tannin in them, and they make the medium cider. Then later on, the end of November to the second week in December, we get the even later varieties of apples – they contain plenty of tannin, and that's the type of apple that makes the dry cider.'

As Bill's ciders vary in sweetness, so they also vary in potency. Take Scrumpy Jack, for instance. 'Easter Monday, we had a local fellow come in who said he wanted to take half a gallon of scrumpy home, because he was going to do some gardening since it was a nice, fine day. He said, "I used to work on a farm as a boy, so I'm used to the old scrumpy!" I said to him as he went out the door, "Now, mind, only have two small glasses of this!" Anyway, he went home, had half an hour in the garden, got a sweat on, so he went into the house, got a half-pint mug and had two and a half pints, then went back out again. A bit later on everything went quiet. His wife went out to see what was happening, and there he was, on his back in the trench. Passed out!'

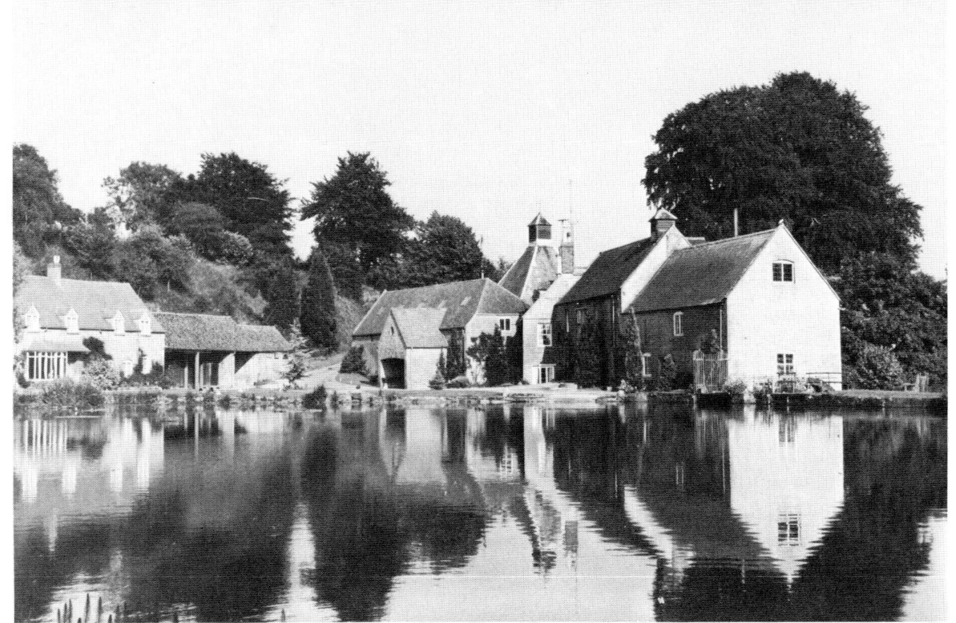

Donnington Brewery, its Cotswold stone reflected in the old mill-pond.

Bill Symonds samples his own produce at Ye Olde Cider Mill.

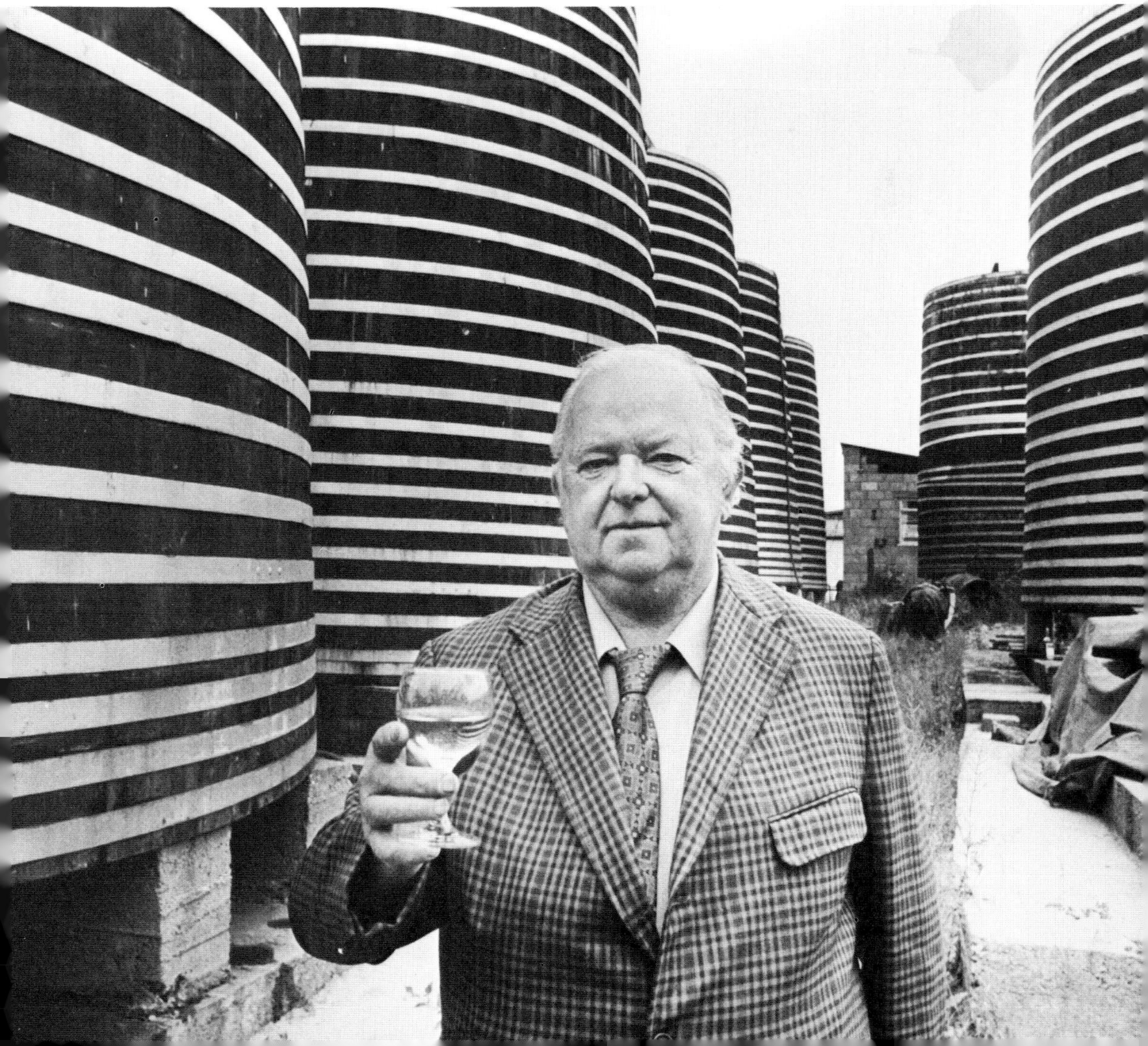

Wine-making at Biddenden, Kent

Compared with brewing and cider-making, commercial vine-growing in this country is a recent development, though there is evidence that the Romans grew vines and made wine here centuries ago. We visited one of the vineyards that have sprung up in the south of England in the last few years – in the Kent village of Biddenden. The Biddenden vineyards were planted in 1969 – on a south-facing slope, for any wine buffs – by Richard Barnes, who had been an apple-grower before he decided to try his hand at making wine.

In a good year he can produce twenty-two thousand, five hundred bottles of wine from eight acres of vines, though he was aiming at producing slightly more – three thousand bottles an acre – to make the venture really viable. 'It's white wine in the main,' Richard said. 'We make a little rosé, but the vines we grow are German vines, which make a crisp, dry white, because in this part of England the climate is roughly the same as the Rhine valley, and those are the varieties that will ripen to a reasonable degree of sugar for good wine-making.'

The grape harvest in Biddenden usually takes place in the third week of October – sometimes earlier, sometimes later, depending on the weather. 'We press the same day as we pick, and the juice from the press is fermented till late November. Then it is matured and fined and filtered in January and finally bottled in February, though it's better kept in the bottle for twelve months prior to drinking. It sells for about £2.40 a bottle in the shops, and "Biddenden blanc" may soon be joined on the wine merchants' shelves by "Biddenden rouge". We're going to clean a nice, southern slope ready for planting red vines next year when we hope eventually to try and come out with a red wine. If we can, it will only be a light red wine, but it will be something different, out of the ordinary!'

Cheers!

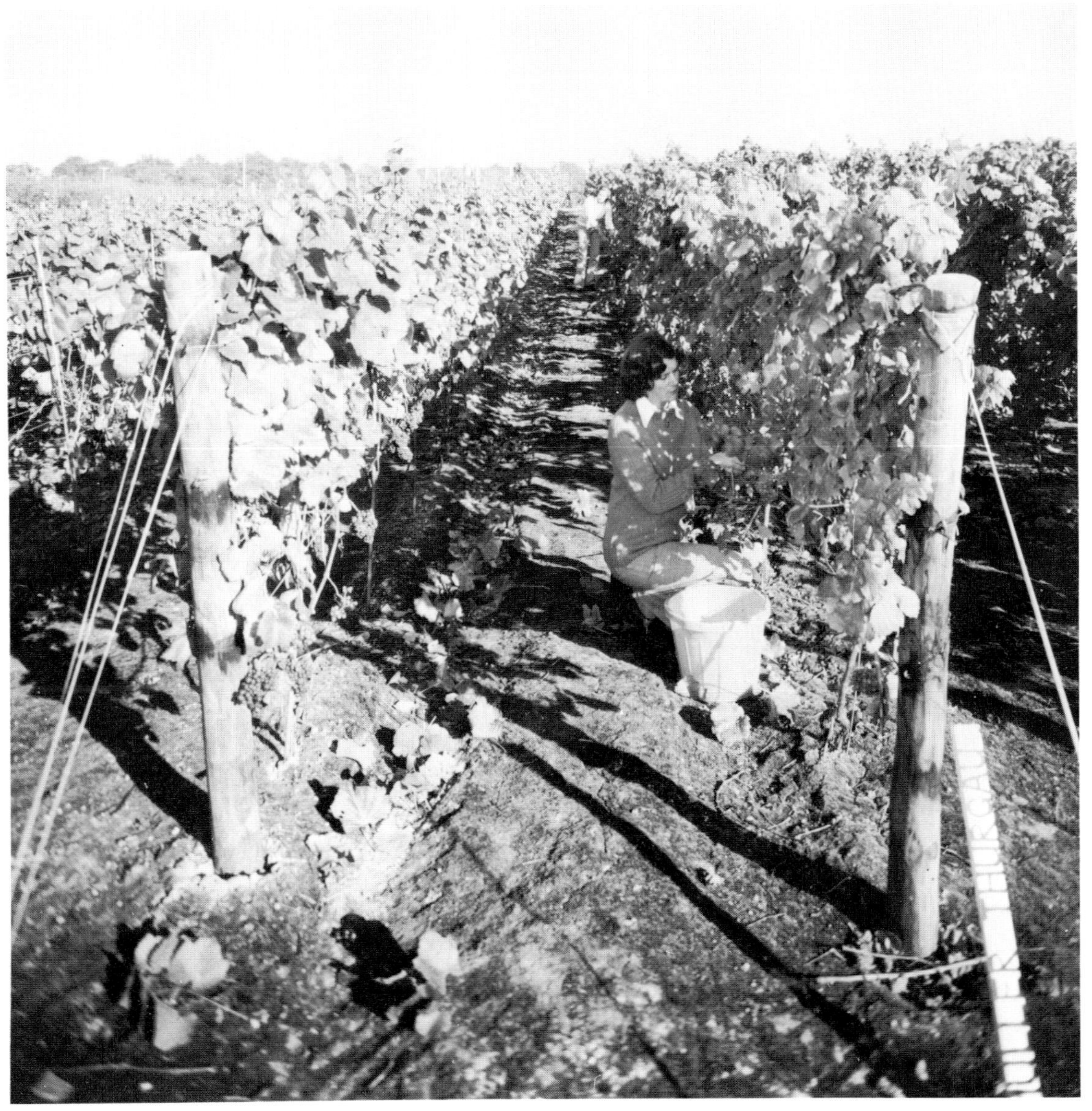

Hardly a typical English scene, but at Biddenden the grape harvest is now a familiar sight.

With These Hands

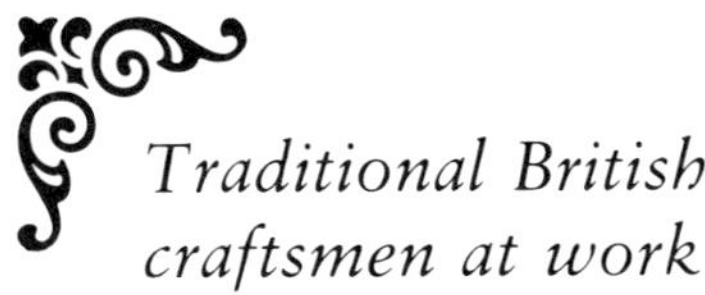

Traditional British craftsmen at work

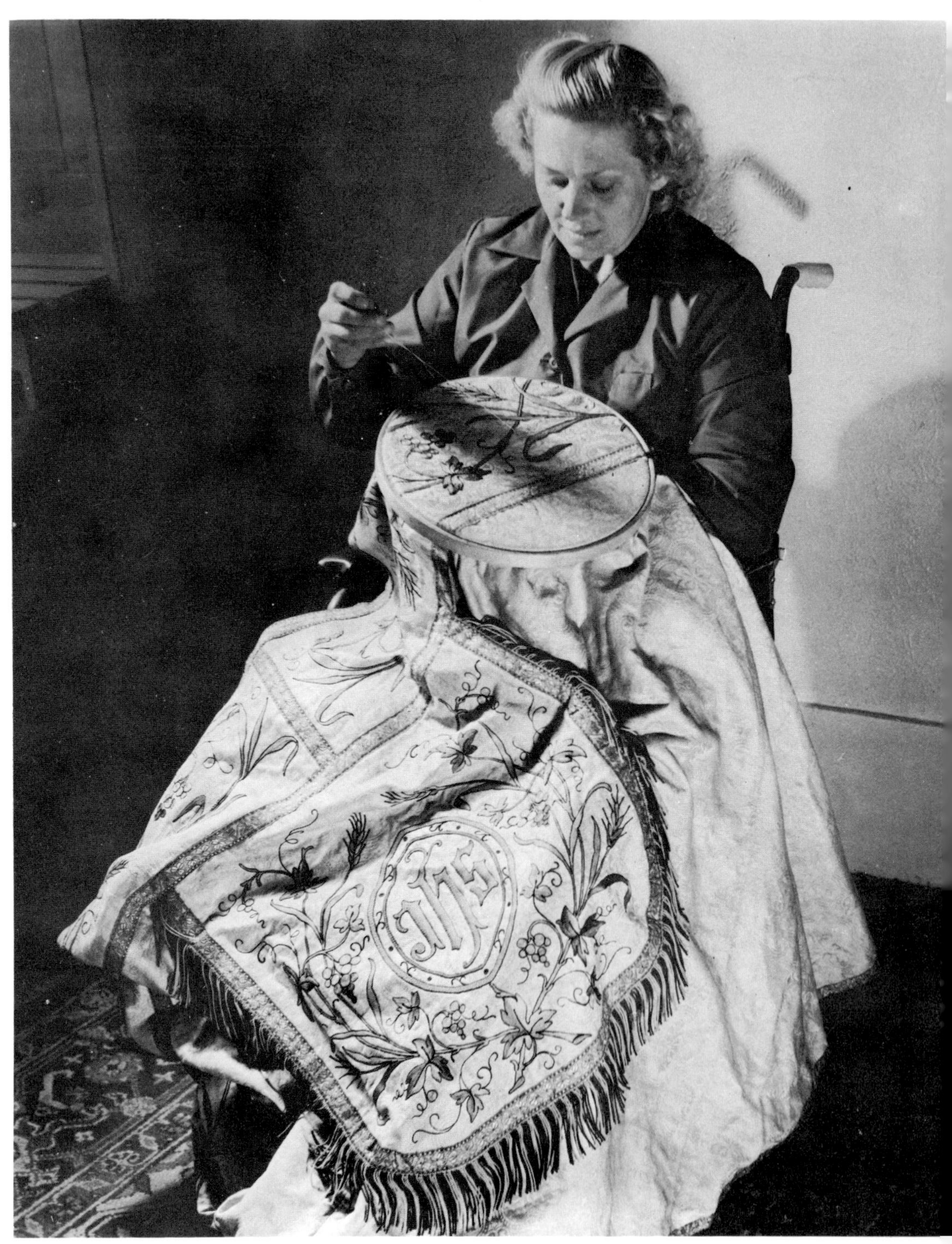

An example of the beautiful needlework produced at the Grange Training Centre at Great Bookham.

Lace-making at Olney, Buckinghamshire

Traditional crafts have been enjoying a well-deserved revival in the last twenty years or so. In the past, craftsmen were part of every small community and their work was more or less taken for granted. But with industrialization and the drift from the countryside to the towns, especially by young people, many of the old crafts began to die out.

Now that trend seems to have been halted, if not reversed. As life becomes more and more complex and mechanical, many people seem to yearn for the simplicity of the past, and are turning away from machine-made, mass-produced goods with their built-in obsolescence to the craftsman's products which still manage to combine beauty with utility.

On our travels up and down the British Isles we have come across all kinds of crafts, some new – to us at least – and some centuries old. Some, encouragingly, are being practised by young people, and others by people who have been working at their craft all their lives. Take Mrs Edith Wetherington who lives in Olney, Buckinghamshire, and who had been making lace, when we talked to her, for seventy years! Watching her work was a remarkable experience. In front of her was her special lacemakers' pillow, pinned in the centre of which was a piece of cardboard with a lace pattern drawn on it, along with the lace she had already made. Attached to each thread she was using, and hanging down around the edge of the cushion, looking rather like Bo Derek's hairstyle in the film *10*, were thirty-two long, cylindrical bobbins, made of bone or wood, with beads on the end to help weight them down. 'If they weren't there,' Mrs Wetherington said, 'when you work with the bobbins, they'd go all over the place and then they wouldn't be in the right place when you need them next time.' To make the lace, she interwove the threads by moving the bobbins backwards and forwards in a set sequence. Different patterns require different numbers of bobbins. ' "Nine Pin" only takes sixteen,' she said, 'but a little pattern called "Crown" takes twenty.'

In the eighteenth and nineteenth centuries, Olney was a well-known centre for making lace known as 'Bucks Point', and Edith Wetherington started to learn when when she was nine. 'There were no such things as woodworking classes and those sort of interesting things to do then, so we just had to go on a Saturday morning and learn how to make lace. Miss Whitmea taught us, and while all the better-off kids went out to play, us poor little kids had to sit and learn it! Then, when we could do it properly, we had to sit in at home at nights and do it, while the other kids were still out playing, because we had to sell it. It was during the First World War when there wasn't very much money – Father was away in the army and Mother was glad for us to help out with this. She used to do it as well, to keep us going.'

The lace bobbins, now quite valuable collectors' items, have all sorts of strange and marvellous names, like 'Dumps', 'Bobtail', 'Cow-in-Calf' and

'Jack-in-the-Box'. They often have quaintly spelt inscriptions painted or carved on them too – romantic ones like, 'I love my love because I no my love lovs me', or, sadder, 'Tis hard to be slited by one as I love'; there were also religious ones like 'Fear God' and 'Jesus Saves', and miscellaneous ones like 'Pop gose the Wesel'.

'I know they used to make them at fairs,' Edith Wetherington told us, 'and chaps used to buy their girls one as a fairing. It was a nice present if you were a lace-maker. There are even some about that commemorated different things – like a hanging.'

Making lace is a painstaking business. A narrow border for a handkerchief can take up to thirty hours, so it isn't surprising that it died out in Buckinghamshire to a large extent when the machine-made Nottingham lace came in at the end of the last century. But Edith Wetherington carried on because she enjoyed doing it. 'You can pick it up and put it down just when you feel like! My eyesight is very good – I'm a bit near-sighted now, but with glasses I can do it. It keeps your fingers from going rheumaticky, too, you know. It's very good exercise for your fingers!'

Embroidery at Bookham, Surrey

They no longer make lace at what used to be called the School of Stitchery and Lace at Great and Little Bookham, Surrey, but at The Grange Training Centre, as it's now called, they still produce some beautiful needlework, as the Centre's bursar, Miss Doreen Caston, explained. 'We make lots of tablecloths, traycloths, morning sets, coffee sets, and cushions. We do all sorts of tapestries, and repair them, and we look after people's heirlooms, like their christening robes when they want a new name embroidered on them, or a wedding veil when it wants repairing and pressing up for the great occasion. We do make wedding dresses too, and children's clothes – little girls' smocked dresses and so on! People do order through the post, or they come here and have a look at what we've got and say, "We'd like that in another colour", or "Can you make me so and so?" and it's done for them.'

The work itself is of an extremely high quality, remarkable by any standards, but the more so when you discover that the forty-five or so women who live in at The Grange all have some kind of physical handicap – polio, spina bifida or epilepsy, for example.

'Each girl comes here initially for a period of three months, to see how she fits in, and if she can learn to sew, and if she's happy and has settled in very nicely, she can go on for a much longer period of training. At the end of that time, if she's been able to train in dressmaking, she might be able to go into open employment, but if she can't, then she can stay here in our own sheltered workshop, and go on living in the flats we have here, where the women live like any working family.'

Cobweb painting at Ruthin, Clwyd

Producing beautiful, delicate embroidery requires great skill, patience and practice, as does another, much more unusual art form we came across in Wales – painting on cobwebs! The artist in question is Patricia Evers-Swindell, who lives in the medieval town of Ruthin in Clwyd, where, apart from her three years at art college in Coventry, she has spent most of her life. Patricia got the idea of painting on cobwebs when she was a child. 'If anyone has ever been to Chester Cathedral, there's a cobweb painting of the Madonna and Child by the choir stalls. It's an old one, done in the eighteenth century, I think, and this is where I first saw it years ago. It just struck me as a good idea to try it as a bit of fun!'

Patricia explained exactly how she goes about it. 'Well, I get a frame, a cardboard frame with a hollow centre, and I scoop down the cobwebs – you can still see the flies and dead insects in there, I'm afraid! I build up a series of cobwebs until it is thick enough to paint on, then I coat the area I want to paint with milk. It stops the brush sticking to the cobweb, and it also gives you a smoother surface to paint on. You have to be more careful than you are on paper, and if you make a mistake, then you either have to utilize that mistake in the painting or start the whole business all over again! After you've completed your painting, you frame it in the usual way, but you have a mount to keep it away from the glass in the front, and you can have a mount to keep it away from the back too, if you want to put glass on both sides of the frame. If you do it that way, and the cobweb painting is held up to the light, it gives it a three-dimensional effect.'

When Patricia wants to make life easy for herself she paints on Jap silk instead, and in fact that is how she earns her living. 'It's easier than cobwebs, certainly, and I think it's just a question of getting used to silk as opposed to canvas!'

Stained glass restoration at Canterbury Cathedral, Kent

The work that Frederick Cole and his team are doing at Canterbury Cathedral is just as delicate in its own way, for they are restoring the magnificent stained glass windows – the largest collection of twelfth-century windows in the country and possibly also in Europe. Although the glass has survived eight hundred years, Frederick Cole told us that it is a 'small miracle' that the windows exist today.

'The glass has decomposed, due to the effects of sulphur dioxide and other pollutants in the atmosphere, which attack the glass and break through the hard, outer skin. Then the glass decomposes into hydrated silica, which forms a hard, opaque crust which in turn acts rather like blotting paper, absorbing more of the pollutants, and therefore the process of decomposition accelerates. The predicted life of the windows when we started this work was about twenty years, but by the time we have finished in another year or two, I think I am safe in saying they'll be secure for another two hundred years.'

The restoration work is extremely delicate and painstaking – rather like taking apart and re-assembling a jigsaw puzzle whose pieces are likely to crumble to dust in your hands at any moment. Each of the vast windows is made in sections which are removed one at a time, lowered to the ground, and taken to the special restoration studio.

'As each panel is taken out of the Cathedral, we make a rubbing of the lead pattern, and that lead pattern is then painted on to a glass-bottomed tray. As each piece of stained glass is removed from its leads, it is put into its correct position in the tray. Each tray is then numbered, and that number follows it through all its processes. Some of the glass pieces are decomposed to the point where they have disintegrated into tiny fragments, and are wafer-thin, and these we preserve by sticking them together again with a silicone resin, and holding them in a sandwich between two very thin pieces of glass. They will still have the pattern of age, and the appearance of age, but much of the pigment has been lost. Where the pigment has been lost and is essential to the iconography, we paint the missing lines back on to the new glass, and put it together so that a face, say, remains whole.'

Love spoon carving at Lampeter, Dyfed

Retired scripture teacher Stan Watkins, who was made a Freeman of Lampeter, in West Wales, eight years ago for his services to the town, doesn't paint on glass or cobwebs, but he does paint on two very unusual surfaces – slate and black velvet. 'Yes,' Stan said with a laugh, 'I've launched into those spheres. As angels fear to tread, so I've stumbled in and they're reasonably successful, I think.'

That is a very modest statement, especially when you consider the difficulties involved. 'On slate, you're apt to leave thumb marks and sweat marks, so you've got to coat it first with linseed oil and let it dry. You have to be very careful when painting on black velvet, too, because once you've put the paint on and it's sunk through the pile, you can't erase it even if you want to! So you have to work from the inside of your drawing out, so to speak, and there are certain disciplines involved that you only acquire with experience. You make a hash of things, but you blunder through.'

Although Stan's paintings would have been well worth the journey in their own right, what took us to his home, with a magnificent view over the River Teifi, was his wood carving, and in particular his beautifully made love spoons. There are both single and double spoons, ornately carved with hearts and lovers'

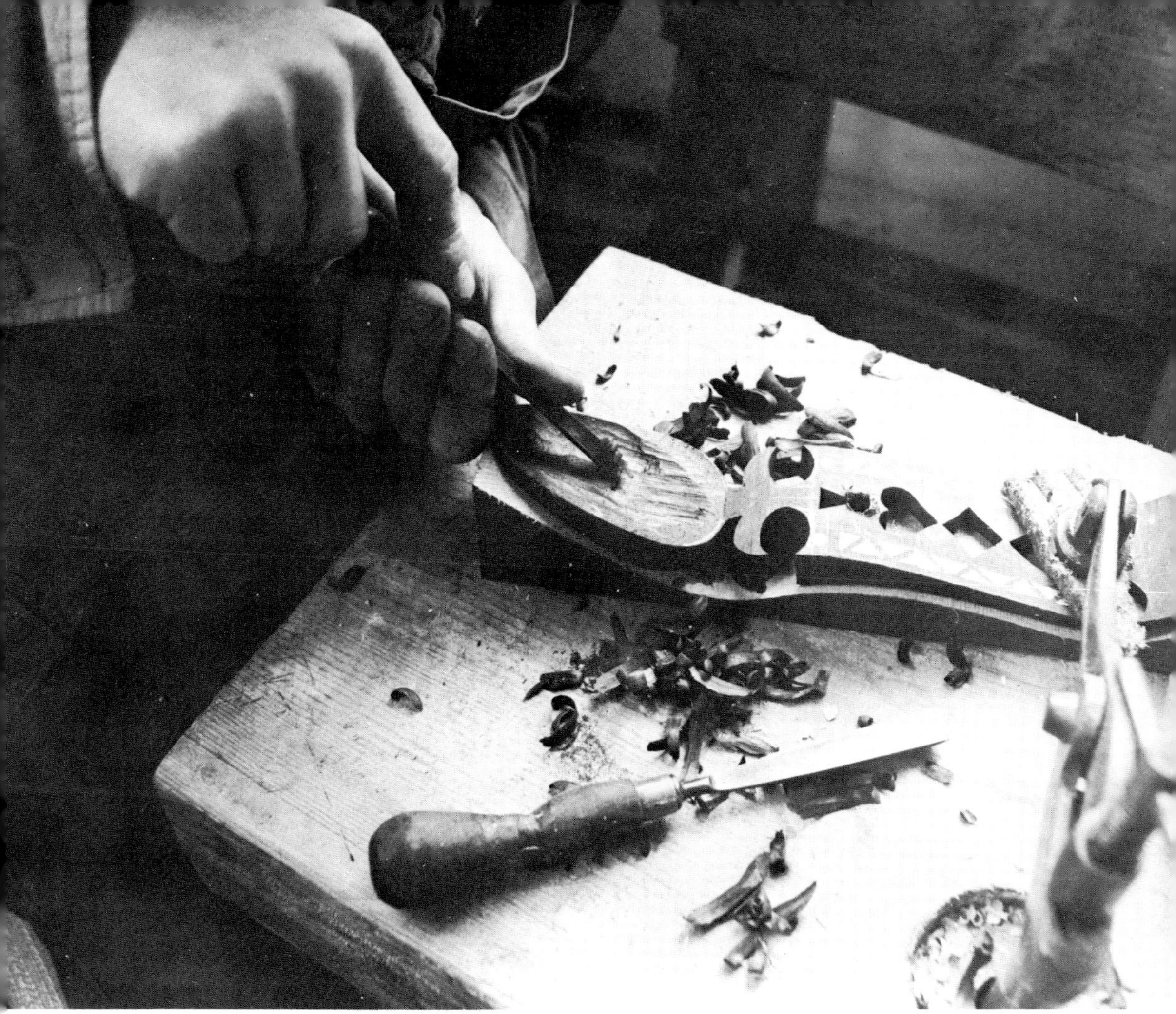

Decorative spoons, carved out of wood, were once given as tokens of love. The greater the ornamentation, the greater the love.

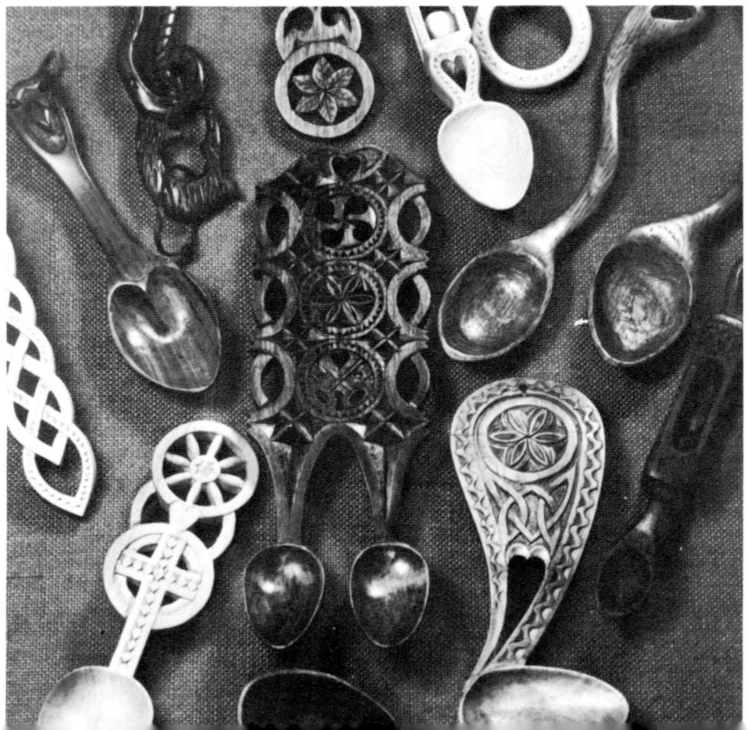

knots and doves. 'In modern times, a man gives silver or jewellery to his beloved, but in the old days they used to make gifts of wood. The swain would whittle away with a piece of wood, and make it as decorative as he possibly could. The greater the ornamentation on the spoon, the greater the love he had for the young girl.'

The hearts and doves made sense, but what about the intriguing little wooden balls in the hollowed-out handle of the spoons? 'If there was just one of those little wooden marbles, that would indicate that the young man wanted one child. If there were two, it meant he wanted two children, and so on!'

Quite why the spoon was chosen as a symbol of love, Stan wasn't altogether sure. 'Possibly it was indicative of the fact that he would be responsible for the girl, that he would feed her. The word "spooning", by the way, came from these love spoons.'

Lute-making at Castle Combe, Wiltshire

The food of love, so Shakespeare said, is music, and chances are that one of the instruments he had in mind was the lute. In these days the lute is something of a rarity, so it was a very pleasant surprise to come across a real live lutier, Charles Ford, still making them in the old, traditional way in the pretty Wiltshire village of Castle Combe. He explained to us how he goes about it.

'I use yew, which is the traditional material. This particular piece I got from the chap across the road who cuts up firewood. I had to get there fairly fast before he cut this piece up! I also used figured sycamore, which is the timber they use to make fiddles, and ebony and ivory, too.'

The distinctive rounded belly of the lute, which looks like a highly polished tortoise shell is made by bending thin strips of wood over a mould, and heating them gently. 'It doesn't take a great deal of heat because the pieces are so thin – I suppose they're not much more than a millimetre in thickness, and with just a little heat they'll bend quite easily.'

Once that process is completed Charles puts on the soundboard, made from spruce. 'This is the life and soul of the instrument. It's the most important thing, and the bars that go right across it underneath discipline the soundboard to vibrate in the correct way. I think it's important to have a musical ear because one has to pick out the right pieces of wood that have a musical note!'

The lutes that Charles makes are eight-course lutes, which means that they have fifteen strings – seven pairs tuned in unison, and one single, top string on which the melody is played. Each lute takes about five weeks to make. 'If I make eleven in a year', said Charles, 'that's good going!' But he can never make enough to fulfil the demand from all over Europe, America and Canada as well as the British Isles. 'We get letters every day asking about lutes – from people wanting to make them as well. A good number play the instrument – lots of young people, too, and it's becoming very popular!'

Ancient weapons at Inverness, Scotland

The sort of music that springs to mind when you visit James McConnell's workshop in Inverness is not the gentle, plangent note of the lute but the skirl of the pipes. For James makes ancient Highland weapons, appropriately enough just a few miles from the battlefield of Culloden, where twelve hundred of Bonnie Prince Charlie's men were massacred in 1746 by the army of George II under the Duke of Cumberland.

Perhaps the most bizarre-looking object James McConnell makes is the targe – from the Gaelic word *targade*, meaning target. It's a small, round shield with an evil-looking spike in the centre. James explained some of the history behind it. 'The stagskin ones go back about five hundred years. They were made of all sorts of wood – obviously anything they could get hold of. There were no specifications or anything like that for their construction. I make them now, basically, of compressed wood which won't warp or split, because I send them all over the world to some very hot climates. The skin covering them is everything that was natural to the region hundreds of years ago – stagskin, sheepskin, leather, all animal skins. Many hundreds of years ago they really didn't know how to cure leather, and the skin was just ripped off the animal and dried in the sun before being sort of nailed on to the wooden disc. That's why some of them were hairy and some weren't.'

The spikes in the centre of the targes in James's workshop all have corks on the end – a very necessary precaution because they were intended to do serious damage to an enemy! 'They were weapons of offence as well as defence,' James said, 'and the spike was, of course, meant for killing.'

So was the *skean-dhu* – the 'Gaelic word means 'black knife' – the Highland dagger which James also makes. 'You can see that from the serrations on the blade. It was no use for peeling vegetables, or anything like that!' It was, James told us, a 'last resort weapon' if you lost your targe and your sword – the Culloden sword which he also makes. 'Those were the swords used by the peasants, as it were. They're not the basket hilts, the swords that were used mostly by the officers and clan chiefs, the nobility of the time. But these were very destructive weapons – you see the two very sharp edges and the very sharp point. And they're very heavy – four pounds in weight.'

Archery and bow-making at Meriden, Warwickshire

Perhaps the most famous of all British traditional weapons is the longbow, with which the English armies finally destroyed the French in the Hundred Years' War. These days archery is an increasingly popular sport, but modern bowmen tend to prefer their bows in materials like fibreglass, sprung steel and aluminium. It was therefore very reassuring to come across Charlie Warlingham in Meriden, the centre of England – Charlie, official bowmaker to the Woodmen of Arden, founded in 1785 and the second-oldest archery society in the country, still makes bows of yew!

One small bit of tradition has disappeared, though, because the yew isn't English. 'Mostly it comes from America now,' Charlie told us, 'because we find it is a better type of yew for the purpose.' The 'nocks' – the hooks at each end of the bow which take the string – are also made from an imported material, buffalo horn. 'A cow's horn wouldn't be any good for this because, of course, a cow's horn is hollow right up to the tip, but the buffalo's is solid.' The handle, or grip, is still bound with string and finished off with gimp, a fine though strong cotton or linen thread, but another tradition has bitten the dust when it comes to bowstrings. They used to be made of hemp, but now they're made from Dacron. In other ways, however, the old bowmaking traditions are still alive and well.

'When the bow is strung up, it is strung so that there's a distance of about seven and a half inches between the bow and the string. As a rough measurement, we use our fist with the thumb extended – that's called a "fistmele".' The bows Charlie makes vary in size, from about five feet six inches for a ladies' bow to six feet long for a man's. The 'pull' varies too – anything from forty-five pounds a square inch for a target bow to about sixty pounds for a flight bow, which is basically a hunting bow and required to shoot arrows longer distances than a target bow.

Arrows, made from Port Orford cedar, pitch pine or Oregon pine, come in different sizes to suit the various bows. They start at twenty-five inches for a ladies' arrow, and go up to twenty-nine inches for the largest man's. Their weight varies, too, and Charlie still uses the traditional method of weighing them – against coins of the realm. 'Ladies' arrows are usually the weight of three and sixpence old money – a florin, a shilling and a sixpence – while gents' arrows vary between three and sixpence and four and sixpence.' The 'pile' – the business end of the arrow – is made of steel, and the flight feathers are always wing feathers from a turkey. 'They're the most suitable for this purpose because they always retain their shape when they are ruffled up.'

Charlie started as a bow-maker when he was sixteen, back in the twenties. 'I was there for twelve years until the war broke out, and then, of course, I was called into the army. When I came back from the war I took over a newsagent's for twenty-four years, and it was only when I retired, about seven years ago,

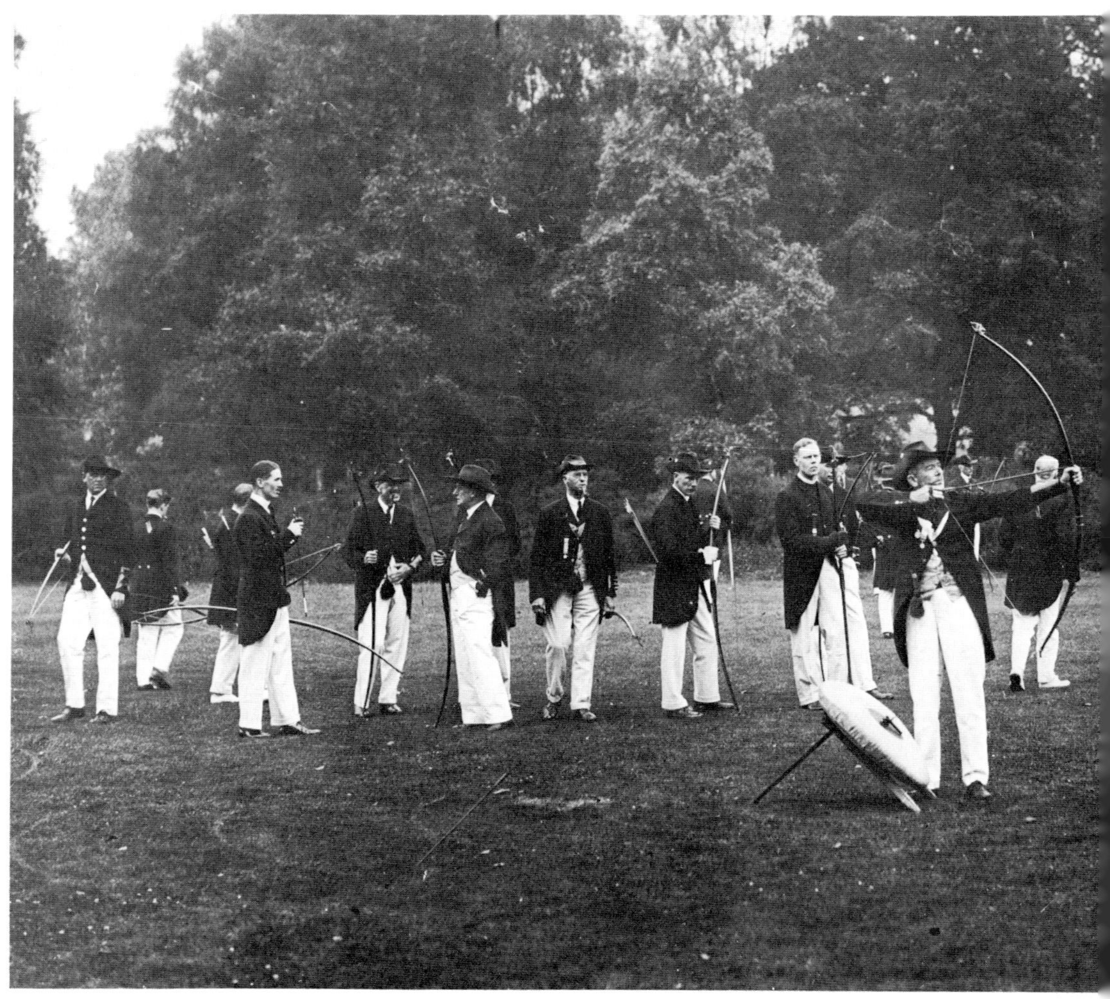

The Woodmen of Arden, an archery society founded in 1785. This photograph was taken in 1925.

that I returned to the bowmaking. These days I do it more as a hobby than anything, but it's very enjoyable work.'

Clogs at Tregaron, Dyfed

Hywel Davies, who is in his forties, lives and works in the small Welsh town of Tregaron, where he has virtually saved an old craft from extinction in Wales. 'I did a six months' apprenticeship with the man who was probably the only clog-maker left in Wales, and now he's retired I'm more or less taking over.' Hywel decided to take up clogging about six years ago, after he'd started wood-carving as a hobby. 'I started carving spoons and crosses and things, and, well, clogs just followed on from there.'

On the floor of his workshop when we visited him were finished clogs, half-finished clogs, rough-carved wooden soles and lots of clog-sized logs. 'I use sycamore and beech, but mainly I use alder. Alder grows in wet ground, and I carve it fresh, straight after felling the tree. I let it dry out before I make the clogs up, and when the alder has dried out completely, it is perfectly waterproof.'

It is only the soles of the clogs that are made of wood – the uppers are leather – and Hywel works from foot-shaped patterns. 'I carve the wood first of all with an axe to get a very rough shape, and then I carry on, basically with three different knives – one to give the shape of the clog, the second one to make the reevage round the edge to take the leather, and the third to hollow out the shape of the sole of your foot. They are very sharp, the knives, and I suppose I sharpen them at least three times a day. If I went through and made a pair of clogs from start to finish, I suppose it would take two and a half hours. But of course normally I don't work like that. I'll carve lots of soles in one go, then put the leather on them all and so on.'

Hywel produces clogs in standard shoe sizes, but he can make them to fit individual feet, '...those that are particularly wide or narrow. Most people want rubber on the heels these days, but if they want iron, like horseshoes, I can certainly do that, too!'

Hedging mitten-making at Montgomery, Dyfed

About forty miles north-east of Tregaron, in the border town of Montgomery, we found another craftsman who may well be the last of his kind in Wales, if not in the whole of Britain. His name is Harold Davies, and among other things he is a hedging mitten-maker. Hedging mittens are, in fact, just what you'd think they are – extremely tough mittens, made from specially treated cowhide, that

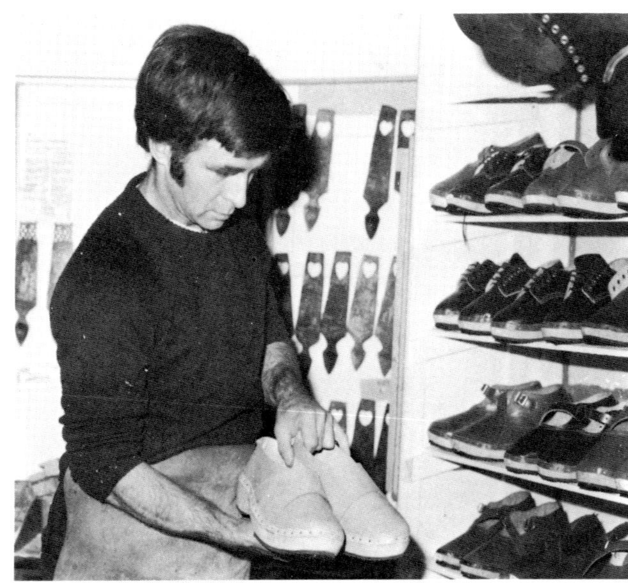

Hywel Davies of Tregaron, one of the last clog-makers in Wales.

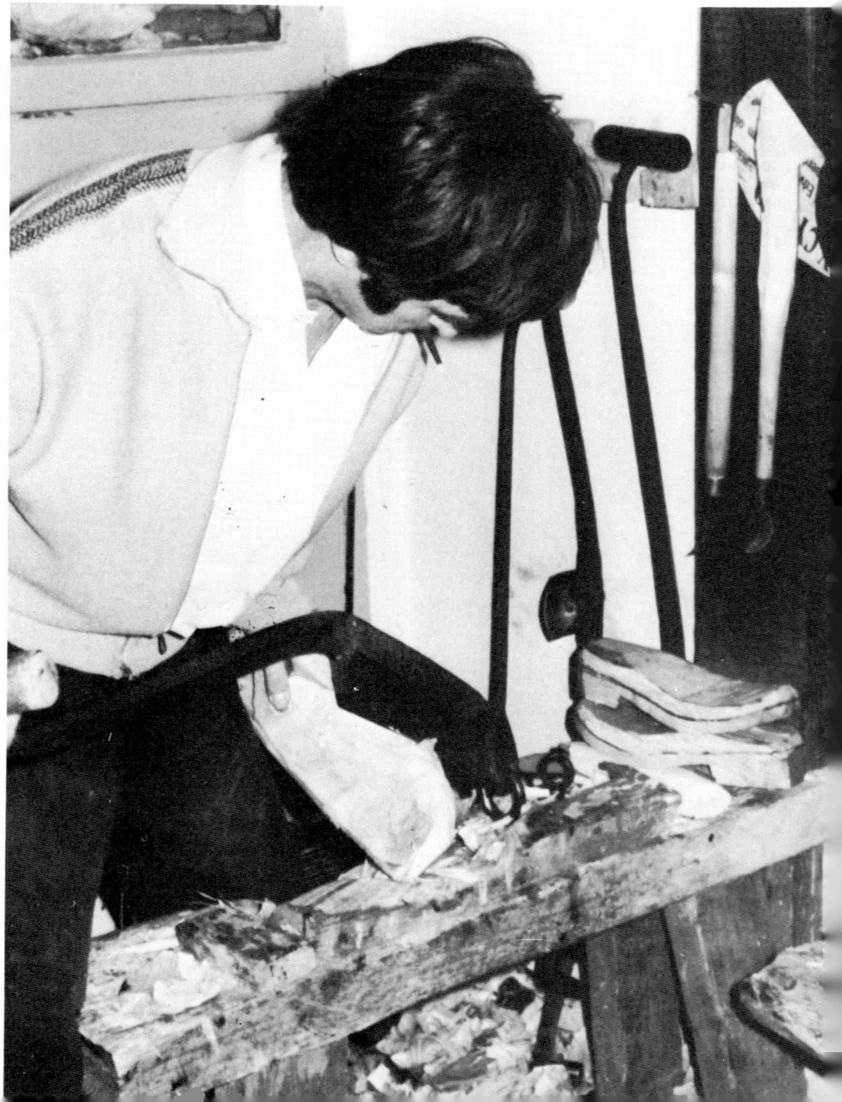

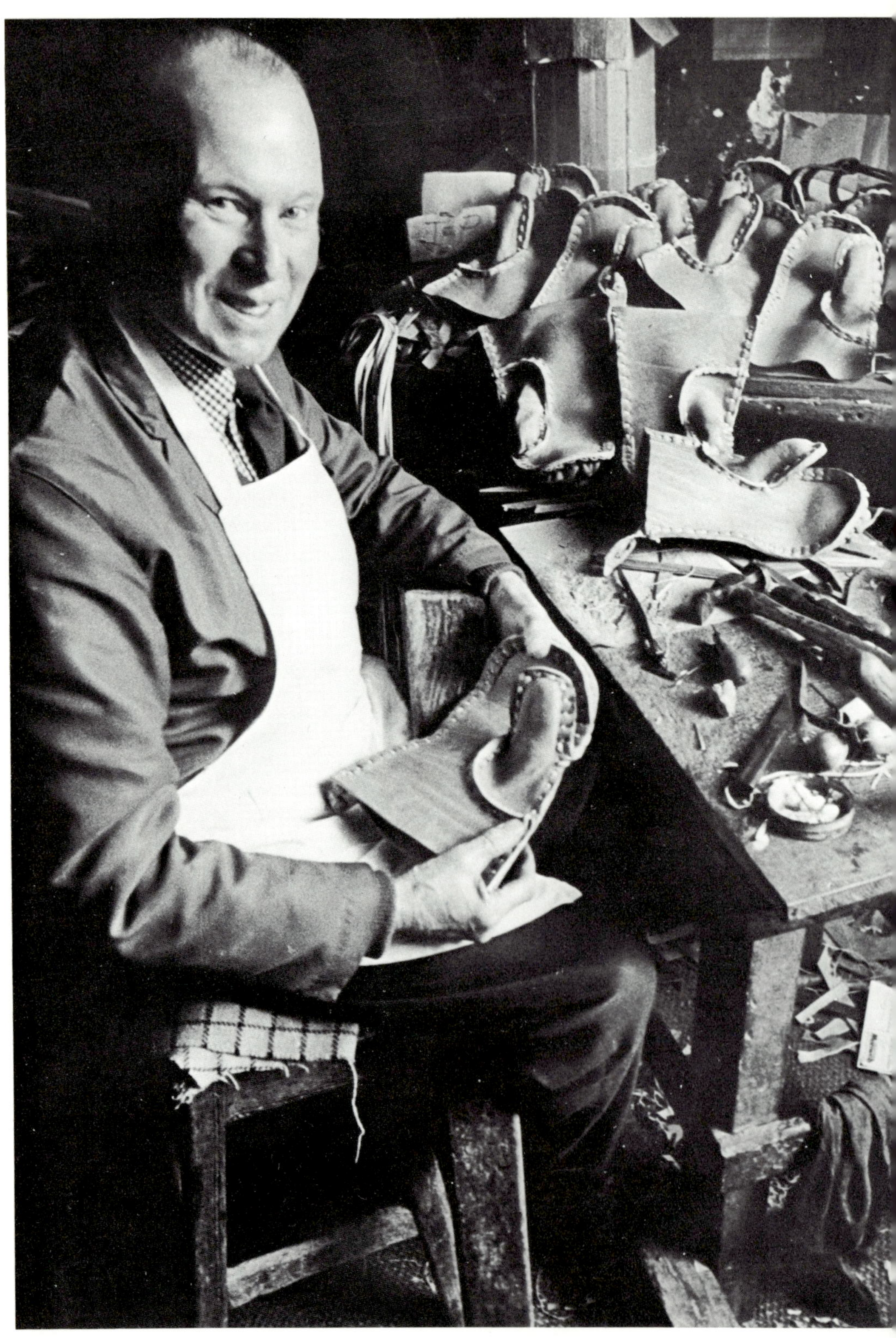

Another member of a rare breed: Harold Davies, who makes hedging mittens.

farmers wear when they are hedging to stop the sharp thorns pricking their hands.

'We're very fortunate in Wales', Harold said, 'that the young farmers still take an interest in hedging, and they're very proud of it. Unfortunately, in other parts of the country, the hedge-cutters have taken over from what we call "pletching", but I think there will always be hedging done.'

Harold makes the mittens entirely by hand – some two hundred pairs a year, and it's clear from looking at them that they are made to last a long time. 'Too long,' Harold said with a laugh, 'that's why I'm poor! I repaired some the other day that I'd made twenty-five years ago! But the average life, I suppose, is about five years.'

Other things that Harold makes in his minute workshop also seem to have the habit of lasting longer than they're expected to. 'Take belts. There was a fellow in the pub the other night who was partly undressing himself! Then he said to me, "Look here, saddler! Look at this belt. You made it for my dad forty years ago." As I say – that's why I'm poor!'

Harold started life as a saddler, but the increasing mechanization of farming over the years meant that the demand for saddles declined. 'We had to turn over to boots and shoes, boot repairing, and mix it together. We've got on very well like that!'

Saddle-making at Malpas, Cheshire

In Malpas, Cheshire we met a master saddler, Robert Jovanovic, who still finds there is plenty of demand for his hand-made saddles, whether they're for general riding, hunting, showjumping or racing. 'I've made saddles for Gordon Richards, Douggie Smith and Lester Piggott.'

Robert came to this country from his native Yugoslavia just after the last war. 'I remember the date very clearly, 20 November 1947, because our Queen got married on that day!' After working as a saddler in Yorkshire and Gloucestershire he settled in Malpas in 1961. His saddles, which are individually tailored to rider, or horse, or both, cost anything from £110, but they are an investment. 'I believe and guarantee that if a person is looking after it – and he can ride as much as he wants – it will last fifty years, and for most people that is almost a lifetime!'

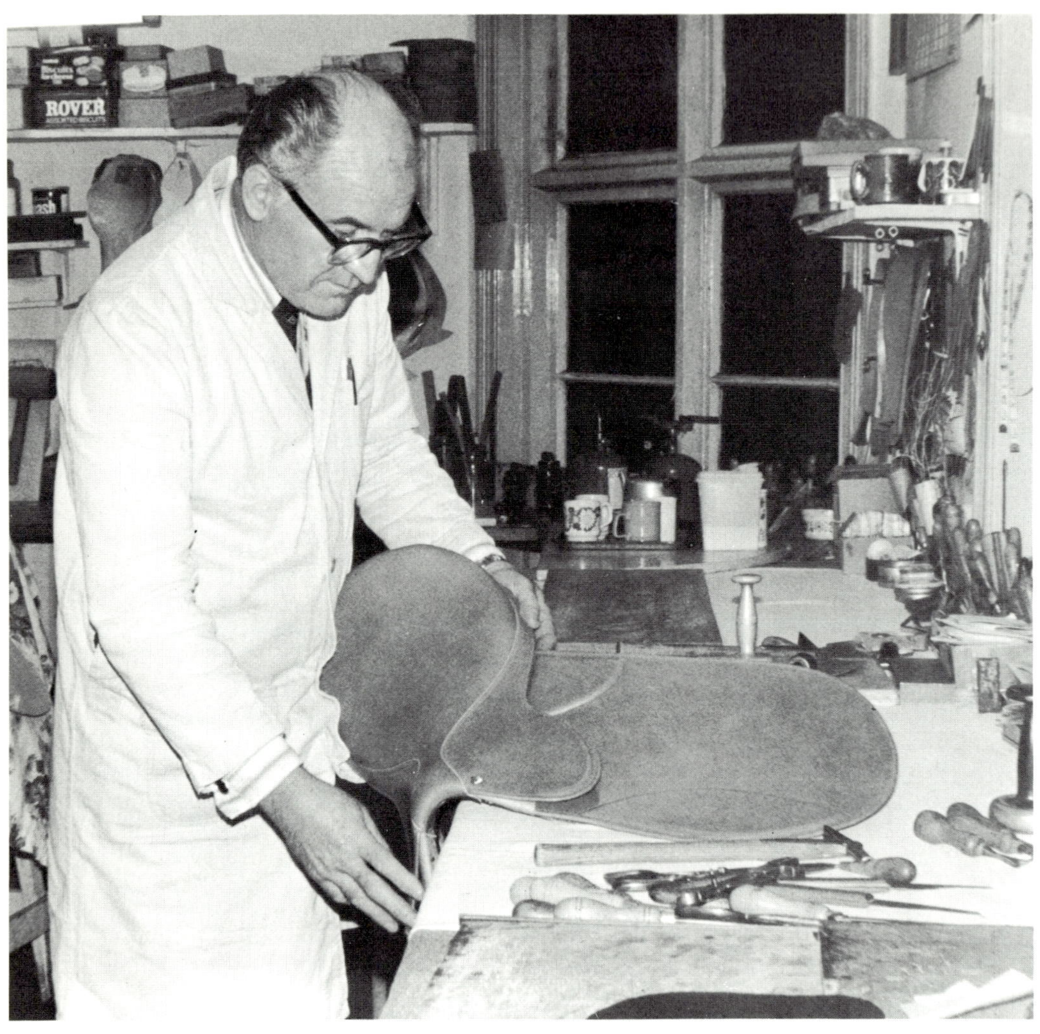

Robert Jovanovic, whose hand-made saddles are used by many top jockeys.

Candle-making at Blaenau Ffestiniog, Gwynedd

Although Michael Rainger, who runs an extremely successful candle-making business in the North Wales village of Blaenau Ffestiniog, only comes from Reigate in Surrey, he is no doubt still looked on locally as a 'foreigner'. He and his wife Rosemary moved to Blaenau nine years ago, basically because they both loved walking and climbing, and having spent holidays in the area they decided that they couldn't think of anywhere better to live.

'But having moved here,' Michael told us, 'we suddenly realized that there was a very serious unemployment problem, and we were just adding to it, and after about six months on the dole we decided we'd got to do something about it. So the idea of our old hobby, candle-making, came up. We decided that we could give it a try, so we got out our old candle-making equipment which we'd brought with us from Reigate and made a batch. Rosemary took them down to the local craft shop, sold them, then came back with £7. We just couldn't believe our luck! We thought, "Well, there's something we can do, perhaps, to create a living for ourselves", so we made more candles, went out and sold them, and to our amazement found that we had a business on our hands! Now we employ four girls from the village working full-time with us, and we make an average of about a thousand candles a week, fifty weeks of the year. The smallest one we make is an egg-sized candle, running up to a large display candle which is about two feet high and about four inches in diameter.'

Michael explained just how they go about making their mottled, multi-coloured candles from paraffin wax, a by-product of refining heavy crude oil. 'The first thing you do is to break the wax up into small pieces and put it into some form of boiler or heatproof container to melt it down. Once you've got it liquid, you then pour it into trays, mixed with wax-soluble coloured dye. You then let the slabs cool down, take them from the trays and break them up into small pieces. You then set a plastic mould up with a metal base with a small hole in the bottom to feed the wick through, with a bar going across the top to hold the wick centrally in place. Having got this in position, you fill the mould with broken pieces of coloured wax up to the top, then pour clear molten wax over the top of this lot which merges all together into one solid candle.'

The candles the Raingers make are mostly tapered or straight, though they do produce one range of geometric shapes – stars, globes, cubes and so on. Many of their candles have pictures on them – of Welsh ladies, railway engines, and maps of the area. They call these their souvenir candles and they are sold mainly to visitors during the tourist season. They also make a range of scented candles, for which sandalwood, jasmine or musk are poured into the liquid wax when the candle is being made. 'They give a nice background smell to a room – not an overpowering one, but one that is very pleasant to sit with.'

Michael admitted with a grin that he's one of the few people who doesn't mind when the power-cut season comes around. 'It's certainly done us a lot of good in the past,' he said. 'It made people candle-conscious in Britain, which I think is a very good thing. Candles give you a romantic atmosphere. I think most people like a living flame, and with the increased use of central heating these days, it's a thing that is lacking in the home, and people enjoy candles for that reason.'

Bee skips at Over Wallop, Hampshire

The Raingers' candles are very much in demand and they make a good living from their craft, but down in Hampshire, in the village of Over Wallop, we found a craftsman who was keeping an old craft going purely for the love of it. His name was Jed Jeans, and he makes bee skips – the old fashioned, sugar-loaf-shaped beehives made from straw, that you tend to see these days only on the labels of honey jars!

'People don't need them these days,' Jed said, in his distinctive Hampshire burr, 'because the wooden beehives have done away with the straw ones, but being an old craft I like to keep it going, so we don't sell 'em. We mainly just give 'em away!'

Jed makes baskets from straw, too, and binds them with split blackberry brambles. 'I go out in the hedgerows and cut them – they come free! But if you go and buy a bundle of thatching straw for this job, it'll cost somewhere about £4!'

The finished product looks sturdy enough – like a rope coiled round and round to form the basket. Jed explained how he managed to get the whole so tight. 'You put all your straw through a ferrel – you'd call it a ring, but we call it a ferrel – so you get all the air out of your straw when the split bramble goes round it, so that your air doesn't get back in, because if it does, it will deteriorate your straw in time.'

One of Jed's sidelines is making spars for thatchers. They look pretty basic, but the skill involved in making them takes years to acquire. Jed took a piece of hazel, and with an exceedingly dangerous-looking bill-hook chopped it in such a way that it split cleanly down the middle. He then split it again, and wound up with four spars, each pointed at both ends. 'It takes months and months to get into it properly. See, nobody can teach you how to do it. You've got to watch people, and then you get into their way of doing it. I watched a chap called Bill Sandy, and that was right back in childhood days!'

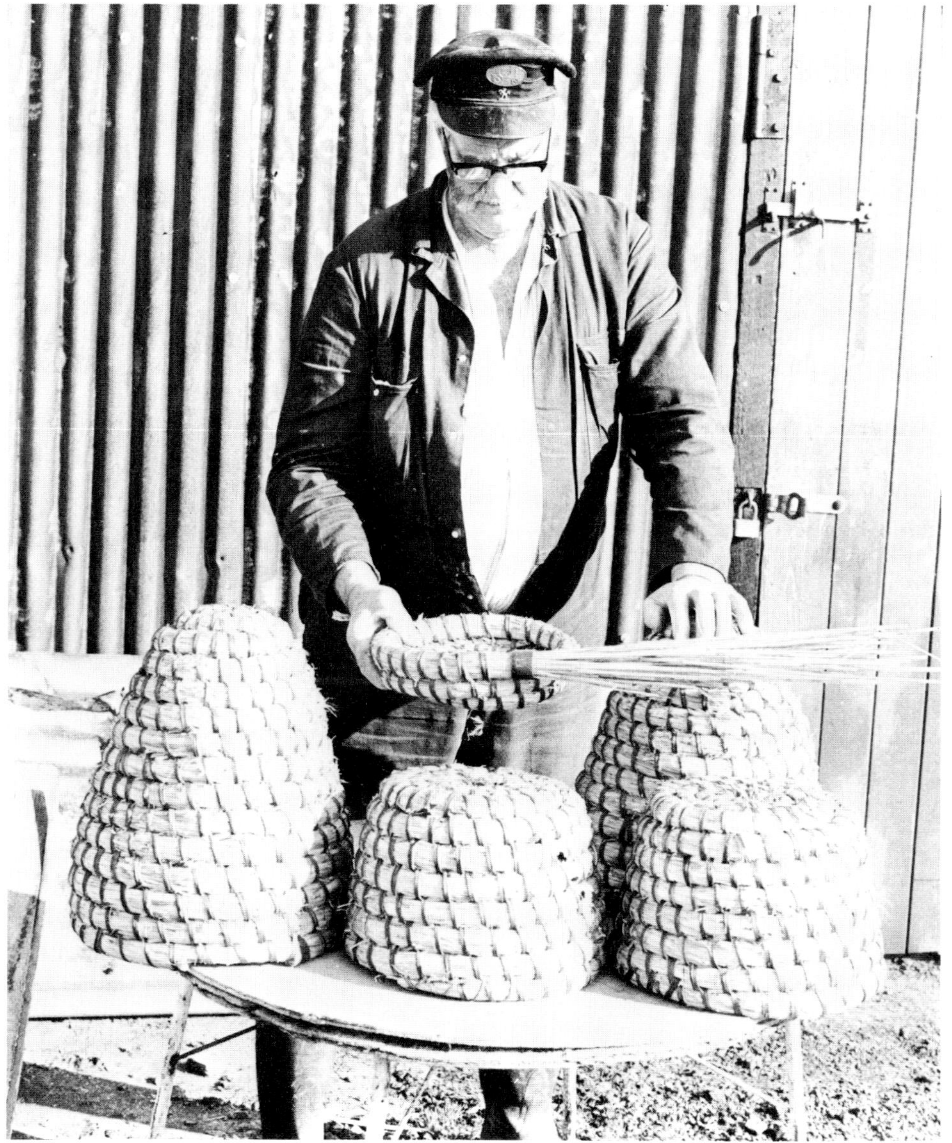

There is little demand these days for the old-fashioned beehive made of straw, but Jed Jeans is keeping the craft alive.

Thatching at Lacock, Wiltshire

In the pretty National Trust village of Lacock, Wiltshire, we saw spars in use – bent in half, rather like giant hairpins, and pushed into the thatch. The thatcher was, encouragingly, a young man in his late twenties called Paul Sugg. He'd come into the thatching business, it seems, just to be contrary! 'I always wanted to be a bricklayer, but thatching seemed like a good trade to go into. Everybody told me it was dying out, but the more they told me not to take it up, the more I thought I would, and I'm very glad I did!'

Paul spent five years learning the craft locally, and although there is only one thatched cottage in Lacock itself, he finds plenty of work in the area to keep him going. Indeed, when we met he had a waiting list of almost a year.

The roof he was working on – an old farmhouse – was being thatched in straw. 'I can thatch in reed, but this is a straw area, so I always put straw on.' That particular roof would need about nine tons of straw to complete, and the work would take him up to ten weeks. 'The first layer of straw is held on with iron hooks made by the local blacksmith, and the second layer is fastened with spars. It may all sound a bit casual, but this roof will still be here when I'm gone! This will go on for about thirty-five years before it needs tidying up!'

Needless to say, Paul is a great fan of thatch. 'It's beautifully warm in the winter – no insulation needed – and lovely and cool in the summer.' Brian Johnston recalled being woken in his mother's thatched cottage by the birds twittering in the thatch. But Paul said that birds needn't be a problem if you wire the thatch – cover it all over with fine-meshed wire netting, rather like a huge hairnet! Paul was obviously a man who loves his work. 'I must do at least seventy hours a week. I sort of live, eat and sleep thatching.' And he doesn't think it is dangerous. 'Most thatchers do fall off some time in their life – I suppose if you spend one-third of your life up on a roof you run the risk of falling off – but touch wood, I haven't yet!'

Cotswold stone walls, Bourton-on-the Water, Gloucestershire

Although these days we tend to associate the word 'stonewaller' with a politician who is reluctant to give a straight answer, or a batsman like Geoffrey Boycott, you can still find the genuine article in the pretty Cotswold village of Bourton-on-the-Water, and he goes by the name of George Martin. Appropriately enough, we talked to George on one of the stone bridges he built over the River Windrush which flows through the village – the New Inn Bridge.

'I built this one in 1954 with money left over from the coronation in '53. There used to be an old wooden bridge here, with a handrail on, but a portion of it collapsed, and hence this bridge was built.' The fact that the bridge has no

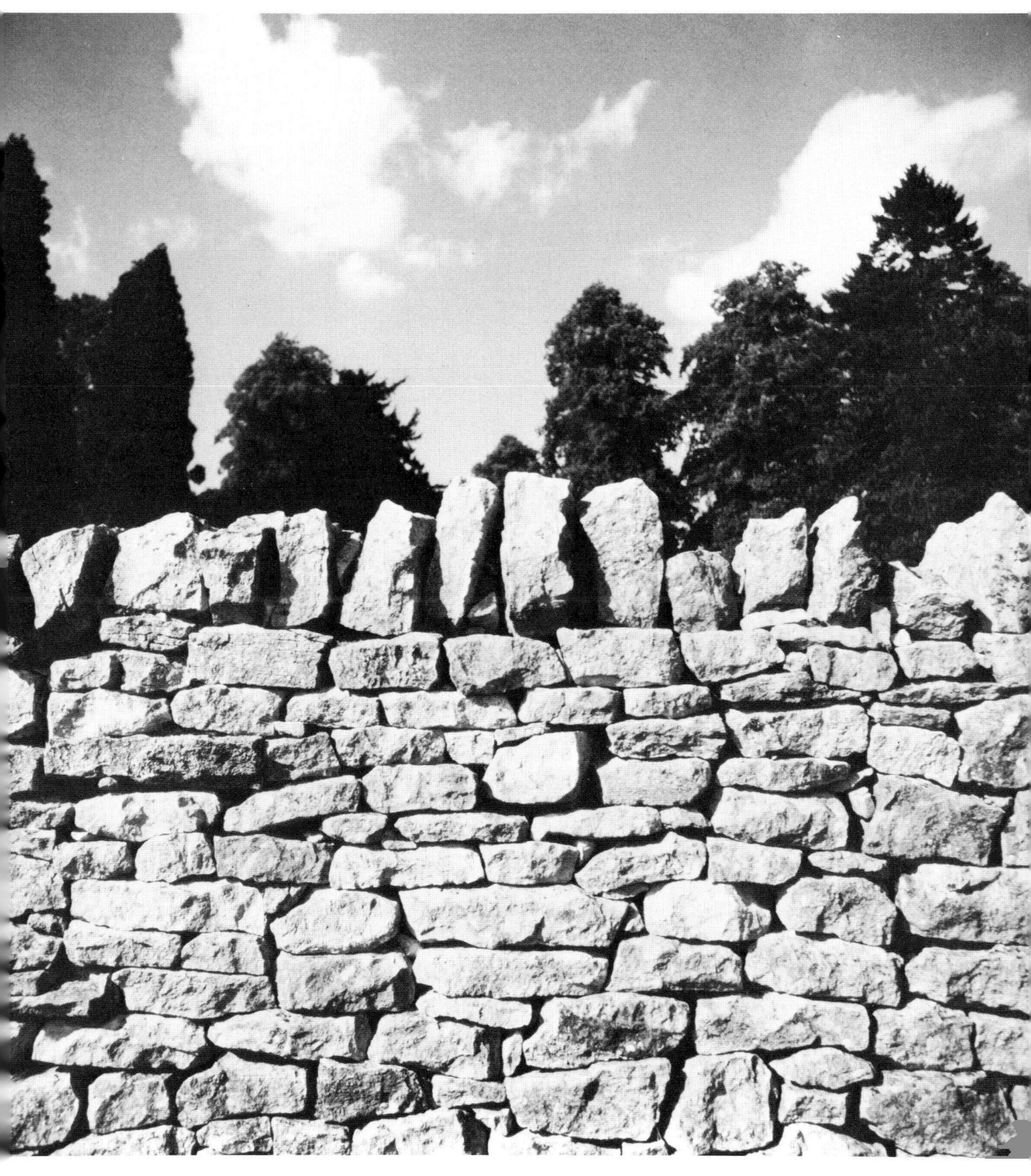

No mortar is used in the dry stone walls they build in the Cotswolds. It is the workmanship which stops them falling down.

parapet prompted the obvious question – do people ever fall in? George chuckled. 'Well, occasionally, but you don't hear much about it these days. But years ago, when we were kids, it was the thing that you weren't a Bourtonian until you fell in there!'

Luckily, the river isn't normally more than a foot or two deep, and in fact used to be the site for one of Bourton's favourite games. 'Playing football in the river used to be a regular event,' George told us. 'They still do it occasionally when there's some money-raising event taking place on the green. It's great fun, and a good money-making event!'

Besides bridges, George also builds Cotswold stone walls. He built his first solo wall back in 1927 when he was eighteen, and, he assured us, it is still as good as new. 'By and large, the stone is so expensive now that there's no new stone walls going up – not in any great quantity, anyway. In fact on quite a lot of farms they're taking the walls down rather than putting them up, to make the fields bigger for arable land.'

The walls are dry stone walls – no mortar is used to hold the stones together – and as George said, with a degree of understatement, 'There's a bit of workmanship involved in making sure they don't collapse! You start with a trench at the bottom – years ago you had to put rough stone in it, but these days you can even put concrete – and then you build one side. Ideally, you've got a mate on the other side, building that. You place your stones with the back slightly higher than the front, and you stabilize them – stop them rocking – by putting what we call a "pinner", which is a small stone, under it. The wall is filled with pieces of stone that aren't any good for the outside wall. You don't just put them in higgledy-piggledy, though. They go in flat, and the way the middle is filled is just as important as the outside.'

All Cotswold stone walls are roughly the same height. 'The average stock fence wall is about three feet six of wall, plus what we call the "big combers", which are the big stones on edge that were stood on the top and made the finished wall about four feet four, or four feet six.'

George has built walls in other parts of the country with other kinds of stone, but he prefers Cotswold every time. 'It's a good stone to my mind. I do classes with it, and I prefer it for that because it's a good demonstration stone. I've taught two courses for the West Oxford Technical College.' It's reassuring to know that yet another of our traditional crafts is being passed on to the next generation. 'It is a very satisfying art,' George said. 'It's something you can see when you've done it. It's not buried in the ground!'

Lawful Business

Ancient rights for ancient wrongs

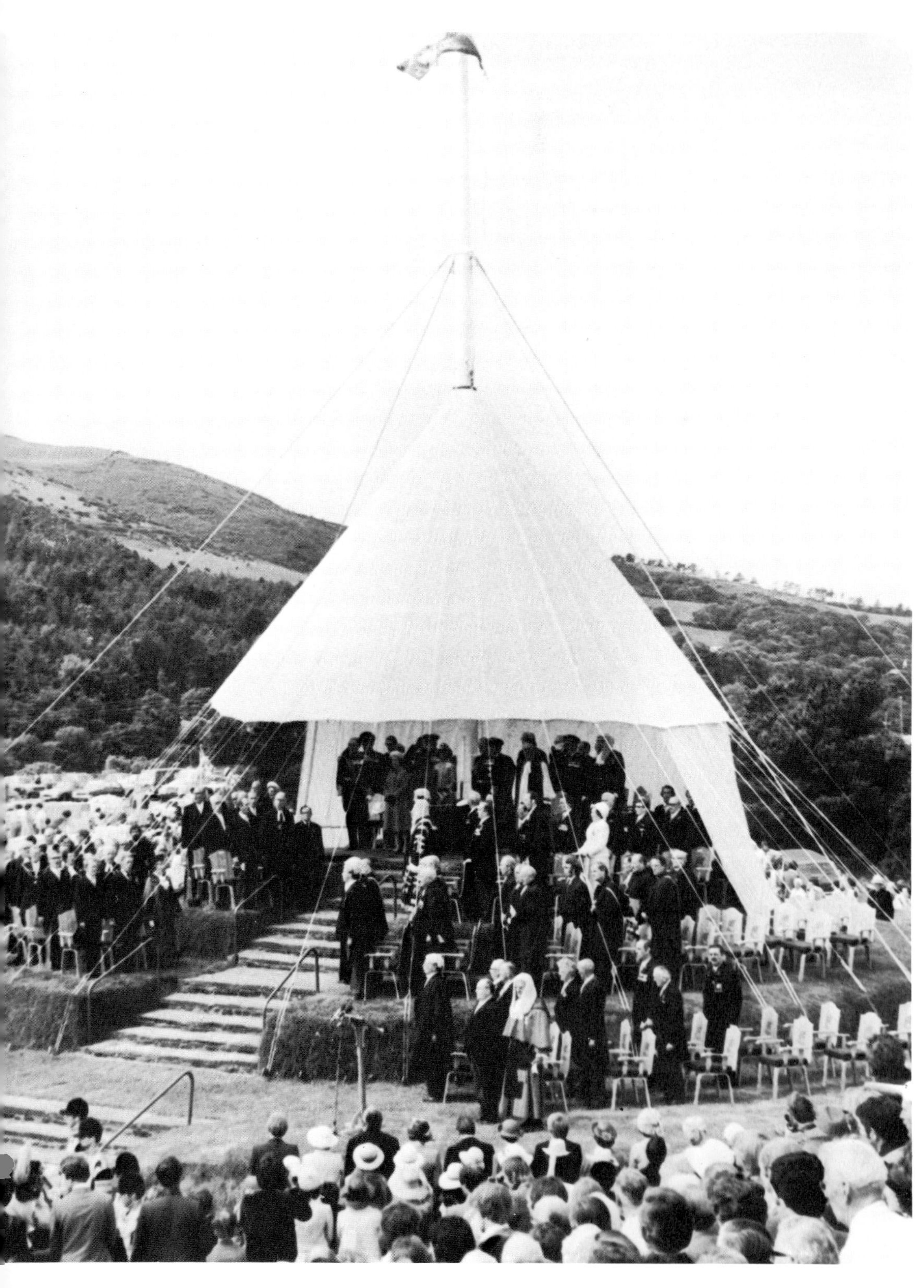

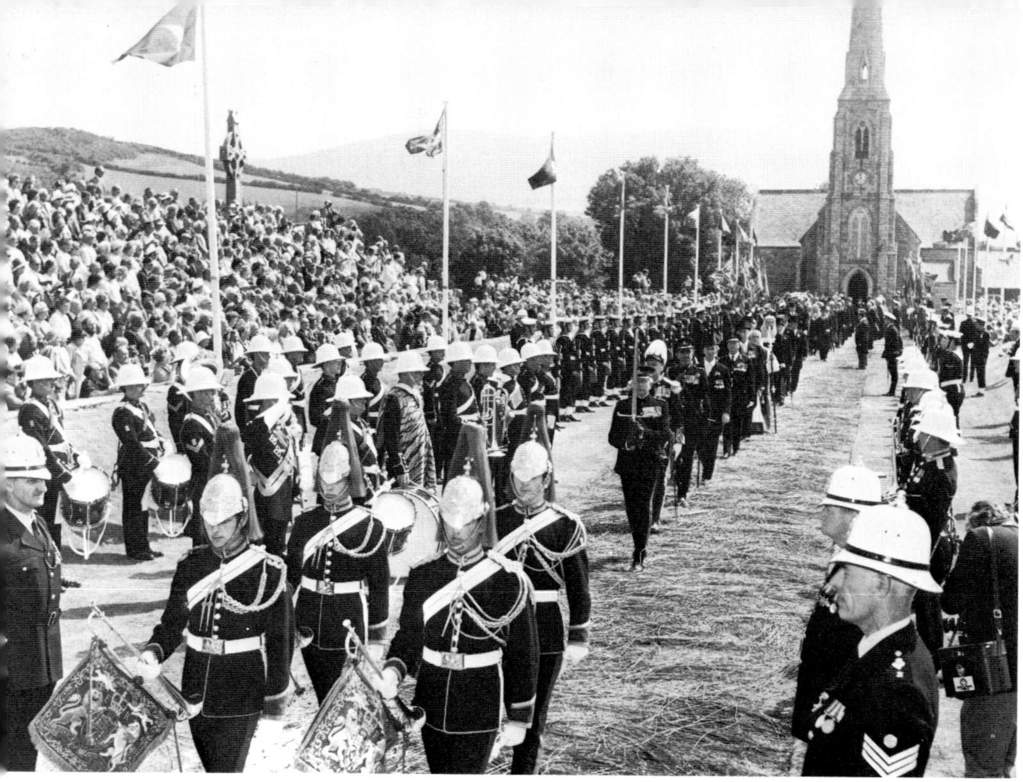

The Tynwald Ceremony, at which the laws passed in the Tynwald during the previous year are read out, and (*right*) petitions are handed in.

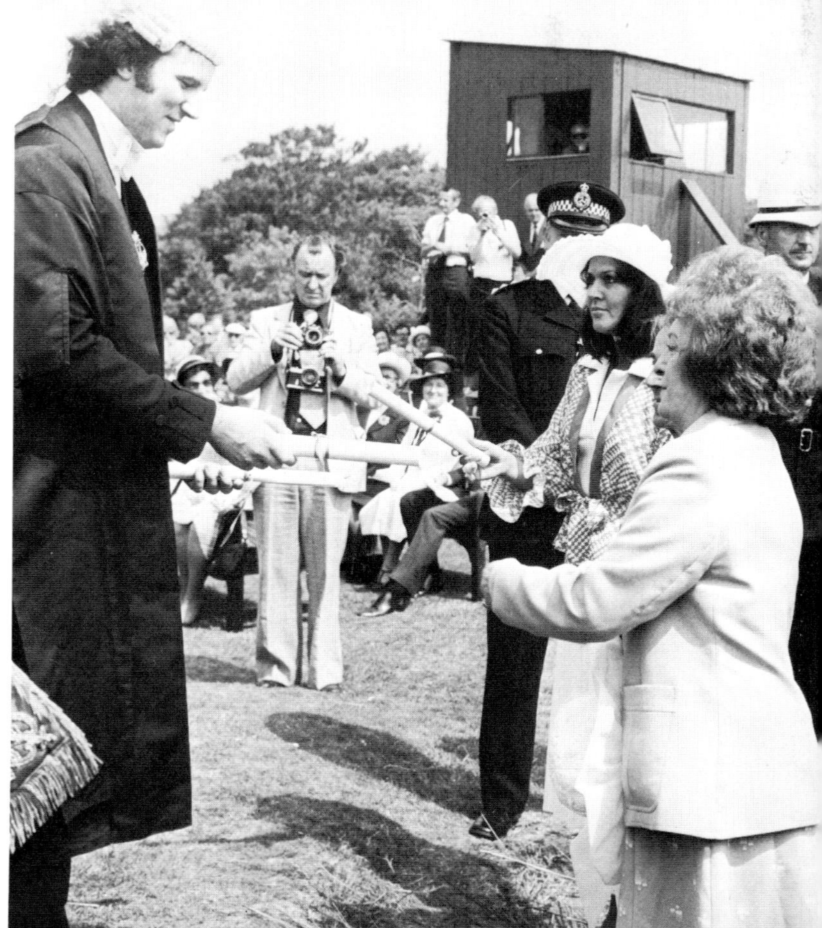

The Clameur D'Haro on Guernsey

As we travel all over the British Isles, we constantly come across relics of our rich and varied past – not just buildings and monuments and landscapes, but the remnants of the legal and administrative system which held sway at various times in the past, long before the words 'crown court' and 'local government reorganization' were even thought of! Although legislation was passed a few years ago to remove, finally, the powers of many of the remaining ancient courts, a good few still survive. And some rights, granted centuries ago, are still in force today and many bodies still have a function, though it is some years since anyone lost an ear or was clapped into the stocks at their behest!

In Guernsey, for instance, there is a traditional right to redress which reveals the island's old bilingual past. It's called the Clameur d'Haro – roughly translated from the old Celtic as 'Cry for help'. Marie De Garis, who has compiled a dictionary of English – Guernsey-French words, explained just how it works. 'It's a way of settling a dispute. For instance, if I thought someone was damaging my hedge or my wall, I would go down on my knees, and with two witnesses beside me, I would call out "*Haro! Haro! On me fait tort!*" And then I would recite the Lord's Prayer in French, and state the nature of the damage being done to what I considered was my property, until the case was settled by the Royal Court. It still happens today, quite frequently.'

The Tynwald Ceremony on the Isle of Man

Another of our offshore islands steeped in history, with ancient rights of its own, is the Isle of Man, as we discovered when *Down Your Way* visited the island during the celebrations for the millennium of the Tynwald, the island's Parliament, in the presence of the Lord of Man, the Queen. On Tynwald Day, 5 July, when all the new laws passed by Tynwald during the previous year are read aloud before they can become law, any subject can petition the Lord of Man, or in her absence her representative, the island's Governor, with any grievance that cannot be resolved in a court of law. In recent years, for instance, the bookmakers petitioned for the betting shops to be allowed to open in the afternoons, two women petitioned against the abolition of the birch, and someone petitioned for the creation of a Manx cultural centre on the island.

'Generally speaking,' the Governor, Sir John Paul, told us, 'there are one or two petitioners who come forward and hand over their petitions to the Clerk of Tynwald, which he will then hand to the Queen. She will say, "I will refer these to the Standing Committee to see if they are in order," and if they are, they will be dealt with by the normal process in the course of the next legislative session.'

Tynwald Day ceremonies take place on Tynwald Hill, St Johns, which is a series of stepped circular grass platforms rather like a wedding cake. Part of the ceremony goes back even beyond the founding of Tynwald in AD 979. The processional way along which the Queen walks to Tynwald Hill is always strewn with rushes, which were the traditional offering made every year to appease the Celtic god of the sea, Manannan.

'When we get up to the top of the hill,' Sir John went on, 'I think the first thing the Queen will say will be, "Learned Deamster, direct the court to be fenced." And Learned Deamster will then "fence" the court in Manx – which means, in effect, that it is closed in, and order has got to be preserved. We have two Deamsters – the equivalent of High Court Judges. The first Deamster is the equivalent of the Chief Justice, and the Second Deamster is a judge of the High Court.

'The next procedure after that is for the Coroners to be given their staves of office. They are not coroners in the sense you would understand in England. They're officers of the court and are really largely there for the enforcement of payment of debts. Then we really get down to the business, the real purpose of the Tynwald Court of St Johns, and that is the actual proclamation of the laws. The Queen would then say, "Learned Deamsters, I exalt you to proclaim to the people in the ancient form the laws as have been enacted during the past year and which have received our Royal Assent." Then the First Deamster will read out the laws in Manx – just the short titles, because it does take up a bit of time – and the Second Deamster will read them out in English. This year there are only eighteen new laws, fortunately. We have had occasions when there have been rather more than that, and it can take quite a little time.

'It stems, of course, from the old days when the Norsemen were here, when they felt that if the citizens were expected to abide by the laws, then they should know what they were!' Once the petitioners have been dealt with, the procession makes its way back down the hill to the Chapel of St John. 'The laws are then "captioned" – that is to say, they are signed by the Queen, customarily with a quill pen, and then they are signed by the Speaker, and that is the end of the proceedings.'

Much of the Isle of Man's present system of government is Norse in origin, dating from the eighth and ninth centuries when the Vikings swept down the west coast of Scotland, through the outer isles, and conquered the island. 'Tynwald' itself comes from a Norse word, as the Speaker, Sir Charles Carouche, explained. 'It is the only remaining example of the once popular '*Althing* of Scandinavian countries, and the word itself comes from the Old Norse expression *Thing Völlr* which means Parliament field, or meeting-place.'

Tynwald, like the British Parliament, is divided into two houses, an upper house called the Legislative Council, and a lower house called the House of Keys. According to Sir Charles, the word 'Keys' comes from the Old Norse-Gaelic word *kjeas*, meaning 'chosen'. 'So my colleagues and I are the chosen representatives of the Manx people.' Other people feel that there is another derivation – since there are twenty-four elected members, they believe 'Keys' comes from the Manx *Yn Kiarelas-Feed*, which means 'The Four and Twenty', and was corrupted by English officials who couldn't get their tongues round it!

On the back of the Speaker's chair is carved the famous 'Three Legs of Man', the island's emblem. 'The original emblem', said Sir Charles, 'was a Viking ship with furled sails, but around 1262 the emblem was changed to the Three Legs of Man, which I believe is Sicilian in origin. Accompanying it is a tag which means, "Whichever way you throw me, I stand."'

The island is divided up politically into six constituencies called 'sheadings'. 'This name goes back to Viking times,' Sir Charles told us, when a sheading was a defensive division in the island, responsible for providing a twenty-six-foot war galley for defensive purposes. The word comes, I believe, from the Norwegian *skeid*, meaning a ship.'

The island's relationship with the Crown and with the Parliament at Westminster is a unique one. Its allegiance to the Queen is through her title of Lord of Man. 'It is a Crown dependency, and as far as Westminster is concerned the relationship is through the Home Office. Internally we have complete autonomy, subject to the proviso that we maintain good law and order and good government. Externally, the United Kingdom looks after our interests in the international field, and for that we pay a contribution to the United Kingdom. On the whole we look after our own affairs, we pay our own way, and we are proud of our independence in that respect.'

The island's government is independent in another respect too, in that political parties have never had much success. 'We certainly have representation here from the Labour Party, and the National Party and so on, but they are not in strength, or such strength as would enable them to form a government. So it is really a government of independents, working on a consensus of opinion.'

The Verderers' Court in the New Forest, Hampshire

The New Forest in Hampshire, given its name in 1079 by William the Conqueror, who hunted there, is also steeped in history. Here you can find the Rufus Stone, which marks the spot where King William Rufus was killed 'by an arrow from an unknown hand', as the history books put it. And in Lyndhurst, the administrative centre of the Forest, is the Verderers' Hall, built in 1388, where the Verderers' Court still sits to administer the laws that to this day govern the Forest. George Cross, one-time Chief Forester, told us that the Forest covers some 97,000 acres, 65,000 acres of it owned by the Crown '... lock, stock and barrel, with powers of management vested in the Forestry Commission ... the rest is Manor ground, private holdings granted in years gone by for services rendered – so you have Beaulieu Manor, Minstead Manor, Brockenhurst Manor, and so on.'

As private citizens, George Cross was quick to assure us, we had absolutely no rights in the Forest at all. 'But you are privileged – privileged to come and park your car in the car park, and then privileged to walk in any part of the Forest you like!' What members of the public are no longer privileged to do, though, is camp anywhere they choose in the Forest. A number of very destructive forest fires, and other damage done by an ever-increasing number of people and cars, has led to camping being strictly limited to officially designated sites.

If you happen to be one of the Forest's commoners, though, you have all sorts of rights, as Hugh Pasmore, one of the verderers told us. 'The commoner has got an inalienable right to ride in the Forest. The public hasn't got that right – they ride in it by courtesy of the Forestry Commission.' A commoner also enjoys four other common rights, as George Cross explained: 'The common right of grazing for commoners' animals, the common right of pannage, which means you can turn pigs into the forest to eat beechnuts and acorns. Then there's the right of turvery, which allows certain people to dig peat turves for their fires, though it's not much exercised these days, and finally there is the right of estovers of wood, for which the Crown has to provide stacks of wood for certain properties completely free, and the commoners can come and collect that wood and take it home to burn.'

The common rights and obligations that go with them are governed by the Verderers' Court, which consists of ten verderers, one appointed by the Queen, four appointed by bodies like the Forestry Commission and the Countryside Commission, and five elected by the commoners. The verderers, who must own at least one acre of land and have common rights in the Forest, all give their services voluntarily. 'We do get a haunch of venison at the beginning of the year,' Hugh Pasmore told us, 'but that's the only thing we do get in the way of recompense. And I hope it stays that way, because people who become verderers are so devoted to the Forest that they are prepared to do this without payment of any kind.'

The Court legislates for all the commoners' animals in the Forest. 'There are three thousand five hundred ponies, two thousand cattle, and one hundred and eight donkeys, to be precise. We make the commoners look after their animals properly, we help them with the annual round-ups and so forth, and additionally and increasingly now, the Court of Verderers is concerned very much with the amenity of the Forest, and we do co-operate very closely with the Forestry Commission over all that happens in the open Forest.'

Clearly, keeping track of some six thousand animals in almost seventy thousand acres of forest is a full-time job, and so the verderers have paid officers called agisters. 'We have three at the moment, but we're proposing to have a fourth, and it is their job to look after all the animals. Each agister, of course, has a horse on which he rides round the Forest, and he also has a car, with a

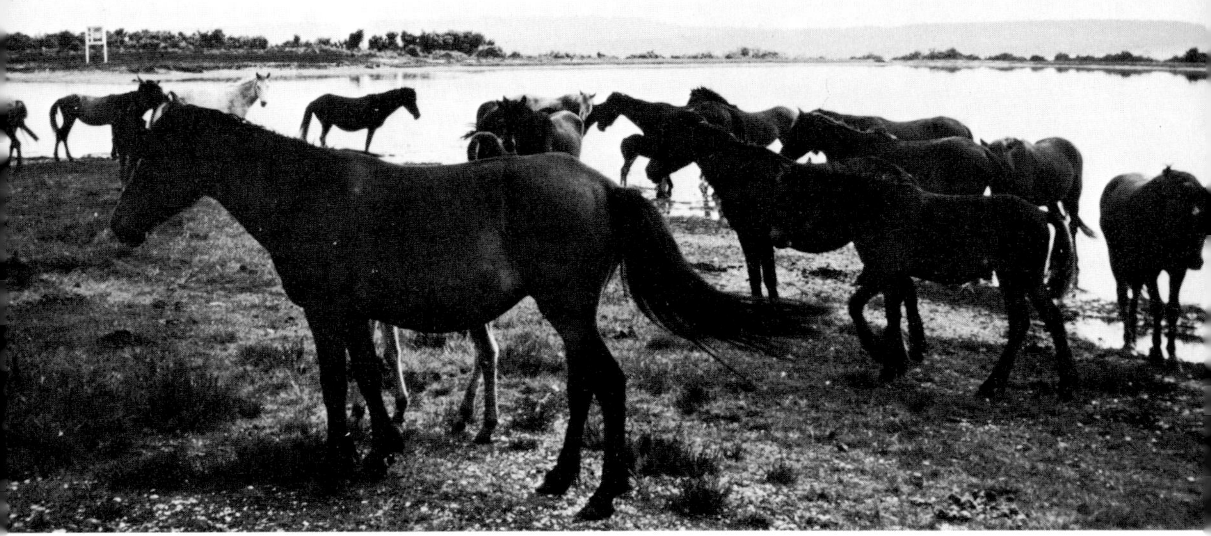

New Forest ponies at Hatchet Pond, Beaulieu. There are some 3,500 ponies in the Forest, under the jurisdiction of the Verderers' Court.

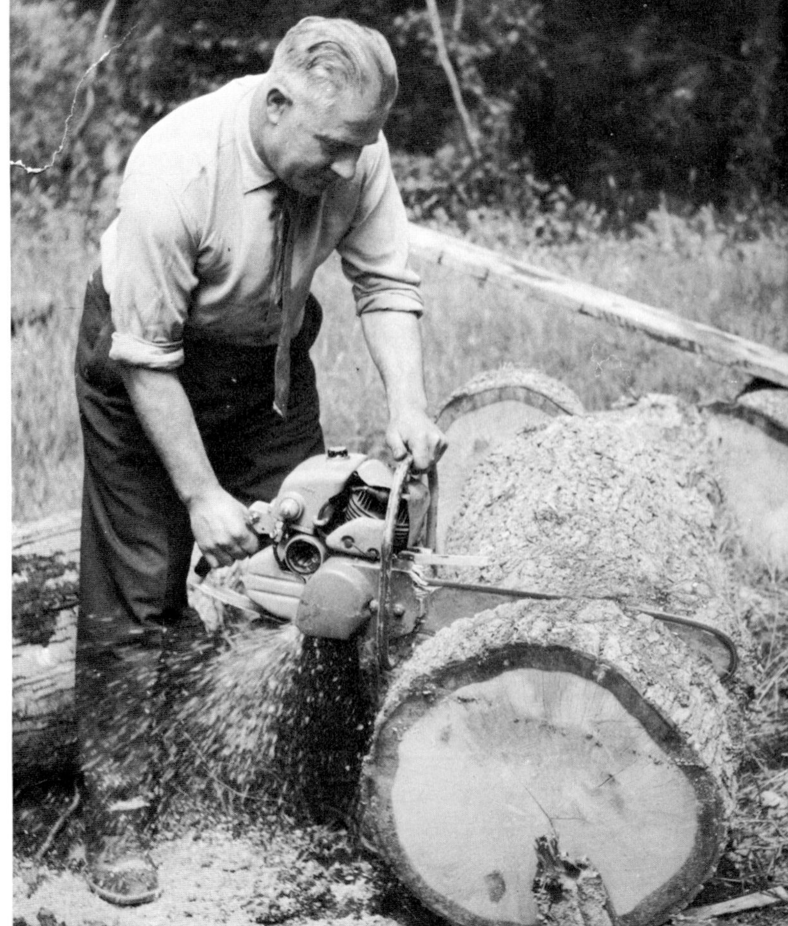

George Cross, former Chief Forester. Private citizens have no rights in the Forest, but are privileged to walk in it freely. However, certain properties are entitled to free firewood.

cattle- or horse-trailer attached, and a two-way radio which is connected to the police, so that if they hear of an accident involving a pony or cattle they merely get on the wireless to the agister and he can be at the scene of the accident within minutes.'

The welfare of the animals is of primary importance. During the winter months, when there is little food around for the ponies, some of them get very thin indeed. 'The verderers are conscious of this, and the agisters have orders to tell a man to remove his pony if it falls below a certain standard.'

The New Forest ponies are famous all over the world, and though they appear to come in all shapes and sizes, there is now an official New Forest breed. 'They've been crossed with many other breeds during the nineteenth century, but now we've got a stud book for the New Forest pony, and for the last forty or fifty years no outside breeds have been allowed to interbreed with them.'

Although the Forest covers a vast area, it isn't as difficult for the commoners to keep an eye on their animals as it might seem. 'When you turn a pony out into the Forest it settles down in a particular position, and from then on, probably for the next fifteen or twenty years of its life, it never moves more than three or four miles. The commoner has, of course, branded his animals before he turns them out, and during the summer that brand is clearly visible, but in the winter the brands are grown over. Even then the commoner knows his own animals!'

Towards the end of the summer the first round-up or drift as they call it locally, takes place. To an outsider it looks like utter chaos, with people chasing ponies in all directions, but it's more organized than that! 'There are about thirty drifts held in the Forest, and the first of the Beaulieu Road sales, at which the animals are disposed of by the commoners, is during August. From then on, till the beginning of November, we have periodic round-ups. Regrettably, now, I suppose, eighty to ninety per cent of them go for human consumption.' The domestic animals aren't the only ones living in the Forest – there are also badgers, foxes and deer. 'I suppose there are about a thousand deer in the Forest,' said Hugh Pasmore. 'They are wild animals, but if they come on to the commoners' land, and are doing damage, they have the right to shoot them under the Deer Act. But that apart, they are nothing to do with the commoners in the way that the ponies are.'

Though the wild life in the Forest is preserved to a degree, some hunting is still done. 'It is an old, traditional area for the purposes of sport,' George Cross told us. 'Hunting, the chase and falconry – they were the very things that started the Forest off in the first place.'

The Verderers' Court in the Forest of Dean, Gloucestershire

The Verderers' Court and the common rights in another of England's great primordial forests, the Forest of Dean, owe their very existence to the royal passion for hunting, as we learnt from Harry Beddington, local poet and author, when we visited the town of Cinderford. Fourteen miles west of Gloucester, the town lies on the side of a steep hill, and to reach it you drive along a lovely, scenic route, winding round the hills and valleys of the twenty-two-thousand-acre forest.

'It belongs to the Crown, and of course their main concern is production of timber now, but back in the old days it was the hunting. You had the Norman kings all doing their hunting here, and driving out the foresters, and when they drove them out they gave the people they dispossessed commoners' rights, which they still hold today.

'They have the right to run sheep on the parts that are not enclosed for the growth of young trees, under mature trees, and on unplanted areas. We call them "shep badgers" – the people who chase after their sheep. They spend as much time driving other people's sheep off their own bit of land! You don't get the pigs run into the Forest like you used to – they used to run them in for chestnuts and the acorns, but pig-rearing is a more commercial business now.'

Since there aren't as many animals in the Forest of Dean as there are in the New Forest, there are only four verderers, thought to have originated in the reign of King Canute, between 1016 and 1035. Although the Court is supposed to meet every forty days, most meetings these days go by default, and it only meets in earnest once a year in the isolated seventeenth-century Speech House in the heart of the Forest, which is now a hotel. Officially it still has the power to try offences 'against the vert and the venison' – against any growing trees and any animals in the forest – though what tends to happen is that the Forestry Commission prosecute offenders in the local magistrates' court.

'The verderers look after the rights of the Forest and the "shep badgers" and the Free Miners (of whom more later), and I think they do quite a bit of good, watching out for the usage of the Forest now that there are many more tourists here.' Progress has brought inevitable changes to the Forest – even the trees are changing. 'Back in the old days it used to be deciduous trees, the beech and the oak mostly, but now they find that conifers are much cheaper trees to grow and the oaks are being thinned out.'

Free Miners' rights in the Forest of Dean

One of the Forest's most ancient surviving traditions is the right of the Free Miners to dig for iron and coal. Ray Wright, the Secretary of the Forest of Dean Free Miners' Association, told us about the miners' history. 'Nobody knows

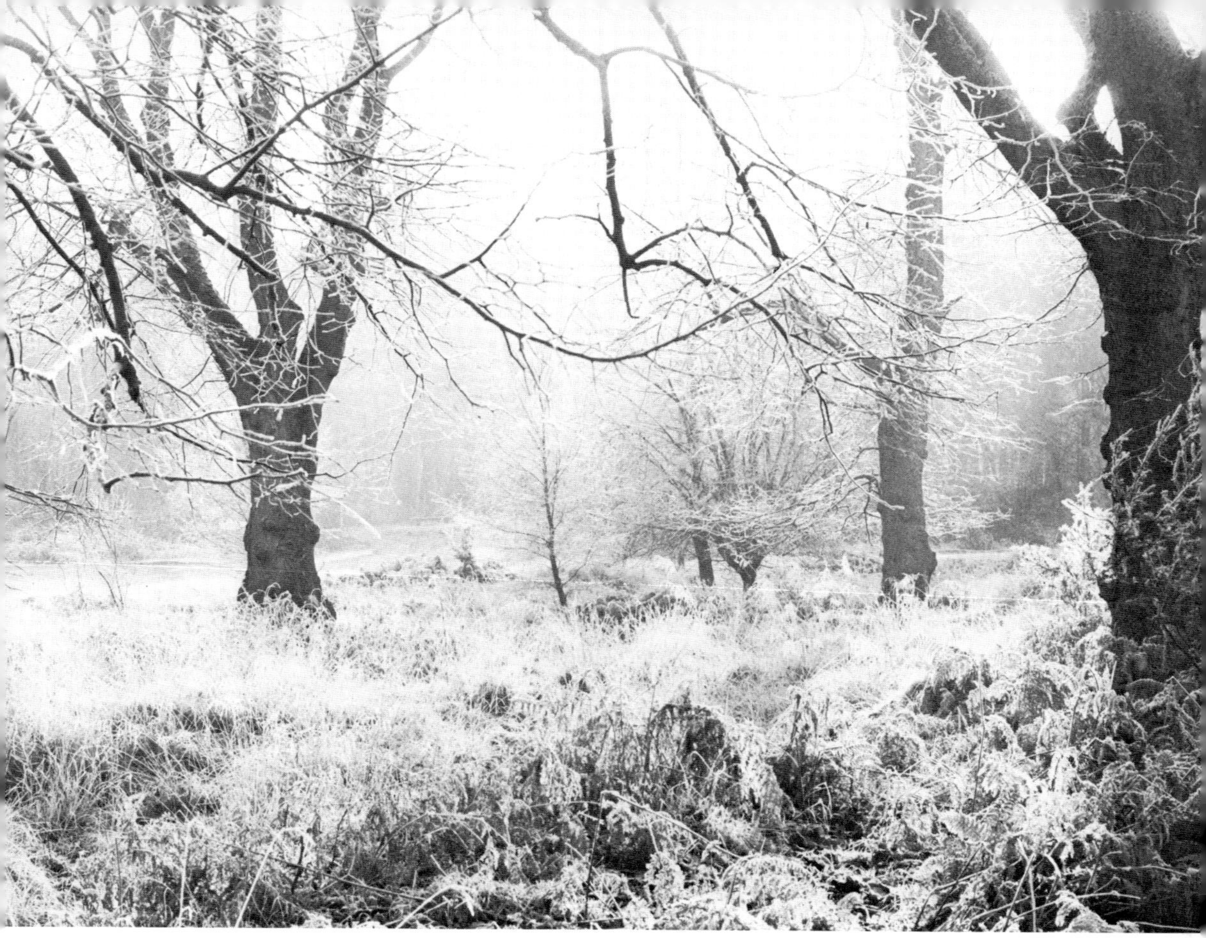

A frosty scene behind the Speech House in the Forest of Dean.

Henley-in-Arden provides a splendid setting for the ceremony of the Bailiff's Court.

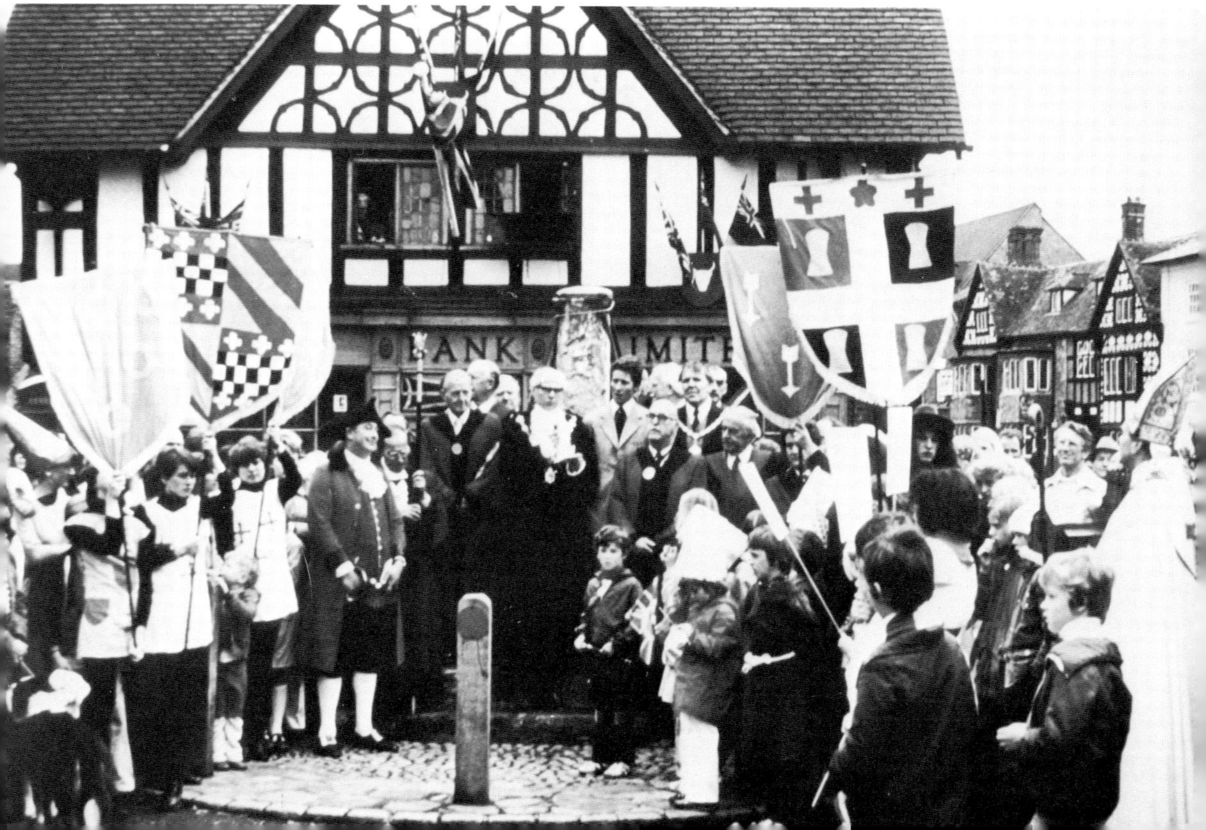

when they started because they go back in time out of mind, as they say, but it's about three or four thousand years ago since the mining industry started here, mainly with iron mining. The original miners were part of the ancient British tribes which migrated across from Europe into this area many thousands of years ago, and a particular Silurian tribe settled in this area. They were a very stubborn type of people, and they hung on to their rights, because they always believed that they owned the Forest of Dean and all the minerals within it.'

The Free Miners have a vocabulary all their own, based mainly, so Ray Wright said, on Old English with a bit of Welsh thrown in. 'There's a "gale", which is a birthright or holding which is allotted to each miner if he wishes. They're all different shapes and sizes, according to how the minerals crop out in the ground. Then there are "churns" – they're large cavities underground – "scowles", which are large cavities which open up to the surface and look very much like deep canyons in the rock. And then there's a "bern" which is a help-mate, or an apprentice Free Miner!'

The qualifications that any would-be Free Miner must fulfil are quite clear. You have to be male and over twenty-one, you have to have served an apprenticeship of a year and a day, and you have to have been born within the Hundred of St Briavels. 'This is quite a large area of land, embracing the whole of the Forest as it exists today. Back in medieval times the kings of England required fighting men, and they split England up into areas known as "Hundreds", where they could get a hundred fighting men from!'

Once you've fulfilled all the qualifications you have to apply to the Gaveller's office. 'The Gaveller is the man who looks after all the rights of the Free Miners. He administers everything connected with Free Mining in the Forest. He gives you a form which you have to go away and fill in, and get someone to sign to prove that you've worked your year and a day in a mine.'

Iron-mining died out more or less completely in the Forest at the turn of the century when all the large deposits were worked out. 'But there is still thousands of tons of iron dotted about all over the place, and during the two World Wars, when it started to get difficult to get iron from abroad and very expensive, they started mining in the Forest again. But it finally finished in 1945.'

Ray himself has an iron gail at Clearwell. 'I mine small amounts of iron – some I sell to the public, and some I send to the local foundry to be smelted down, mainly to make Free Miners' plaques. I also open the gail up occasionally to the public to show them how they mined iron in the old days!'

The Barmoot Court at Wirksworth, Derbyshire

Up in Wirksworth, Derbyshire, they mined for lead, not iron, and although there is very little done these days, everything connected with lead-mining is governed by the Barmoot Court, which still meets twice a year – in April and October –

at the one-hundred-and-fifty-year-old Moot Hall in the town. 'The Court itself', said Horace Ellam, who was unofficial organizer of the Court for over thirty years, 'is far, far older than that, though. So old that nobody knows the exact date.' They do know for certain, though, that the Court was meeting at the beginning of the sixteenth century, for in the Moot Hall there is a ceremonial brass dish, used for measuring lead ore, which bears the date 1512 and which was presented to the court by Henry VIII in that year.

'The object of the Court', Horace said, 'was to register the claims for any lead found in the district, in the "King's Field". That's the ground surrounding here, which is owned by the Duchy of Lancaster – or in other words, the Crown. Anyone prospecting for lead and finding it had to come to Court and stake his claim.' Although these days lead-mining is only done incidentally – it is sometimes found when people are mining for fluorspar and barytes – they register the claim just in case, and, as Horace Ellam explained, the old miners' rights still hold good.

'As long as you aren't in a churchyard, or on the highway or in an orchard, you could stand up in any farmers' field, and if you could prove that there was lead there, you could stake your claim. And one-thirteenth of any lead you got out of the ground would go to the Duchy of Lancaster.'

In the old days the Court had powers to punish anyone trying to defraud the Duchy of its thirteenth share, or stealing lead. If you were caught three times, on the third occasion your hand would be pinned to the wooden winding-shaft, and you either pulled yourself free, obviously injuring your hand in the process, or you starved. These days offenders are still summoned to the Court, but all they're likely to get is a rap over the knuckles.

The Steward and the Barmaster are appointed by the Queen as Duke of Lancaster. The Barmaster chooses a jury of twelve local men from a list he has of miners – of any substance – or quarry-owners.

Before the Court is convened, what is known as "Miners' Refreshments" are served – bread, cheese and beer, a relic from the old days when the jurymen might have had to travel some distance to get to Court. When the Court is formally convened the jury elects a chairman, and then they are all formally sworn in – a much longer oath than the traditional jurymen's oath, and unlike other juries they are not discharged when the Court rises. They remain on call till the next jury is sworn in, and can be summoned by the Barmaster at any time to view a claim.

The Steward then gives 'the charge to the jury', which means that he goes into great detail about their duties in old, formal English, before any claims are dealt with. If there are none, the sessions last about half an hour, after which all the members retire to the Hope and Anchor for the traditional banquet – tomato soup, roast sirloin of beef, Yorkshire pudding, horseradish, cauliflower cheese, green peas and baked potatoes, followed by college pudding with rum sauce, and washed down with a special punch, made from rum, brandy, black beer and some secret ingredients known only to the Barmaster and the man who makes it!

'After lunch is over,' Horace Ellam said, 'and you get permission to smoke, there's a very light shag tobacco put on the table, and all the jurymen and guests are issued with a clay pipe. The lead-miners used to smoke small clay pipes, and they still find them in the old lead mines sometimes.'

The Bailiff's Court at Henley-in-Arden, Warwickshire

There was a time in Britain when every Manor, in legal terms anyway, was an independent body with its own courts meting out its own often very rough justice. Two of those courts still survive today. Over fifty towns have a Court Leet, and some also have a Court Baron. Henley-in-Arden, in the heart of Shakespeare country, has both.

Walter Collins, who was High Bailiff when we visited the town, explained the difference. 'The Courts Baron were concerned with land and property, and the Courts Leet were concerned with law and order, fair trading and so forth.' These days the courts and their officers no longer have any legal powers, but, as Walter Collins pointed out, that is not to say that they are without influence.

'We are quite active, but we do rely very much on our prestige. The fact that the Court Leet is recognized locally as a very important body gives it enormous influence. One recent example was a river improvement scheme that the Severn and Trent River Board wanted to carry out. The Court Leet was very active in the public outcry, and the Board did modify its plans as a result.'

The High Bailiff and the other officers are elected annually every November at the town's Guildhall, by the jurors of the town – people who live here and are virtually the descendants of the original Freemen. The Lord of the Manor – a young man called Timothy Robinson who lives in France and trains racehorses – plays a very important part. He attends these meetings and actually places the chain of office on the shoulders of the elected High Bailiff. 'He wears a black robe with white cuffs and cravat, while the other members of the Court wear red robes, trimmed with black. We meet in full robes certainly at the annual meeting, but otherwise we meet and parade in the major town and church functions during the year. I would think the nearest description of the High Bailiff's function is that of first citizen, and the job does involve a lot of attendance at local functions – very enjoyable it is, too!'

Besides the High Bailiff, the Court also appoints a Low Bailiff, mace-bearer, constable, a butter-weigher, an ale-taster, a town crier, chaplain, steward, two affearors – who set fines and collected the money in the days when the court levied fines – and two brook-lookers. 'This is still an important office in the town, but was even more so years ago. The River Alne, which we call "the brook'', runs just behind the High Street, and the brook-lookers take a great interest in seeing that it is cleared and kept in a nice-sweet condition. These days they function unofficially – we mustn't forget that there are official bodies who do a good job – but our brook-lookers are still quite active in that respect!'

The Court Leet at Alcester, Warwickshire

They have brook-lookers – or brook-watchers – in the nearby town of Alcester, with its beautiful old timber-framed buildings, where they also have a Court Leet, or, to give it its full title, 'The Court Leet, Court Baron and View of Frankpledge of the most honourable Hugh Edward Conway, Marquis of Hertford'. Quite how old it is no one knows for certain, but by the time it is first mentioned in the Alcester Manor Rolls, kept at Warwick Castle, in 1299, it was already so well established that it had secured a customary right.

The Court Leet, as Aubrey Gwinnett, the town's Constable, told us, was a Court of Record. 'It could fine, but it could not imprison, and though it could try people accused of capital offences, like sheep-stealing, it could not hang them, so they had to be referred to the Sherriff's Court to be hung!'

In the old days the Court Leet used to be held every three weeks to deal with all the petty offences that had been committed – failing to move a privy, for instance, selling 'flesh corrupt', playing unlawful games like quoits, bowling, or dicing, and stopping up ditches and not scouring them. The Alcester Manor records also reveal the kind of punishments handed out – 'Blanche, wife of Richard Hasuhold, fine four pence for assaulting the Bailiff. Richard, servant of Richard Preyers of Evesham, fined two shillings for selling stock herring putrid and unfit for consumption.' And it wasn't only the poor who fell foul of the Court either. The Alcester rolls also record that the Lord of the Manor was fined five pounds for failing to provide the Bailiff with a dinner.

These days the Court Leet meets once a year in October, summoned by the Steward of the Manor, who is still appointed by the Lord of the Manor, the Marquess of Hertford, who lives at Ragley Hall just outside the town. The Leet's chief officer, the High Bailiff, is elected, though, '... by common consent of the township', to be chief citizen and superintend the '... peasantry's labour, and to account at the annual audit as to all the financial dealings carried out by him or on his behalf for the residents'. Besides the High Bailiff there is also a Low Bailiff, as in Henley-in-Arden, a town crier and beadle, ale-tasters – 'They go round with the other officers of the Court Leet twice a year, and taste the ale at the various pubs and declare that it is fit for man to drink!' – fish- and flesh-tasters, affearors, a hayward in charge of fences and enclosures, and of course a constable.

In the old days, Aubrey Gwinnett told us, his predecessors were responsible for arresting offenders and putting them in the stocks. 'I have a truncheon which is dated 1722 with the initials "IM", or possibly "JM", on it. I'm sure it's an original one because I rescued it years ago from a very old man, and it had belonged to another person's family in Alcester who was constable in 1799!'

Down in his cellar Aubrey has another relic from the bad old days – the old town stocks. 'They're the original ones that my father rescued many years ago. They were going to be chopped up, and my father begged them from the man who owned them! They're most unusual. I should think they're unique in this country because they were originally on wheels. The chap was pushed round the town, and the old people said that they were even pushed in the river sometimes!'

Planting the Penny Hedge at Whitby, Yorkshire

In Whitby, Yorkshire, they still go through an ancient rite every year on the eve of Ascension Day, which originated in Norman times to right an ancient wrong. It's called 'Planting the Penny Hedge', as Bill Slater, former editor of the *Whitby Gazette*, explained.

'It originates from a legend that the Hermit of Eskdale Side was set upon by three Norman nobles for giving sanctuary to a boar they were hunting. The hermit received fatal injuries, and before his death he imposed the penance that the hedge, made of "stowers and yedders" – in other words, branches and twigs – should be built in Whitby harbour on the Eve of Ascension at nine o'clock in the morning. If they failed to build the hedge, or if it failed to stand three tides, they forfeited their lands to the Abbot of Whitby.'

Today, nearly eight hundred years later, the hedge is still built by a member of the Hutton family, descendants of the three Norman nobles. 'At the end of the ceremony, an ancient horn is sounded three times – it's rather like a hunting horn and has been in use for five hundred years. In addition, the Bailiff of the Manor of Fyling will give the rebuke, "Out on ye! Out on ye!", which is how the Hermit of Eskdale Side rebuked the noblemen at the time of his death.'

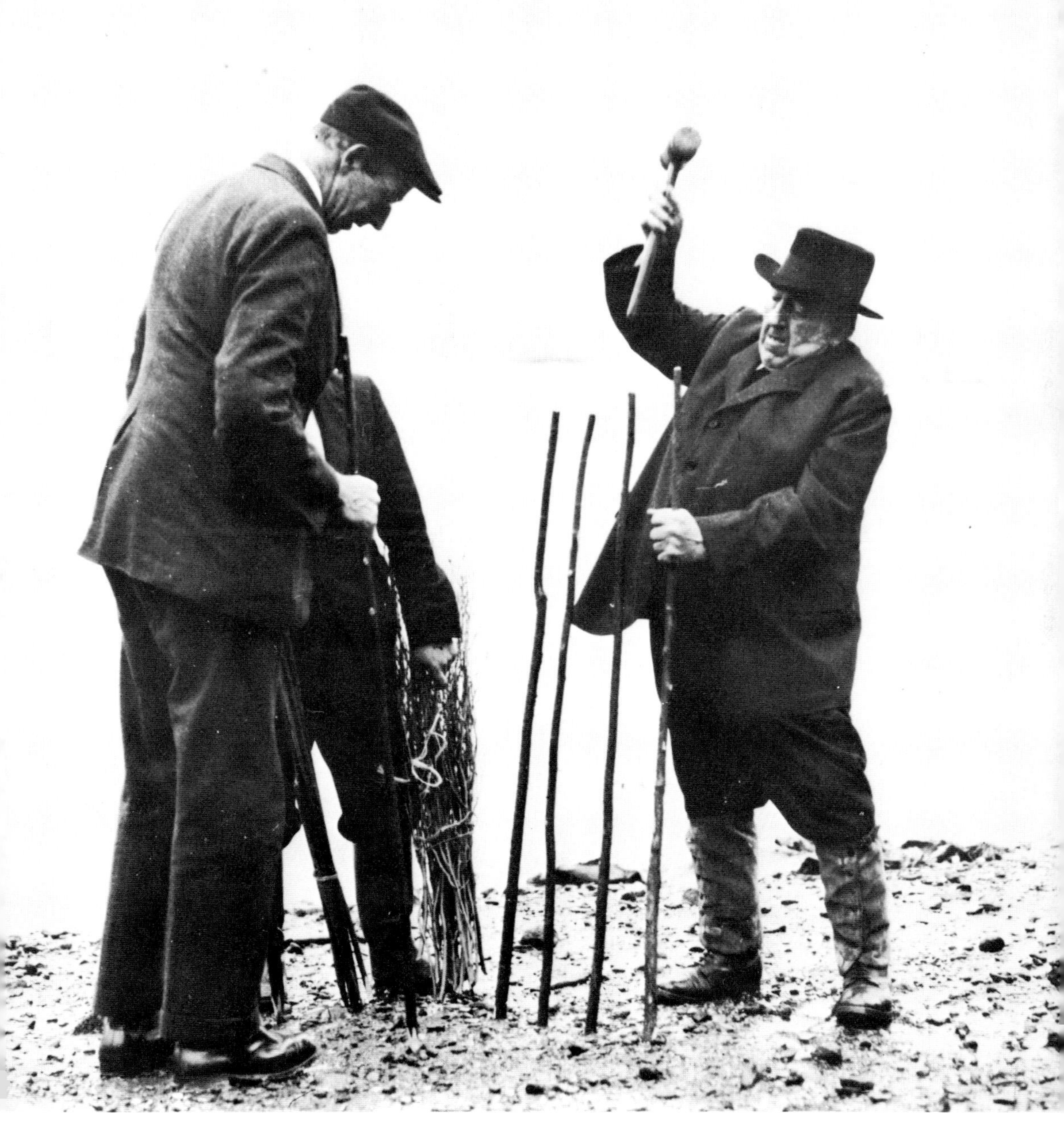

The 'Penny Hedge', planted every year in Whitby harbour in accordance with the dying words of the Hermit of Eskdale Side.

At the Water's Edge

Life on the seashore and the internal waterways

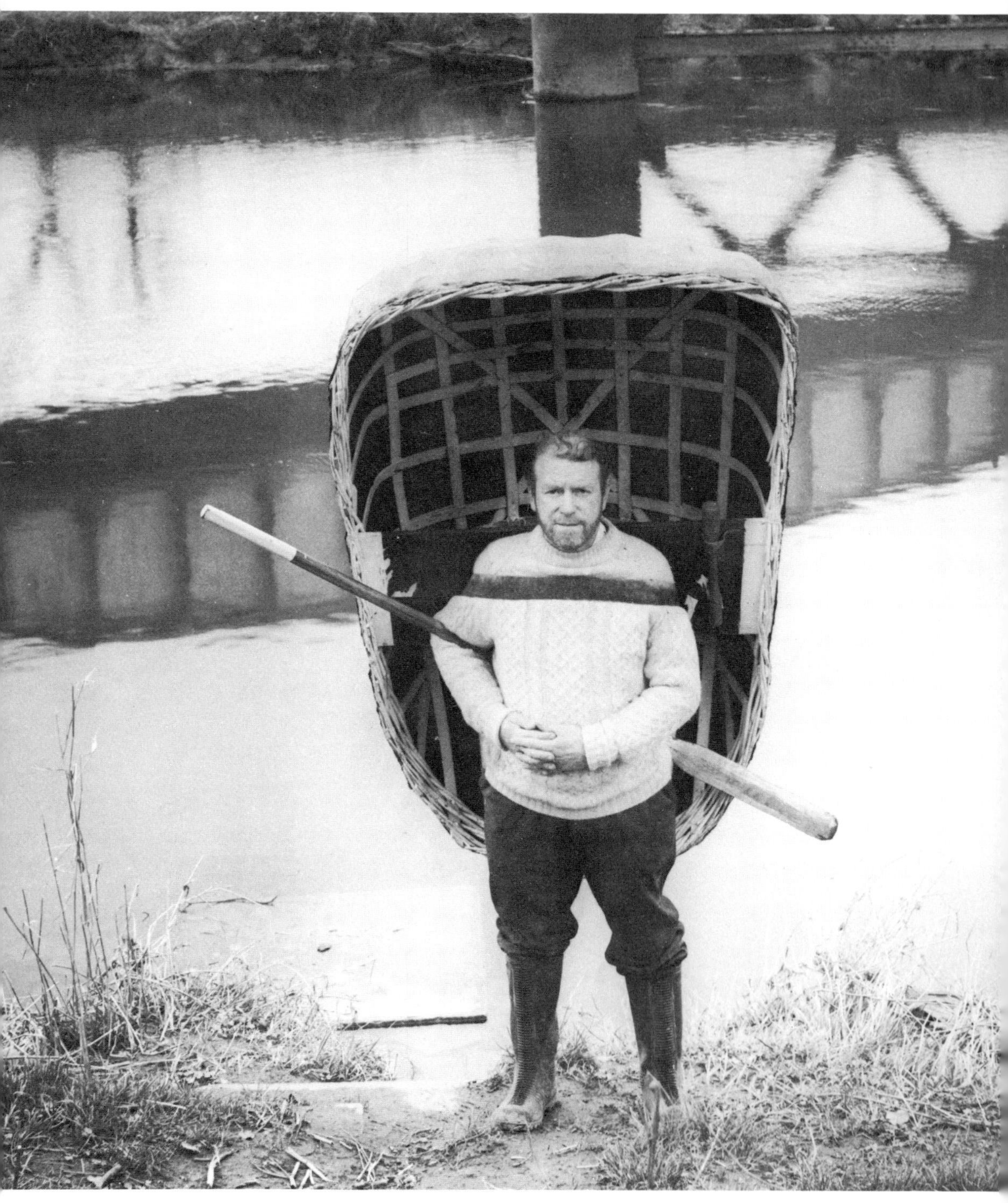

Ray Rees, coracle fisherman on the River Tywi. The manoeuvrability of the coracle is an advantage in salmon-fishing.

Coracle fishing at Carmarthen, Dyfed

Even though Britannia no longer rules the waves, the sea around our shores is still fundamental to our way of life, The Channel, for instance, has been our last, or best, line of defence since 1066, not only against foreign armies, but against foreign viruses like rabies, too. We are still a maritime nation, even though, these days, it manifests itself not in the might of our navy or the size of our merchant fleet, but in the hundreds of thousands of us who regularly make our way, lemming-like, down to the water in every conceivable kind of small boat and craft.

The sea that surrounds us has traditionally been a rich source of food, too, and although sadly our fishing industry is in decline in many places, owing to new rules and regulations and the competition for the same, limited stocks of fish from foreign fleets, less scrupulous, perhaps, than our own, British fish is still among the best you can get!

In the face of so much change, it was extremely reassuring to come across a form of fishing – and fishing craft – that has remained virtually unchanged for thousands and thousands of years – coracle fishing on the River Tywi in Carmarthen, Dyfed. We called on Ray Rees, one of the coracle fishermen still active on the river, in his hut down on the river bank, and asked him first of all to tell us about the small boat that no Ancient Briton would have any difficulty in recognizing – the coracle.

'It's rather like half an Easter Egg, a chocolate Easter Egg, with a seat across the centre of it. It is three feet four inches wide and it's about five feet six inches long, but coracles are made to suit the person who is going to use them, so they are tailor-made, in fact.' The most modern of Ray's coracles are made of fibreglass, but he still has one made on more traditional lines, which looks rather like an outsized shopping basket.

'In Carmarthen we've attempted three types. The first traditional kind was ash laths, formed into a framework. Then using willow or hazel, we put a basket weave around the top of the coracle to form a gunnel. Originally, the outside covering was animal skin. The cow played a very important part in the coracle man's materials because the hide was used to cover the coracle, the fat was used to make it waterproof, and the cow's horns, which are hollow, were cut up into rings for the top of the net – the net is like a purse and it runs on these rings – and we used the cow's tail to spin the main ropes, the hand ropes and the foot ropes. Although it's more convenient now to use polythene and nylon, there is really no substitute for the old cow's tail!'

Ray demonstrated for us just how manœuvrable the coracle is, though Brian Johnston felt sure that the only manoeuvre he'd execute successfully, should he set foot in it, was a capsize! 'Yes, they are very manœuvrable,' Ray confirmed, 'and of course we need that. If you've got a struggling twenty-five-pound salmon, he can spin you all ways round, so the thing is you need something that will give with whatever you're going to catch. We use a paddle in one hand to control the boat, and a very strange feature about the coracle, you know, is that it's got a blunt end, and a pointy end, but unlike other boats, the pointy end is the back and the round end is the front. And having said that, I'm sure you noticed that we go sideways in it.'

It's that very sideways movement that makes the coracle ideal for the kind of fishing that Ray and his colleagues do. 'We fish the river in pairs. We trawl for salmon and sea trout, with a thirty-three-feet-long net, and we drift downstream with the outgoing tide, hoping to catch the salmon on their journey up to the spawning grounds about thirty miles upstream. 'The net actually fishes the first eighteen inches from the bed of the river, so if we're fishing in twenty feet of water, there's eighteen feet six inches of water without any net, so the fish have to be on the bottom if we're going to catch them. The thing is that, if you used an ordinary boat with two oars, every time to you took a stroke it would jerk the net off the bed of the river. But by using the coracle, which has survived all these years, we just drift with the tide, and the net just stays on the bottom of the river all the time, where we want it.'

Although Ray and his fellow fishermen are allowed to fish by law at any time, they choose to fish in the evenings or at night, and keep fishing till they've caught enough. Since their method is designed only to catch one fish at a time, it can be a lengthy business. 'That's because there is only one and a half pounds of thread used in the net, so once a fish hits it he tangles it up, so it's virtually impossible to catch two – unless you're lucky enough to take two fish travelling together at exactly the same pace.'

At one time, Ray told us, there were over two thousand men working on the River Tywi catching salmon. 'These days there are just twelve working the Tywi, two pairs working the Taf, which is about eight miles downstream, and five pairs working the Teifi.'

Putcher fishing at Berkeley, Gloucestershire

On the estuary of the River Severn, at Berkeley in Gloucestershire, they also catch salmon in a traditional way, using the tide to help them, but there the similarity ends. On the Severn they use large baskets – or putchers as they call them locally, which look like giant ice-cream cornets, about the size of an average man. Maurice Haines, who has spent his whole life as a fisherman on the Severn, explained in his soft Gloucestershire burr just how it's done.

'We put them in the river on 15 April and leave them till 15 August – that's the season. We place them with the broad end pointing upstream, and when the tide comes back – when it's going out, in other words – that's when you catch the salmon. The tide is running so fast that they go into the basket, and can't get

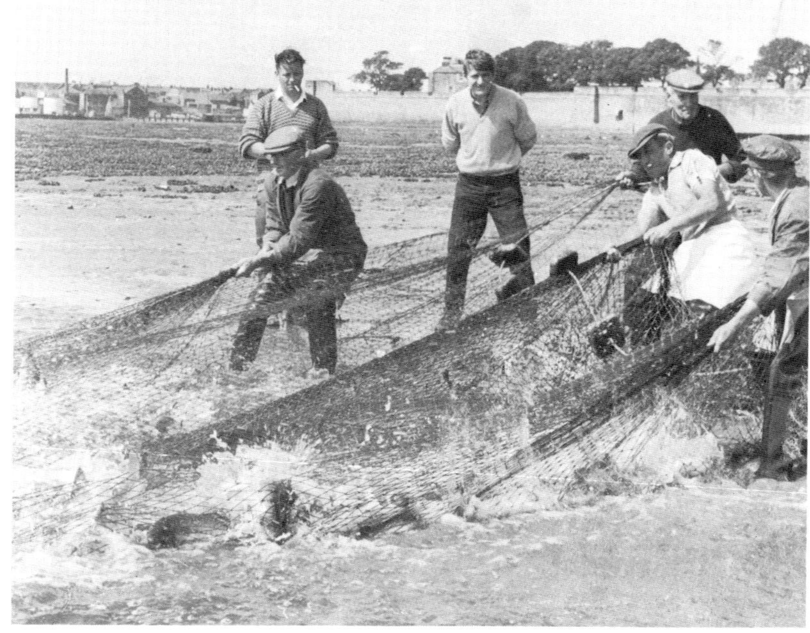

Net and cobble fishing consists of teamwork. *Above:* The net is pulled in. *Below:* Not a bad catch!

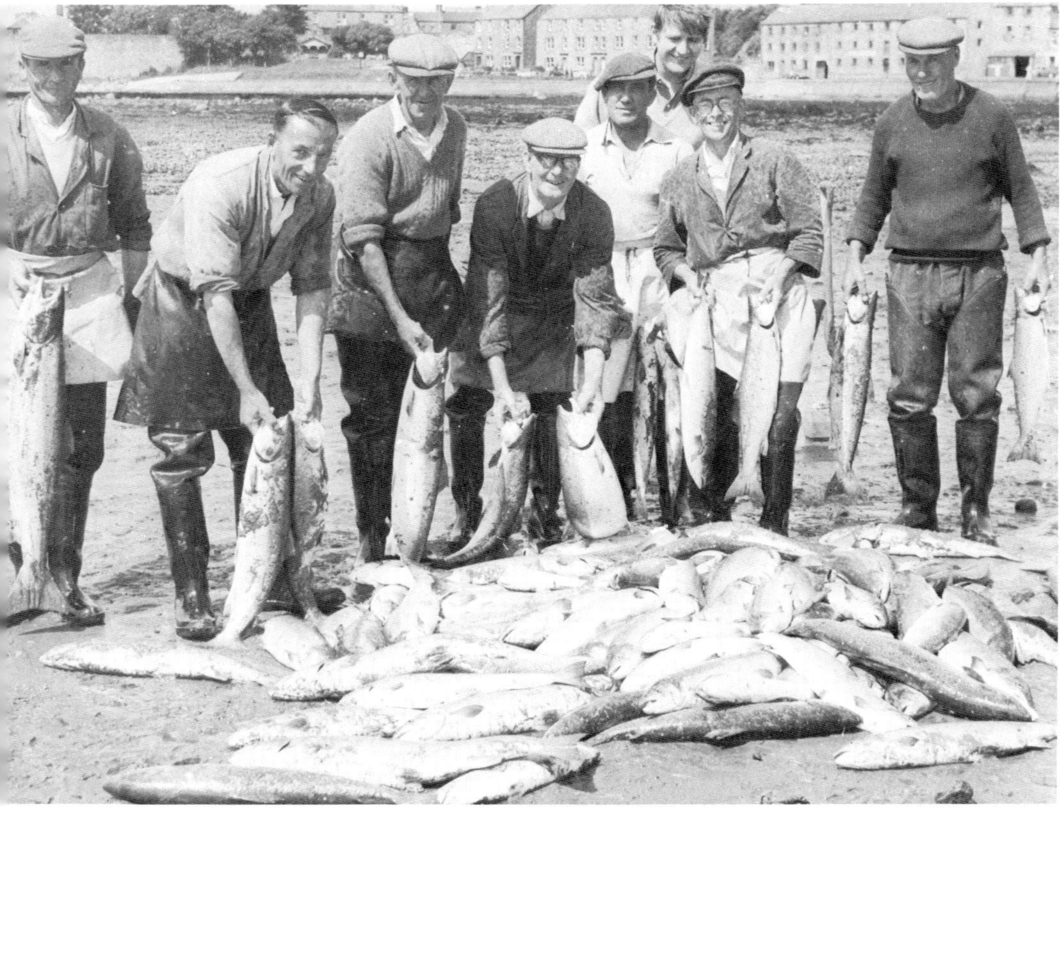

out again. The biggest fish I've ever caught here was forty-seven and a half pounds, but they come in all weights, anything from five pounds up to forty.'

The tide was in when we talked to Maurice, and the Severn at the point where we were standing was a good mile wide, so it was hard to imagine how the fish are retrieved from the putchers. 'We go down twice in twenty-four hours at low tide. When the tide's right out, there's just a small channel out in the middle and you can walk down to them easily enough, so long as you've got a pair of wellingtons on!'

Slightly bigger than a putcher, though built along the same lines, is a kipe. 'They're six foot across, some of them,' Maurice said, 'and besides salmon you can get shrimps, eels, flat fish, whiting, and I've even caught pilchards in them. Kipes are really three baskets in one – you make a big kipe, then another basket goes in that, and an even smaller one goes inside that. The smaller baskets are very tightly woven and so, although the shrimps could get out of the bigger kipes, they can't get out of these.'

Maurice and his fellow putcher fishermen make their own baskets during the winter months. 'They're made entirely from the willow we get from farms round here. It's got to be two years old. You start with a frame and you just work 'em up, you know, binding them together. You get so used to it that you can make about eight or ten in a day!'

Net and cobble fishing at Berwick-upon-Tweed, Northumberland

In Berwick-upon-Tweed, the historic town on the border between England and Scotland, which was fought over by the two nations for centuries and changed hands no less than thirteen times, they catch salmon in yet another way. Jim Reid, managing director of the Berwick Salmon Fisheries, who is also a Harbour Commissioner and a Tweed Commissioner, explained just how it is done.

'The actual process is known as net and cobble fishing – a cobble being the flat-bottomed fishing boat that is used locally and in some parts of Scotland. The boat with two men in it goes out with the net, and describes a semi-circle. One man remains on the shore, holding on to one end of the net, and walks along the shore towards the boat as it comes back in. Then the whole crew, seven men in all, gradually pull both ends together and bring the net ashore. A good catch would be about fifty or sixty salmon. The biggest I've seen weighed was forty-six pounds, and it was actually caught very close to where we're standing now, just the other side of the river.' The spot where we were standing with Jim Reid was called Hallowstell, which has an historic derivation. 'It is said that there was definitely salmon fishing here during the time of William the

Conqueror in 1066 when this actual fishery was operated by the monks. Therefore the derivation is the "hallowed stell".'

During the season, from 15 February to 14 September, the fishermen go out twice a day at low tide and fish for about four hours at a time. The catch is sent off to Billingsgate and to provincial fish markets. 'At the moment we send them away fresh, boxed in ice. Later on, of course, it's possible when the peak comes that some of them will be frozen and dispatched later. If they are frozen the way we do them – blast-freezing at forty degrees below – there's really no difference in taste between frozen and fresh.'

Salmon fishing at Fochabers, Morayshire

The purists would argue that if you're a sportsman there is only one way to catch a salmon, and that's with a rod and line, not to mention a great deal of patience and no small degree of skill! Undoubtedly one of the finest salmon rivers in the world is the River Spey, which rises in Inverness-shire, then runs through Strathspey, Aviemore and Fochabers before it runs into the North Sea at the Moray Firth.

It was at Fochabers that we met Willie Gordon, who had been a gillie (the fishing version of a gamekeeper) on Sir George Gordon-Lennox's private estate, Gordon Castle, since 1962. He looked every inch the part, too, in his plus-fours and jacket in the estate tweed, and his gillie's hat, which looks like a deerstalker. There are, he told us, no formal qualifications for the job. 'You just ask the employer if there's a vacancy, 'Willie said in his strong Highland accent, 'and if you're nae good, you dinnae last long!'

A gillie's job covers everything to do with the fish and the fishing on his stretch of river, including taking care of any newcomers to the sport. 'We concentrate on the person, if the lady or the gentleman is a beginner, you see. You have to attend to them until you think they're getting it, but it never does to stand guard on them, you see, because they begin to get a wee bit upset if they think you're watching them! But you've got to be pretty firm, you see, because the River Spey is dangerous – she's the fastest-flowing river in Scotland – and they're inclined to wade out too far, so that's what you've got to watch first. They'll maybe wade one day and it'll be all right, and then overnight you get a heavy thunderstorm, and the river will be maybe about three feet up on the day before. They might try to wade in the same place as they did yesterday, and it could be fatal!'

A good teacher helps, of course, but Willie said that teaching alone can't produce a good fisherman. 'It's sort of born into you, that! Some people will never be good fishermen, just like anything else. Take good drivers – you can teach plenty of people to drive, but that's not to say that they'll be good drivers.'

In summer, Willie told us, the best time to fish is in the evening when the sun

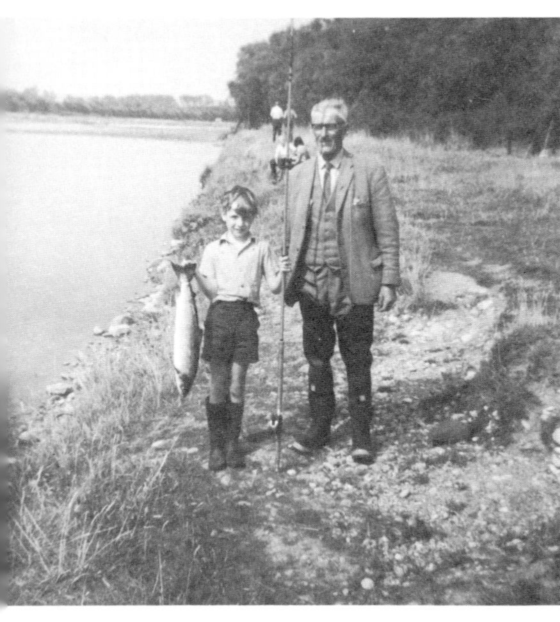

This fine salmon was caught single-handed, with rod and line, by the eight-year-old Edward Gordon-Lennox – under the watchful eye of Willie Gordon, gillie at Gordon Castle.

On the peaceful mill-pond at Nether Wallop, Dermot Wilson gives instructions on the delicate art of casting for trout.

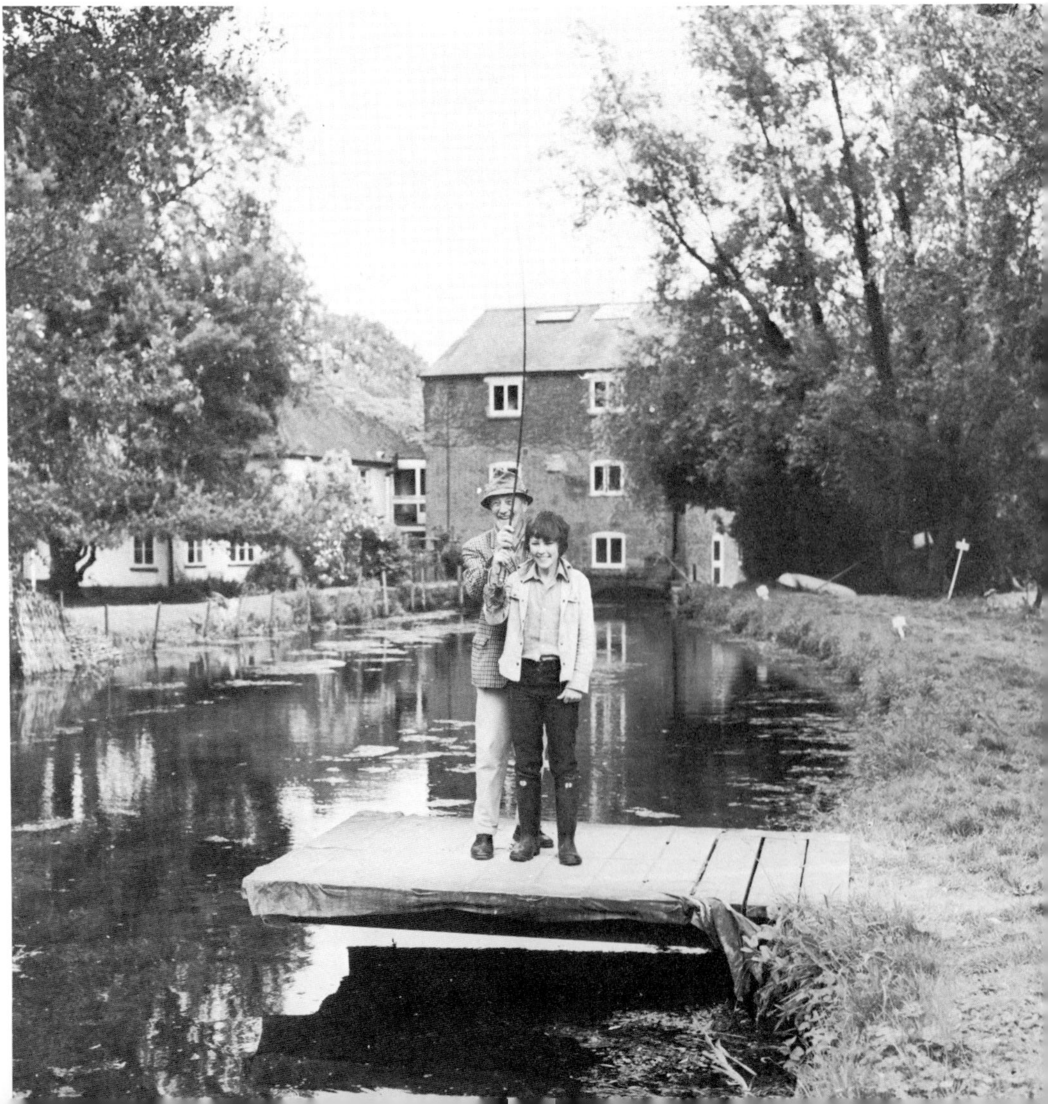

is off the water. That particular summer the fishing hadn't been very good, and Willie thought the unusually warm weather had probably had something to do with it. 'If the weather is too warm, the fish are inclined to stay out at sea until they get rain. Then, when the river is up, they'll come.'

Naturally Willie believes that the Spey is without doubt the finest salmon river in the world, though when he told us that the biggest salmon he had ever seen caught in the river was a fifty-six pounder, Brian Johnston couldn't resist asking whether that was just a fisherman's yarn. 'No, no, no, 'Willie said, with a laugh, 'we don't tell nae stories! No, no, no!'

The piece of music Willie chose for *Down Your Way* was 'The Star of Rabbie Burns'. 'He was a right lad! He stayed at the Castle once, you know, although there's no record of him catching a salmon!' He chuckled, 'He might have poached one, though!'

Fish fly tying at Tutbury, Staffordshire

Think of fishing for salmon, or for trout, and you automatically think of flies. Not the real thing, but those brilliantly coloured miniature masterpieces that deceive the fish into taking the hook. They are made – or tied as they say in the trade – by hand, and Rosa Smith, who lives in Tutbury, Staffordshire, makes them on her kitchen table in what really is a cottage industry. When we called on Rosa her table was covered with reels of differently coloured silk, bits of twine, tinsel, raffia and feathers in almost every size and colour you can imagine. She explained where they all came from.

'That's from a jungle cock – they're not obtainable now, but we've got just a few left. And that's from a golden pheasant. Those are from cockerels' necks, from starlings' wings, from crows, peacocks, pheasants, moleskin – we've used practically everything you can think of!'

There are two main kinds of fly – wet flies and dry flies. 'A wet fly sinks,' Rosa said, 'and a dry fly floats – that's the difference. To make sure it floats, you put on nice, stiff hackles.'

The range of different flies that Rosa makes is enormous, from the smallest, which looks rather like a large full-stop – the size 18 black midge, which, she told us, is one of the easiest to tie – right up to the extremely life-like daddy-long-legs, one of the largest and most complicated to tie.

'The legs are made from a strand of pheasant tail, and you tie two knots in them, to make the joints of the legs. You then tie on two hackle points for the wings, and we make them "spent" – to look like a real fly after it has laid its eggs and collapsed on to the water with its wings out. We then make the body of raffia, ribbed with gold wire, and then we tie in the legs – two over the bend of the hook, two over the eye of the hook, and one on each side as on a natural fly. Then you wind on the feather – just an ordinary blue cock hackle – and that'll make it float.'

Because the daddy-long-legs is such a complicated fly to tie, Rosa can tie only three or four dozen in a day, compared with ten dozen of an easier fly. They cost anything from 12p to 15p, and most of them are sold, mail order, to fishermen in Ireland and Belgium.

Casting for trout at Nether Wallop, Hampshire

Even if you couldn't buy Rosa Smith's flies in Dermot Wilson's shop in the pretty Hampshire village of Nether Wallop, if you were a keen fly fisherman you'd be able to find just about anything else you needed. Apart from selling you the gear you need, Dermot will also teach you how to cast for trout, even if you are greenest of newcomers.

'We've got a millpond here, with two casting platforms on it where we send pupils with one of our instructors, and teach them how to cast. It's fairly still water, and fairly unencumbered by trees, so it's easy to cast. They take lessons of about an hour, and after about forty-five minutes they're usually pretty tired, so then they go on to the little artificial lake which we have here. Then with the instructor's help – and sometimes it needs more help than at others – they actually catch a trout!'

Dermot Wilson gave us a demonstration of casting for trout by aiming at a leaf floating on the water about fifteen yards away, and landed his fly within inches of it! Before he had actually cast, he had moved the fly backwards and forwards through the air a few times – what's known as 'false casting'. 'The theory is that as you go backwards and forwards, you get a better sense of aim, and also, because you're fishing with a dry fly, you dry the fly in the air so that it will float all the better when it reaches the water. You aim to drop the fly just in front of the trout. The trout's head stays in the same place, and the river acts as a sort of conveyor belt, bringing the food over him. The idea is to put your fly just upstream of him, so that it floats down over the trout on the conveyor belt, looking like a natural fly, and with luck he'll take it!'

The best time of day to fish for trout, Dermot told us, is when you get what's called 'a hatch of fly'. 'That's a lot of flies all hatching out at once, and then your rather lazy trout who's been sleeping away on the bottom for the last half hour or so will come up and start feeding on them, and that's the time when you can catch a trout on a dry fly.'

The river which runs between the mill pond and the lake is the Wallop Brook, which trickles through the village, but is about ten feet wide at the point where we were standing. 'About six or seven miles downstream', Dermot Wilson said, 'it joins the River Test, which is probably the most famous trout river in the world.' The reason it does provide such good fishing, Dermot explained, goes right back to its source. 'Really, the water comes straight out of the chalk, carrying with it the salts that are absolutely necessary for the plant growth, and you do get aquatic plants growing like anything in the Brook, and indeed in all the chalk streams in this part of the world. They get covered with algae, and the algae are the food of insects and crustaceans, which are the food of the trout, on which they will grow big and fat, and that is the food chain. So you get very good trout, and plenty of them!'

Trouting farm at Stow-on-the-Wold, Gloucestershire

Trout fishing is first and foremost a sport, with a delicious, edible bonus at the end of the day. If you want trout primarily for food, though, you have to set about it in quite a different way, as we discovered when we visited the Donnington trout farm at Stow-on-the-Wold in Gloucestershire.

Again the waters of the local river, in this case the River Dikler, have an important part to play, as the farm's manager, Peter Austin, explained. 'We chose this site because we have the head waters of the River Dikler, and out of the ground here issues a beautiful, clear stream – about fifty thousand gallons an hour in the winter, going down to about twenty thousand in the summer. This clear water is what is absolutely necessary for the intensive trout production. Trout must have running water all the time to survive. They are very delicate fish.' The water isn't heated at all. Fortunately for Peter Austin, it comes out of the ground at a constant 50 degrees Fahrenheit, winter and summer.

Breeding trout is obviously the foundation of the business, so the difference between male and female is not something that matters only to another trout! 'In summer they look very similar,' Peter told us, 'but in winter the male goes very dark in his spawning trim, and grows a very long kype, or jaw, while the female has a little, round jaw.' The breeding of the fish takes place under carefully controlled conditions. 'We take the female, and when she is ready to lay her eggs, which only happens once a year, we "strip" her, which means, basically, that we squeeze her underside, and the eggs are then ejected into a bowl. We then take the male fish, and squeeze him, so that the sperm runs into the bowlful of eggs, which are then fertilized within two or three minutes. We get about a thousand eggs per pound of fish, so a five-pound female will give about five thousand eggs.'

The fertilized eggs are then transferred to small hatching troughs, where they take about twenty-one days to hatch into tiny fish. 'They hatch in very much the same way that chickens hatch. It cracks the eggshell, and after that it lies on the bottom for two or three days, absorbing the yolk sack. Then it will eventually swim up and then it's ready to start feeding, and the process of trout farming

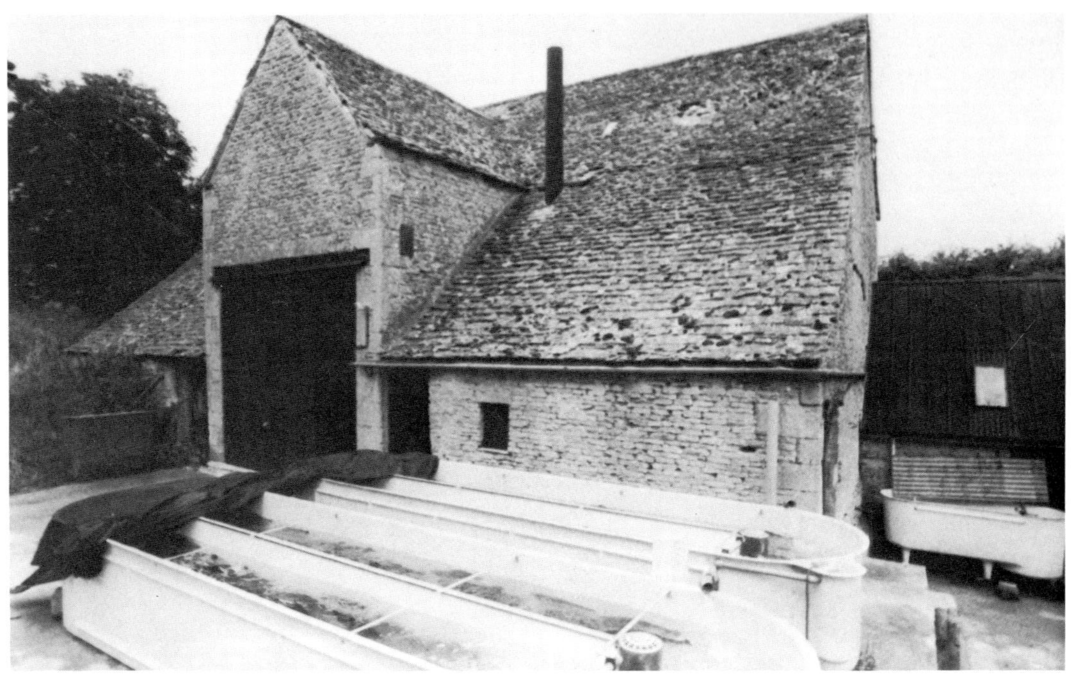

The trout farm at Donnington, where the head waters of the River Dikler provide beautifully clear water at a constant temperature.

Under farming conditions the fish grow much larger than they would in the wild.

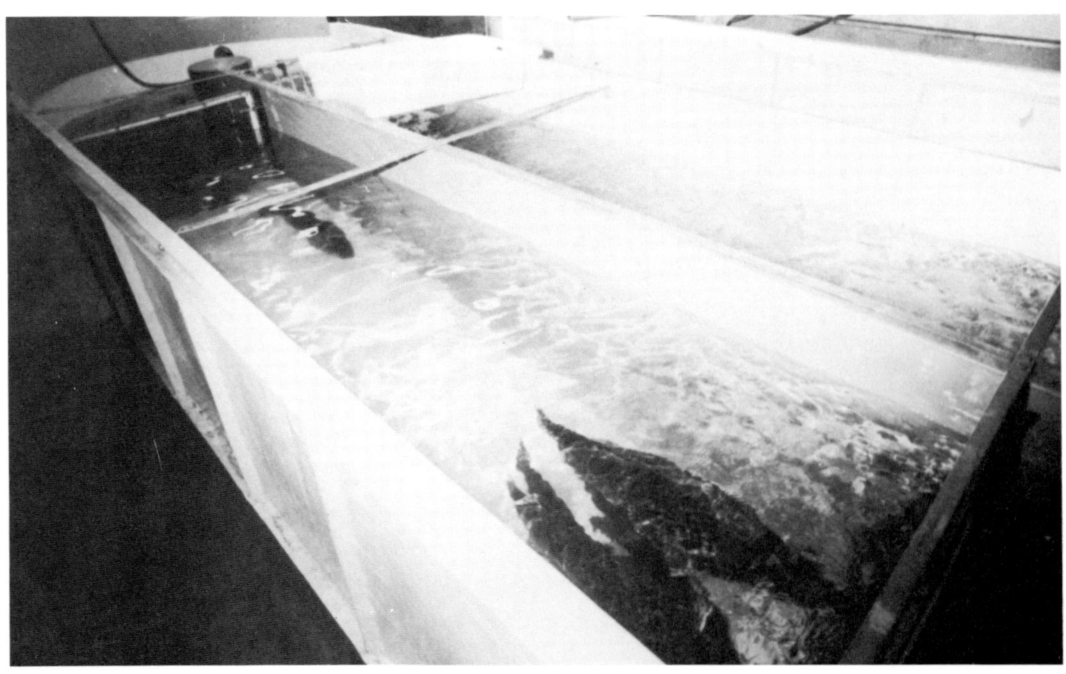

proper begins. It's crucial to start feeding at exactly the right moment when the yolk sack has been absorbed.'

Under these conditions the fish grow much larger than they would in the wild. 'Here, it will grow for the whole of its life. It will grow to forty or fifty pounds, perhaps more, and up to two and a half feet long, like a salmon. In a river, the fish normally die after four or five years and the river food isn't sufficient for it to grow that much in that space of time.'

The fish from Donnington are sold in a number of ways – as small fish to other trout farms, or, when they are larger, to stock trout rivers, as well as to hotels and shops, either fresh or smoked. 'We smoke them here in a kiln – cold smoking for larger fish, which is the way they smoke salmon sides, and hot smoking too, for the small, half-pound trout.'

With some twenty thousand trout being reared for the table at Donnington alone, was there any chance that the price of trout would come down in the next few years? 'Relatively speaking,' Peter Austin said, 'I'm sure that trout will remain more stable in price than other fish.' Or, to put it another way – no!

Oysters at Orford, Suffolk

Perhaps the last notion you'd connect with fish is fashion, and yet as in everything else there have been fashions in fish over the years. It's hard to believe today but, in the early nineteenth century, London servants made it a condition of employment that they wouldn't have to eat oysters more than twice a week! Now they're in the luxury class, and along with champagne are some people's idea of the ultimate celebration meal. Just outside the small Suffolk town of Orford we visited an oysterage run by the Pinney family, who also run the justly famous sea-food restaurant in the main market square. Although there have been oyster beds in Orford for hundreds of years, they had died out until they were revived twenty years ago by Richard Pinney.

The oyster beds, as his son Bill explained to us, are situated in Butley Creek, five miles from the sea. It is a tributary of the River Ore, and at high water it is one hundred per cent salt water. 'It's always been a well-known fattening ground for oysters, 'Bill Pinney told us. 'The reasons are not always straightforward, but generally speaking there's good food and good water here for oysters.'

They produce two kinds of oysters at Butley Creek – the native oysters which have been grown on the coast for hundreds of years, and the Japanese oysters which the Pinneys introduced about ten years ago. The fact that the two types are produced means that oyster-lovers can eat their favourite food three hundred and sixty-five days of the year, whether there's an R in the month or not!

'The reason you can't eat the native oysters in May, June, July and August is that they carry their eggs inside their shell and they become a blacky colour, and therefore the oyster doesn't look very presentable during the summer months, and you have to wait until spawning has finished before you can start eating them. The Japanese oysters, though, have a very small, fine, white egg which is not visible, and doesn't blemish the taste at all.'

The Pinneys breed their oysters in a special hatchery close to the river. 'We bring the oysters in, and actually breed from the eggs and the sperm inside them. We mix the two together, and after about twenty-four hours they turn into freely swimming larvae. They are very tiny – about fifty microns, which is far, far smaller than a pinhead. They free-swim for about twenty-one days on average before they change into what would be recognizable as oysters, complete with shell, if you looked at them under a microscope. They settle on a piece of black perspex, and immediately they settle we scrape them off, so that they are individual oysters.

'We then feed them until they're large enough to go into the river. We put in about ten thousand oysters in each plastic bag, and suspend them in the river from wooden trestles. They stay in there for about a fortnight, and then as they grow we thin them out again and again until there are only about five hundred oysters in each bag. When they are large enough to look after themselves on the bottom of the river, we throw them out into the river and leave them there for a year or eighteen months, until they are large enough. Then we come along with our dredger and harvest them.'

In the wild, only a very small proportion of the larvae would survive. As it is, the only hazard the Butley Creek oysters face is being crushed by a carelessly dropped anchor, or a boat running aground, since the area is very popular with pleasure sailors. 'At high tide, though, the creek is deep enough for boats to go safely over the top!'

Sea fish farming at Loch Creran, Argyllshire

At Loch Creran, just north of Oban in Argyllshire on the beautiful, rugged west coast of Scotland, we came across a rather unusual scheme. The Sea Life Centre is part aquarium, showing the public the marine life of Scotland, and partly marine fish farm. 'It is very new,' the Centre's manager, David Mace, told us. 'There are only a couple of companies operating in Great Britain at the moment, but we think it's something that is going to be very exciting in the future. After all, the fishing industry is not in a very good state, and fish farming is going to have to take over from it.'

When we visited the Centre they were concentrating on the luxury fish – salmon, turbot and Dover sole. Unlike Donnington or Butley Creek, where the small fry develop in unheated water, the tiny turbot at Loch Creran are reared in water that is heated. 'If we don't do that,' David Mace told us, 'their development is so slow that it would take months and months for them to reach the size they're reached here in just four months.' They've also had some success in farming Dover sole, though with some unexpected results. 'You see the coloration on those fish? They are black and white, and that is not the normal coloration of Dover sole. This is because we've produced them in the hatchery, though no one knows why. But they're good fish to farm, and they seem to thrive on captivity!'

Clam fishing at Oban, Argyllshire

As yet, they haven't started farming clams at Loch Creran, so there is still work for Oban Divers, a company run by David Tye from his home just outside the town. He told us just how to fish for clams in an aqua-lung. 'You find them in the sand, upside-down, with the flat point of the shell upwards. We go down to about fifty or sixty feet with a bag, and collect them one at a time. When the bag is full we come back up the rope, which is connected to a buoy on the surface, and swim to the boat. The boatman pulls the bag with the clams in it on board, and empties them out, so we can go down again.'

But clam fishing is really only a sideline for Oban Divers. 'We work on piers – we're working over on Iona and Mull at the moment. We're doing a slipway there, putting the concrete down. And we've just been laying telephone cables over in Uist for the Post Office. Our boat's been over there all week.'

During the summer months David and his team also organize holidays for diving clubs and individual divers. 'We've got the whole thing sorted out to accommodate divers, and to give them a jolly good time, letting them get around the waters of Oban to dive, because the water round here is absolutely superb for diving, whatever the weather. If it's blowing a force ten gale the visibility under the water just doesn't change.' The life David Tye leads makes him pretty unusual, but he may in fact be unique, for he is in a wheelchair, paralysed from the waist down. 'It happened over ten years ago now. I was called to do a job for a fishing boat, looking for some clam dredges that had been dropped over the side in a hundred and twenty feet of water, just off Tyree.

'I'd had a very hectic winter down in Derbyshire, enjoying myself, over-eating and what have you. So when I came back up here to do the first job of the season I wasn't feeling particularly well. I went down, and used up one bottle of air looking for the dredges, but without any luck. I came to the surface, swam to the boat, and an hour later I went down again. This time I found the dredges right away. I brought them up, and was taken on board, straining my back in the process, because I had all my weight belts on and my air bottle.

'The combination of everything went to the weak part of my back, and the nitrogen I must have had in my system from the first dive actually attacked my

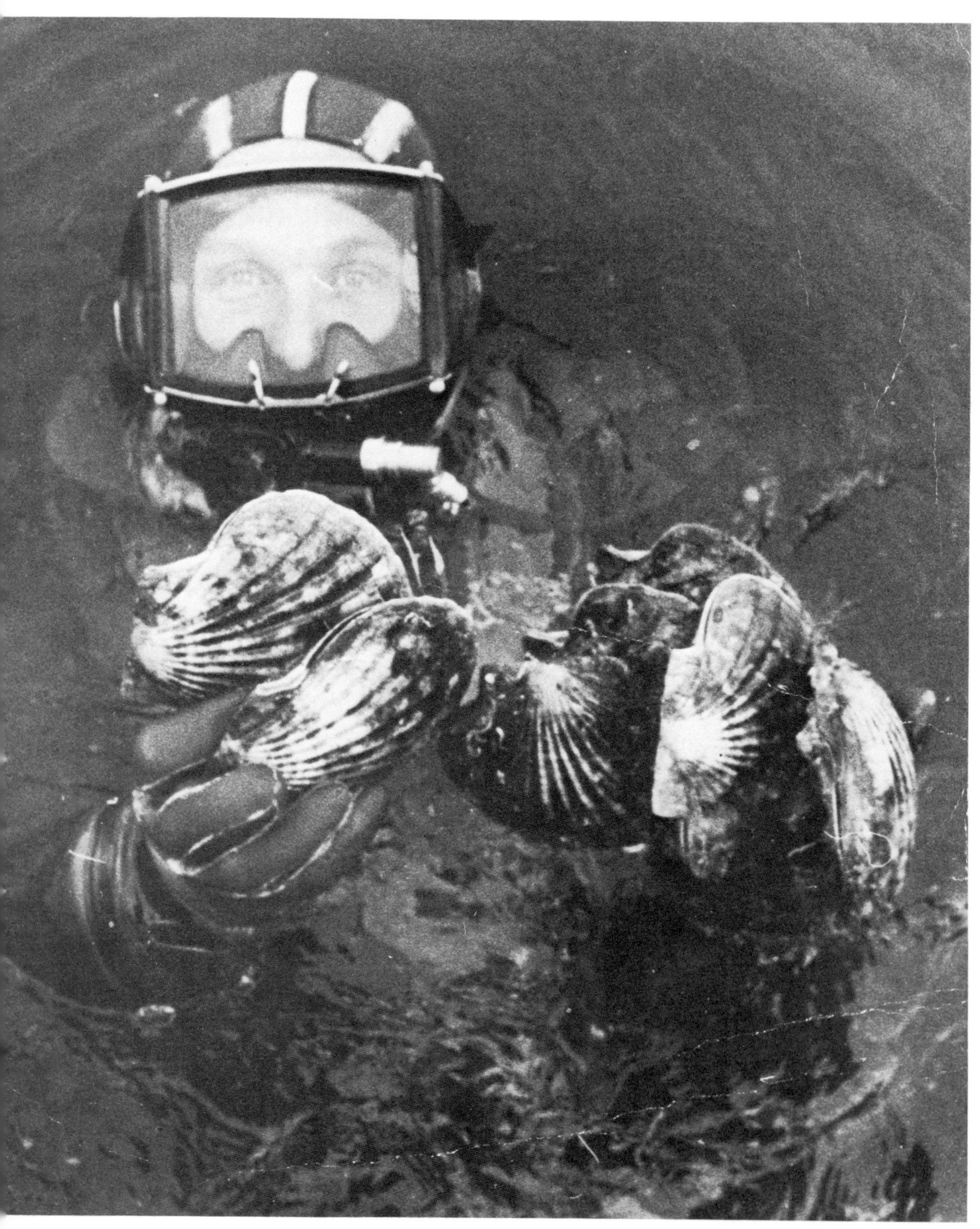

David Tye demonstrating a recent variation on an old theme: fishing for clams in an aqua-lung.

nervous system. Two or three hours later I got this trouble with my legs, and that was that!'

Now he directs operations from his wheelchair, and, as he puts it, acts as a constant reminder to his divers about how careful they must be. 'They say to me sometimes, "I had a fright today. I did this or that, and then I thought of you, and thought 'God! I wouldn't like to be in that thing.'" David's next venture, he hoped, was to get involved in flying ultra-light aircraft which are, he said, rather like hang-gliders with small motors. And when he said 'get involved', he meant personally. 'Definitely! Why not? You don't need a rudder on those things, so I don't need my feet!'

Long-line fishing at Inverbervie, Kincardineshire, and at Southwold, Suffolk

On the other side of Scotland, in the small fishing town of Inverbervie about fifteen miles north of Montrose, we met Andrew Cargill who still fishes from his boat *The Reaper* in the traditional way that has been practised locally for generations. It's called long-line fishing, and Andrew, who has been a fisherman since he was fifteen, explained what it is and just how it is done.

'A long-line is a nylon cord, about two or three millimetres thick, and anything from three-quarters of a mile to a mile long. From this hang snoods, lengths of line about three feet long, on the end of which is a hook. You bait each of the twelve hundred hooks with mussels, two mussels per hook. Each boat has a crew of four, and each man carries line, so you wind up with about a four-mile stretch, and forty-eight hundred baited hooks.'

The line isn't towed behind the boat. It's laid on the bottom for about forty-five minutes, then hauled back on board – all four miles of it – by hand. 'We look for banks, hard ground banks, with roughly twenty fathoms (about a hundred and twenty feet) of water over them. Anything up to thirty fathoms is good enough fishing ground. We really don't know whether the fish take the bait while the line is on the bottom, or when it's going down or coming up. Sometimes you think that they take it on the way down, and yet in winter it could possibly be proved that the bait lies on the bottom, and they'll take it on the turn of the tide.'

Andrew caught a wide variety of fish, he told us – haddock, whiting, codling, some plaice and lemon sole, but no herring. 'No, there hasn't been any herring fishing in my time. There was before, at the turn of the century, and up to the First World War, but after the First War it died out.'

The advantage of long-line fishing, so Andrew said, is that each fish is caught individually, and doesn't get damaged the way it would if it was caught in a net. As the fish come aboard, they are selected according to size and species and put

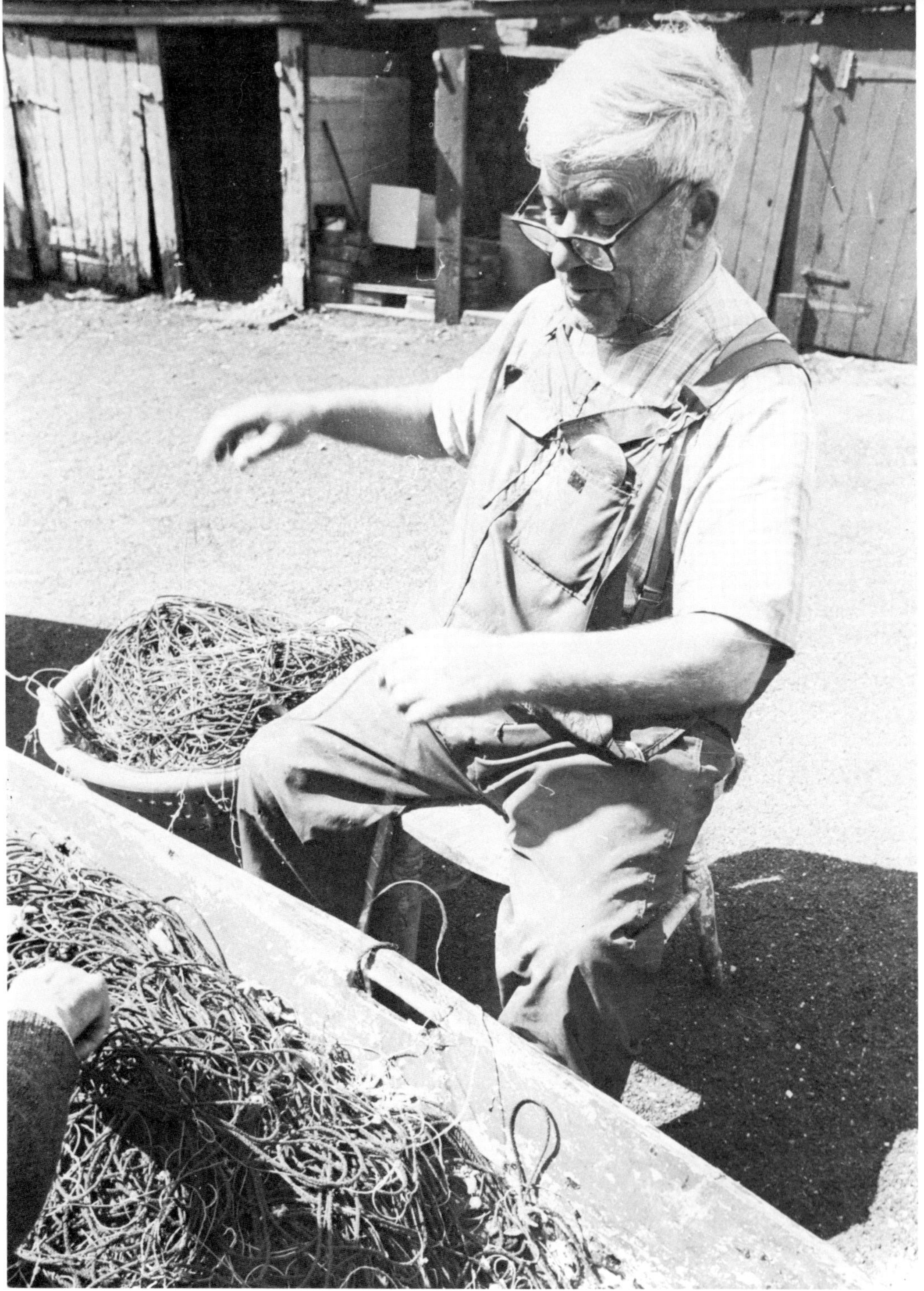

Andrew Cargill, long-line fisherman of Inverbervie. The twelve hundred hooks on the mile-long line are baited every day with mussels – usually by the fisherman's wife.

into boxes, but no gutting is done on board. On a good day Andrew will catch one fish for every six hooks. 'My father used to say that one in six was good enough fishing – above that, you're getting better, and under that it's all touch and go.'

They fish five days a week, weather permitting, and will spend anything up to twelve hours at sea, depending on how far from port they have to travel – between sixteen and nineteen miles in summer, but only six or eight miles in winter. Since Andrew and his crew are out at sea all day fishing, the obvious question was, who painstakingly baits those four thousand eight hundred hooks with mussels every day? The answer – as you might expect – was 'the wives'.

'Each wife baits twelve hundred hooks a day, which takes her approximately eight hours, sometimes more, sometimes less – it depends.' What would happen, Brian Johnston asked him, if he were a bachelor and wanted to join the crew? 'You've had it!' Andrew said with a laugh. 'It's always been a sort of family thing, where your wife, or, if you were a single man, your sister or your aunt or something would do the baiting. To employ what we'd call "outsiders" would be impossible, you see. They just wouldn't do it! It's always been a real partnership. It has to be. The boats were all family-owned, and it was fathers and sons, uncles and nephews. In the old days you'd get about thirty boats in the harbour, with about a hundred and twenty men working them. Now there are only twelve, and forty-eight men. It's a tough life, but I don't regret it. I don't think I'd be happy doing anything else!'

'Dinks' Cooper, who's been long-line fishing from the east coast town of Southwold, Suffolk, for over fifty years, feels the same way. He loves the sea and his way of life, though he has no illusions about it. 'You'll never make a fortune in inshore fishing. You'll just live comfortable!'

'Dinks' goes long-line fishing for cod and whiting from his boat *Expectation* during the winter months, baiting his hooks with Norfolk lugworm, though in the summer he trawls for sole, plaice, flounders and dabs. Like Andrew Cargill, 'Dinks' has watched the local fleet getting smaller and smaller. 'In the old days you'd get sixty or seventy boats going out. Now there are only about ten or twelve, though you generally only get six or seven of you together fishing.'

'Dinks' began fishing when he was a boy with his father in his eighteen-foot sailing boat. 'A sailing long-shore punt, they call them, with sail and oars. You had to do a bit of rowing as well. You had to, or else you'd get an oar round your head or something from the old man! You had to do as he told you! He taught me how to fish, and how to scull a boat, before he taught me how to row. He always made me scull the boat with one oar, because if you lose one of your oars and you can only row, you can't get back, but if you can scull you can always get ashore. He was right!'

Living on the east coast, exposed to the North Sea, 'Dinks' has developed a healthy respect for it, and still remembers vividly the floods of 1953. 'Nearly everything was washed away. A lot of the fishing boats were lost, and the water came right up into all these houses, and into the pub. I was in there at the time, and I had to go upstairs because I couldn't get out!' It might not have been such a calamity if all the beer hadn't been washed out of the door! 'All we could rescue was one carton of Woodbines between five of us. We were in there from Saturday night to Sunday night before they came and got us out!'

Sea salt collection at Maldon, Essex

Further down the east coast at Maldon, Essex, on the Blackwater River, there is one company that is extremely grateful for the extra-high tides, the spring tides which they get once a fortnight. The Maldon Crystal Salt Company produces sea salt, the finest, many gourmets would argue, in the world. Cyril Osborne, who has been with the company fifty years and is now semi-retired, explained just how they go about producing the salt.

'We take in the water on the spring tides which are every two weeks, and the water flows across acres and acres of saltings – land which over hundreds and thousands of years has become impregnated with salt. The salt which is in these saltings is automatically taken into the river water as the tide flows in, raising its salt content. When the tide is at its highest, within about an hour of full tide, we open our reservoir sluices, and allow the water to flow in from the river. When the tide turns, we close the sluices. This traps the water in our reservoir, and we then have sufficient water to keep us going till the next spring tide in two weeks' time.

'We then pump this water through what we call the filter beds – large, underground concrete tanks, where it is filtered and circulated to the point of almost complete clarity. Once the water has been cleaned, it is then pumped into the evaporating tanks, and the temperature is brought up to boiling point. The salt then begins to crystallize on the surface of the water. As the crystals form they become heavier and sink to the bottom, and immediately other crystals form in their place. This process goes on over a period of roughly twenty hours until practically all the water has been boiled away.'

The finished salt, piled high in what looks like gleaming white snowdrifts, is then sold to the public as it stands, with no chemicals, no additives, nothing. Its taste, Cyril said, is instantly distinguishable from that of ordinary salt. 'This has a soft, mellow taste, as opposed to a hard, shall we say, "attacking" taste.' Although sea salt is produced in other parts of the world – for instance in Spain, in Lanzarote in the Canary Islands, and in the south of France – the Maldon method is unique.

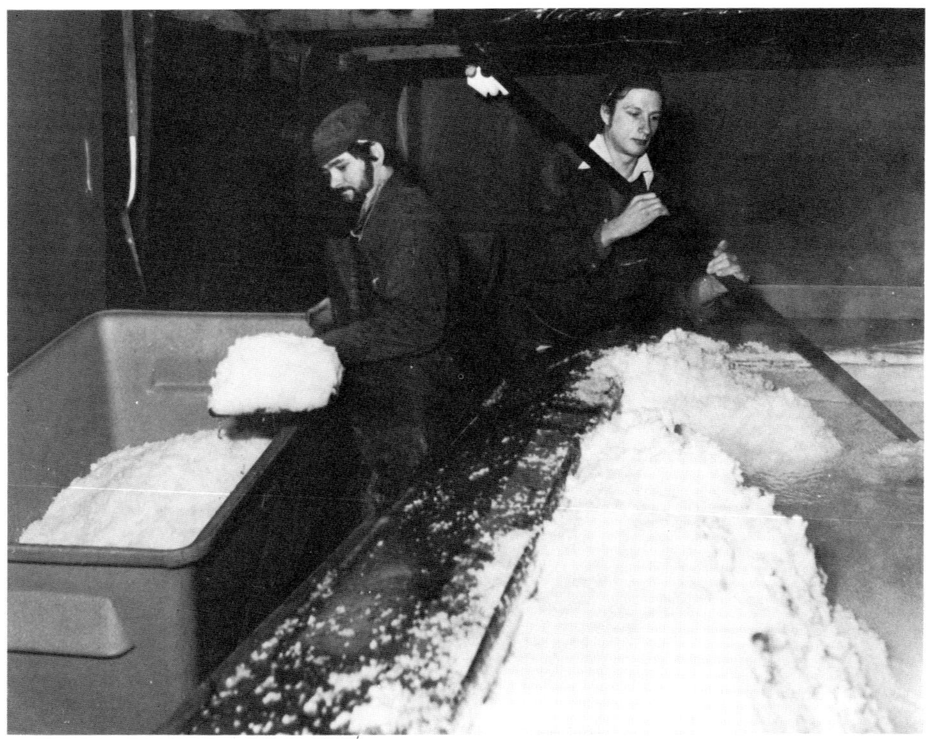

The collection of sea salt. As the water evaporates, the salt crystallizes on the surface.

The finished salt is shovelled into piles like snow.

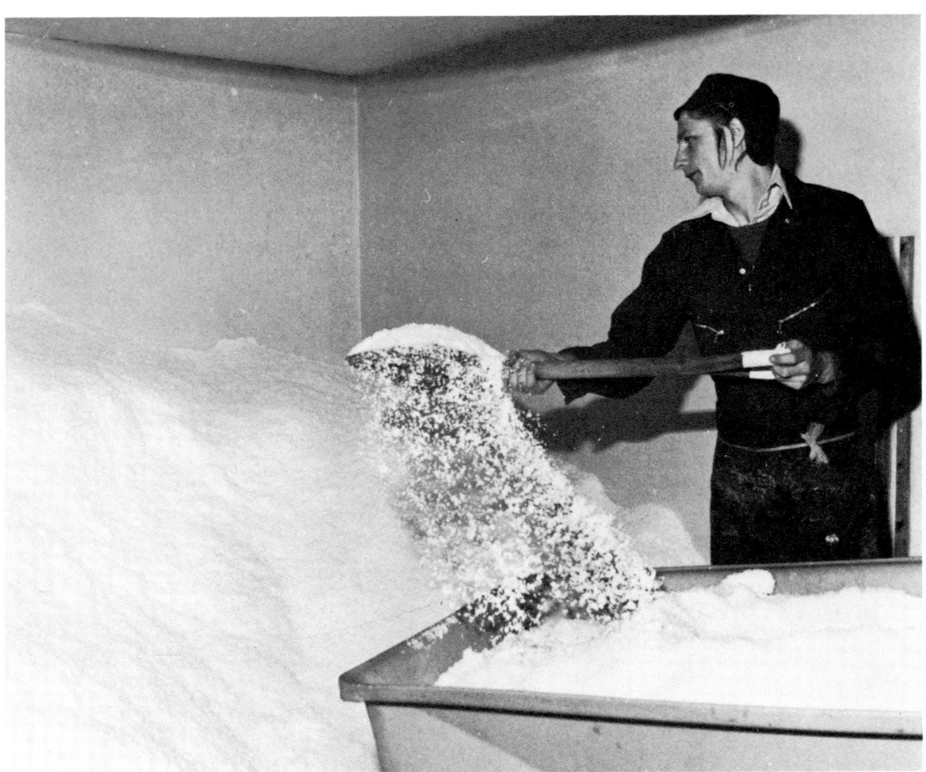

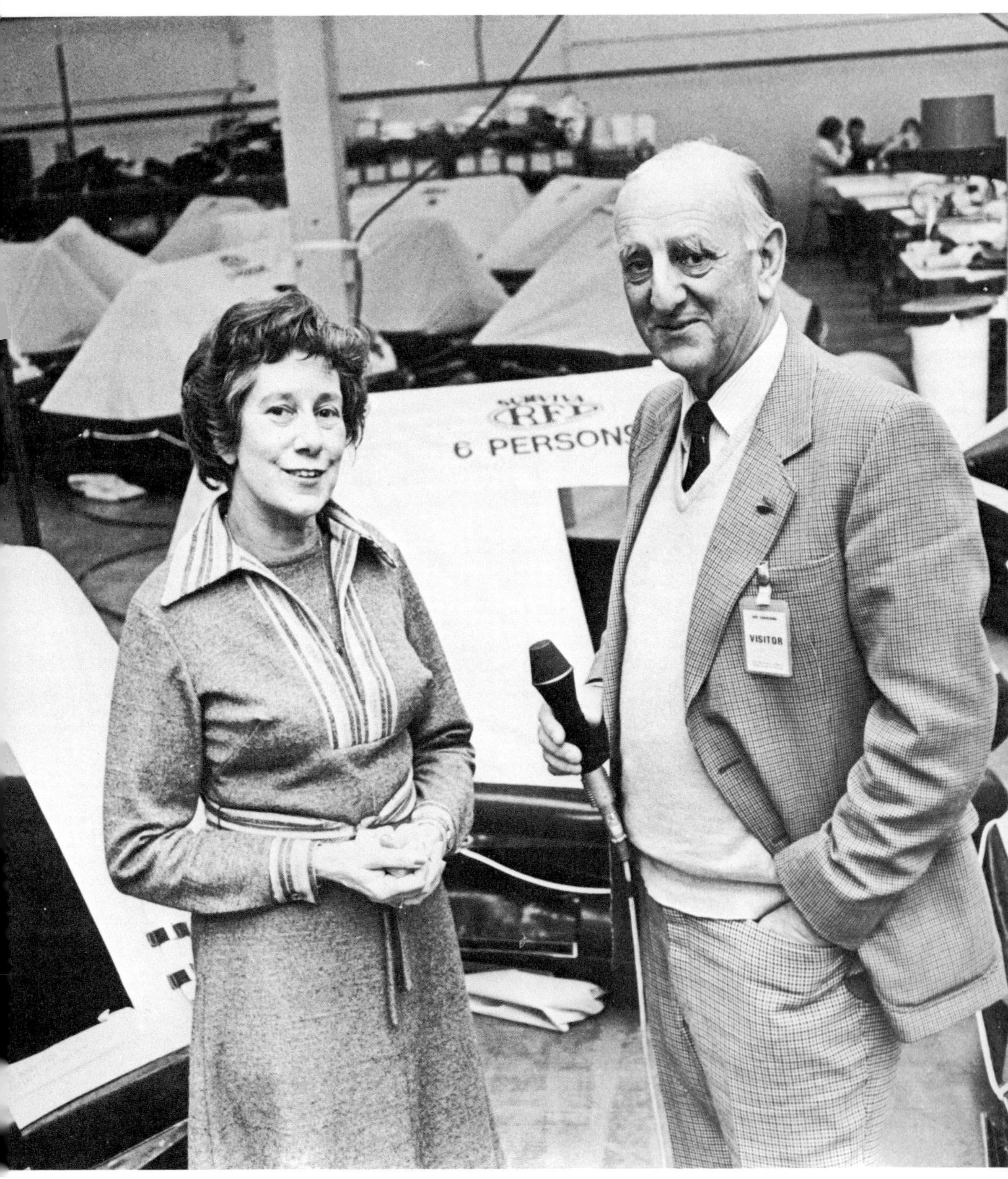

Brian Johnston interviewing Betty Moat at the RFD Inflatables factory at Godalming. Their life-rafts have saved nearly three thousand lives.

Making dinghies at Godalming, Surrey

Even though Godalming is by no stretch of the imagination near the sea or any major river, it does have a strong seafaring connection. It is the home of RFD Inflatables, who make the sort of life-rafts which have saved the lives of many sailors, as Betty Moat, the firm's public relations officer, told us. 'We've kept records actually since 1954, and since then we know that our life-rafts have saved getting on for three thousand lives!'

The initials 'RFD' stand for Raymond Foster Dagnall, the founder of the company. 'Mr Dagnall was a sort of balloonatic,' Betty Moat said with a laugh. 'He was very interested in airships and balloons and gliders, and allied himself to the aeronautical industry right from its early days. RFD made lots of barrage balloons for the defence of London and our other major cities during the Second World War.'

These days they concentrate mainly on making life-rafts – from the small 'Survivor' life-raft for the small boat owners, yachtsmen and inshore fishermen, to the vast, thirty-six-man aircraft life-rafts which Concorde carries, along with six inflatable escape-slides, three of which convert into life-rafts.

Whatever the size, though, all the rafts are designed to inflate automatically within seconds. 'Our founder discovered and patented quick, automatic inflation with carbon dioxide from cylinders. I know that the Concorde rafts inflate very quickly, because the airworthiness test stipulates that you must be able to evacuate the aircraft in the dark, using only half the exits, in ninety seconds.'

RFD also does business with the aircraft industry in another, even more spectacular, way. They manufacture those huge, inflatable bags that can lift almost any aircraft, up to and including a Jumbo jet. 'When the aircraft overshoots the runway, or loses a wheel, or gets into any difficulties at all at an airport, this equipment will lift the aircraft and enable it to be moved and repaired with the least possible secondary damage, and in the least possible time.'

Games People Play

Some funny ways that people have fun

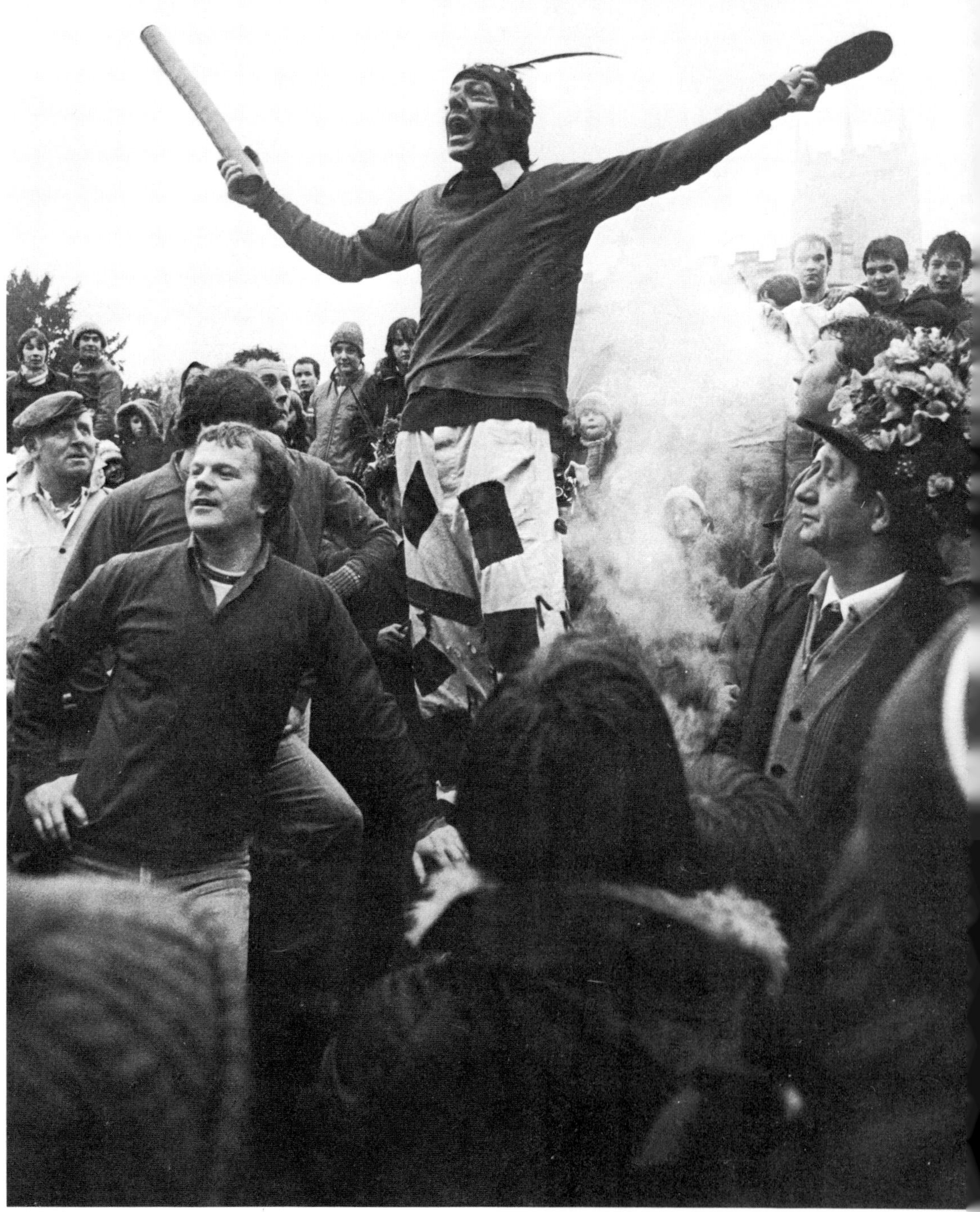

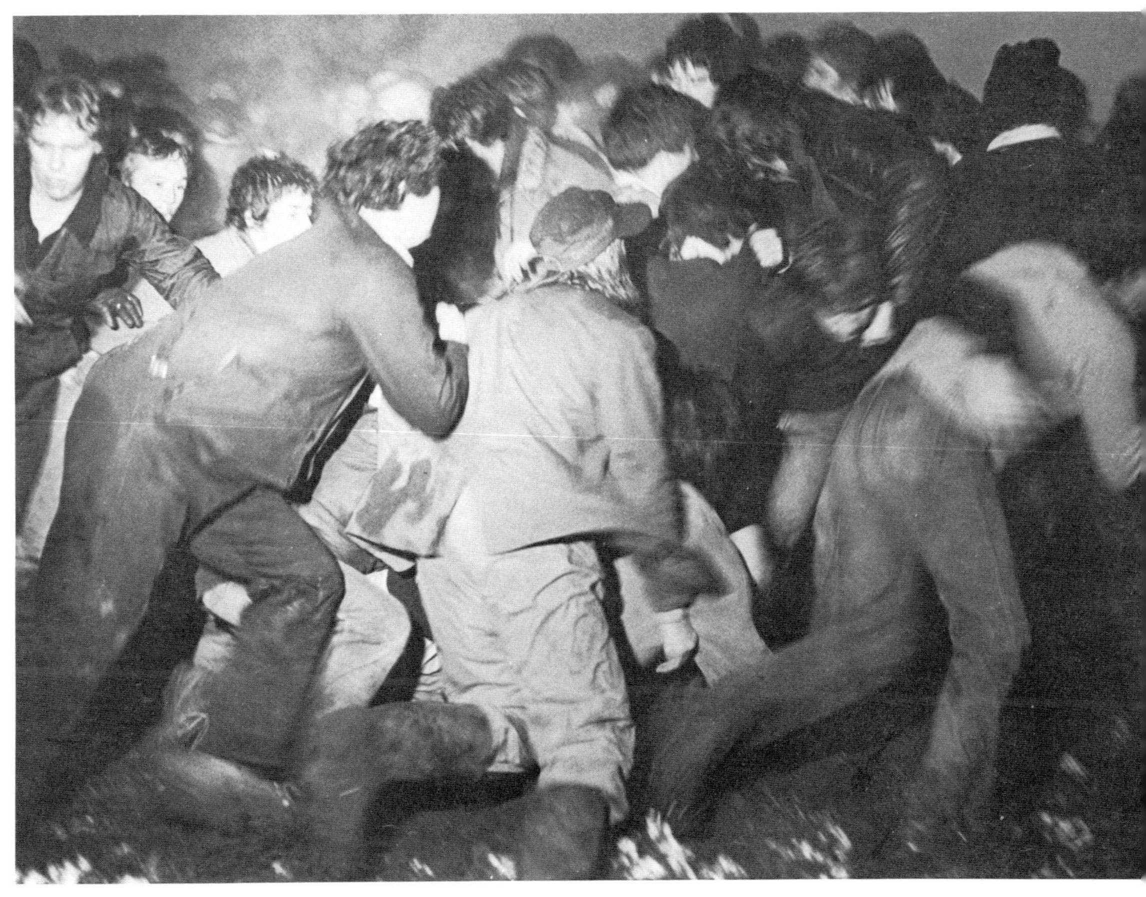

The Haxey Hood Game begins in a pub, after which the Fool makes a speech of welcome. It ends in a pub, too, though which pub the hood is taken to is decided by the 'Sway' (*right*).

The Hood Game at Haxey, South Humberside

We British have always been a sporting nation. After all, we invented most of the world's most popular games, even if everyone else now beats us hollow at all of them! From the time when records were first kept, there is plenty of evidence of just how popular sports and games were everywhere. In medieval times the one officially encouraged sport was archery – the king and his barons wanted a ready supply of trained archers for use against an enemy, or against each other. But inspite of – or perhaps because of – that, many people preferred other ways of passing their time, such as football, quoits, bowls, and dice, with the result that, in the reigns of Edward II, Edward III, Richard II and Henrys IV, VII and VIII, laws were passed making them illegal! It's quite common to find references in old manor records to people being fined for playing quoits or dice or bowls, and attacks on the gambling that was an inevitable part of the literature of the time. Take, for example, Stephen Gosson's *The School of Abuse*, published in 1579: 'Common bowling alleys are privy moths that eat up the credit of many idle citizens; whose gains at home are not able to weight down their losses abroad: whose shops are so far from maintaining their play that their wives and children cry out for bread, and go to bed supperless often in the year!'

One ancient game we came across in our travels with *Down Your Way* that did not involve gambling was the Haxey Hood Game, played in the village of Haxey in that area of very flat, fertile farmland on the west bank of the River Trent near Doncaster, curiously named 'the Isle of Axholme'. Stan Boor, who rejoices in the title 'Lord of the Hood', explained how the game originated.

'It started six or seven hundred years ago when Lady Mowbray, wife of a very powerful local landowner, was riding across the fields and lost her scarlet riding cap, or hood. There were thirteen men working in the fields nearby, and they had a real, good scrummage to have the privilege of picking the hood up and returning it to Lady Mowbray. At the end of the scrummage the largest and strongest man had the hood, or what remained of it – but he was too shy to give it back to Lady Mowbray, so he gave it to one of the other men to give to her. Lady Mowbray thanked them very much and said she'd enjoyed it that much that she'd like to see it again the next year. She called the man who'd been afraid to give the hood back to her a Fool, and the man who did, a Lord.

'Ever since then, the game has taken place every year on 6 January (or 5 January, if the next day is a Sunday), and so far as I know it's had no break, neither for the First World War nor the Second World War. Weather hasn't put it off at all, either. It's never been stopped.'

Apart from the Lord and the Fool, there are eleven 'Boggans' to make the number up to the original thirteen men. 'We think "Boggan" comes from when they were scrummaging for Lady Mowbray's hood. As it took place in January, it was very muddy and they might have been saying "Bog'er down" or "Bogged in'', something like that. And once a Boggan always a Boggan, until you either become too old or move out of the district!'

Since Lady Mowbray's hood was supposed to have been scarlet, red features largely in the Haxey Hood Game's costumes. The Fool, for instance, has his face smeared with red ochre and soot, and wears sackcloth trousers patched with red; the Boggans wear something red, even if it's only a patch or a band round their arm; and the Lord wears a red hunting coat. 'I also wear a tall silk hat, decorated with jewellery and flowers. In the past they were crêpe paper, but these days they're plastic!'

The day itself begins about lunchtime, when the Lord, the Fool and the Boggans meet in a local pub. 'We have a song or two, get lubricated, and then we go up to the stone outside the church where the Fool stands up and makes a speech of welcome to all that's come into the village.'

In the old days, according to an account of the game in 1896, the Fool, was then 'smoked' - suspended from a tree over a fire of damp straw,' . . . and swung backwards and forwards over it until almost suffocated; then allowed to drop into the smouldering straw, which was well wetted, and to scramble out as he could!' An early example, perhaps, of how smoking can damage your health! These days, the Fool is 'smoked' by standing in front of the fire! 'As the flames creep up and the smoke gets going, you'll hear the Fool say:

Hoose agin' hoose
Toune agin toune
If thou meetst a man
Knock him doone,
But don't hurt him.

'After he's said that, we proceed up to the fields between Haxey and Westwoodside, the next village, where the game begins. We have twelve dummy hoods - they're made of rolled-up sacking that's stitched into a cylinder - and the one big sway hood, which is a stitched-up leather cylinder twenty-four inches long and two and a half inches in diameter.'

Then the Boggans space themselves out round the field, and the first hood is thrown up for the spectators to scramble for. If the person who picks it up and prevents anyone else taking it from him can get through the ring of Boggans and make his way to one of the local pubs, he'll be rewarded with a free pint. If he doesn't manage to get through, the hood is returned to the Lord who throws it up again, and the whole business starts again. This carries on until all twelve dummy hoods have been disposed of, and then, at a quarter to four, they get down to the real business of the day.

'The sway hood is thrown into the air by some local dignitary, and everyone who wants to take part gathers round in an extra-large rugby scrum. There could be anything between fifty and two hundred people in the 'Sway' as we call it. The hood is in the middle of all this, and it's just pushed along, held by the men in the middle, until it gets to one of the three local pubs – the Carpenters' Arms at Westwoodside, the Duke William at Haxey, and the King's Arms. All the local lads that use each public house push towards the one of their choice. There's no organized teams as such – there could be fifty pushing for one pub and a hundred pushing for another – and eventually (it could take anything up to two hours) sheer weight of numbers decides where it winds up.

'When it gets to a public house, the rules are that, if the landlord is stood on his own property and reaches out and touches it, it is "dead" and it goes into that public house and stays there till New Year's Eve the following year, when the Lord, the Fool and a few of the Boggans will collect it. Then we tramp round the neighbouring villages, visiting forty-odd pubs and a few private houses, singing the traditional songs – "The Farmer's Boy", "John Barleycorn" and "Cannons". When we've sung them, we make a collection in the pubs to defray any expenses for the Hood game!'

The number of injuries sustained in the 'Sway' each year is surprisingly small. 'Well, we do get the occasional breakage of limbs, but mainly it's sprains, bruises or a cracked or bent rib. On the whole the injuries aren't too bad, though I wouldn't advocate anybody to take part unless they're on the lower side of thirty!'

Quoits at Wallsend, Tyne and Wear

Even though quoits was one of the sports banned by law hundreds of years ago, it has survived in many places in one form or another. Up in Wallsend in Tyne and Wear, for instance, they play the game with circular steel quoits nine and a half inches in diameter, with a five-and-a-half-inch bore, weighing between five and a quarter and five and a half pounds. Jimmy McKeown, who is the manager of the Lindisfarne Social Club's team, told us exactly how the game is played.

'The pitch is thirty feet long with two beds of clay, one at each end, which are two feet in diameter, with a steel pin called a "hob" in the middle of each. The object of the game is to be nearer the pin than your opponent. If you touch the pin you score one point, and if you "ring" the pin you score two.'

There is no set way of throwing the quoit, though underarm seems to be favourite. Whichever style you choose, though, you are only allowed to take two steps before delivering the quoit. We watched one of Lindisfarne's players demonstrate the technique, though instead of trying to ring the pin he stuck his quoit into the clay in front of it.

'That's to spoil his opponent from gaining the shot,' Jimmy McKeown told us, 'so what he has to do then is to knock it out, or carry it over the hob, with his own quoit on top. The quoit that's on top is always the winner.'

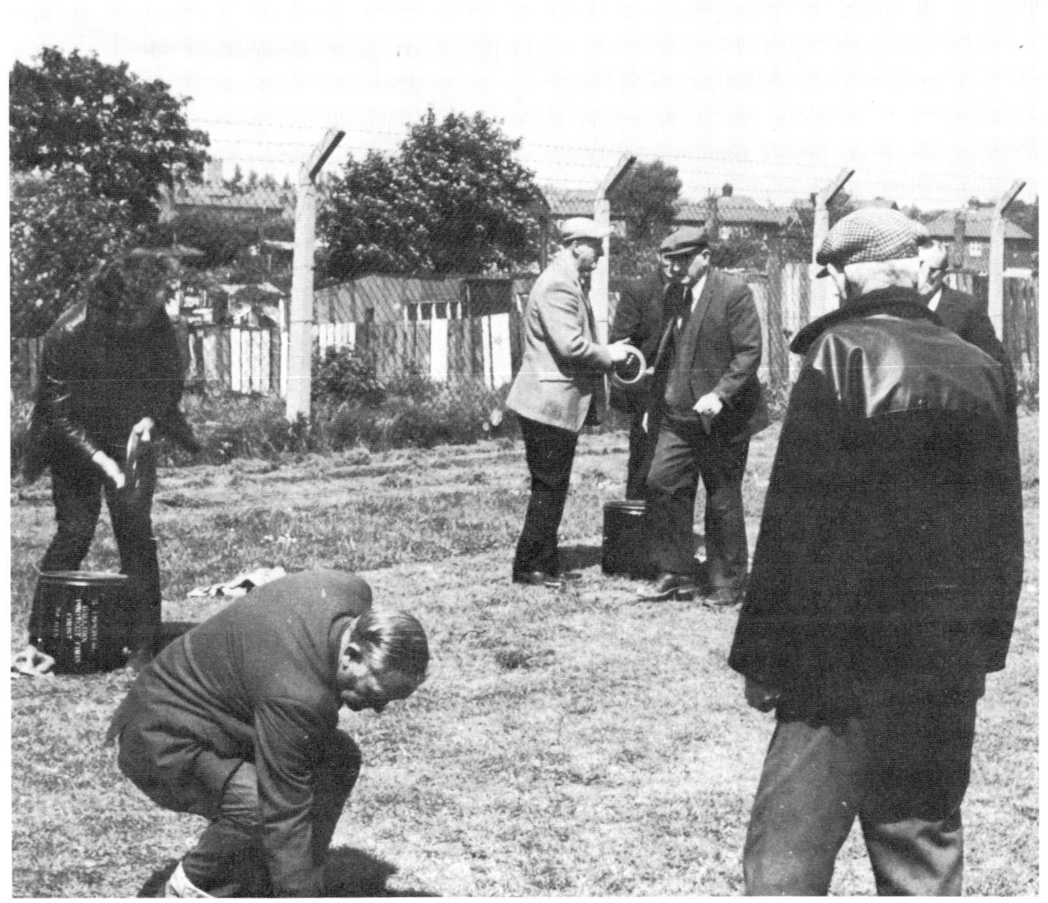

At the Lindisfarne Club in Wallsend they use circular quoits made of steel – and callipers to settle the arguments about whose is nearest to the pin.

When nobody manages to ring the hob, the winner is the player whose quoits are nearest to it, which leaves plenty of scope for ... debate! 'Oh, arguments all the time!' Jimmy said, cheerfully. ' We used to use a piece of grass or a piece of straw – anything that was straight, you know – but then we decided that the best way to measure was a calliper, so that's what we use now!'

When we visited Wallsend, the club had just completed an extremely successful season in the local leagues and competitions. 'We've won everything except the singles championships and my captain got beaten in the final of that. If he hadn't, we'd have done the grand slam! I hope we might pull it off next season, though – don't see any reason why we shouldn't!'

Stoolball at Midhurst, West Sussex

In the West Sussex town of Midhurst we came across a game which dates back at least to the sixteenth century, and which many people say is one of the forerunners of cricket. It is called stoolball, possibly because in its earliest days the wicket was a milking stool, and as Mrs Gladys Werry, president of the Midhurst Stoolball Club, told us, these days it is played mainly by women. It is played by two teams with eleven players aside. The bat, with a handle very like that of a cricket bat, is about half the size of a tennis racquet, with a solid wood face slightly rounded at the back. The ball is about half the size of a cricket ball, and although the famous seventeenth-century diarist John Aubrey wrote that it was 'as hard as a stone', these days it is made of cotton and paper and covered with white kid.

'When the men do come and play with us sometimes,' Gladys Werry said, 'they don't like the size of the ball that we play with at all. They're cricketers, you see, and they drop it quite easily.'

The wicket in stoolball is a pole with a piece of wood, one foot square, fixed to the top. The whole thing is four feet eight inches overall, and the bowler's task is to hit the square, while the batsman tries to ensure that she doesn't!

'The bowler stands ten yards away from you, and bowls underarm as fast as she can. It could be dangerous, I suppose, but then you do have the bat!' Given that today's cricketers – both batsmen and fielders – go out to play padded up like American football players, don't the stoolball players wear any protective clothing at all? 'Oh, no!' Gladys Werry said, shocked at the very idea. 'Nothing like that!'

In fact these days the players wear '... the shortest shorts you can imagine'! In the old days the players used to wear long dresses, but that led to a certain amount of unsporting behaviour! They used to hold their dresses out from the bottom and catch the ball! That's why the rules then said you had to have a clean catch in your hands. 'You can't knock the ball on to another player, like you can in cricket. It can't run up your arm either, or anything like that. You have to catch it.'

The pitch is shorter than in cricket – sixteen yards as opposed to twenty-two – but runs are scored in exactly the same way. You get out in pretty much the same ways, too. 'You can be bowled, or caught, or you can play on. The only thing that isn't like cricket is that you can't be stumped.' Stoolball is still a very popular game in the Midhurst area. 'We play about twenty-eight matches in the season.'

Grasmere sports in Cumbria

Many of Britain's traditional sports and pastimes took account of the local conditions, and the skills that a working man in the area would acquire. Take the famous Grasmere sports, held in the Lake District village of Grasmere on the Thursday nearest 20 August every year, beginning at noon and finishing at about half past five. Josh Hardisty, a hill farmer in the area, told us about some of the events.

'Well, there's fell-racing, Cumberland-Westmorland wrestling, pole-vaulting, the hundred yards, the three miles and, of course, hound trailing. That's really a race round the fell. There's two trailers who set off to lay a trail with aniseed and oil and various stuff. They go to the half-way mark, then one sets off and comes back to the field where the hounds are slipped, and the other one goes the opposite way to where the hounds will finish. They do about ten miles in all. I'll be laying the trail again this year. I'm not going to tell you how old I am, but this will be the forty-first year that I've done it!'

Many local people own hounds – not unlike foxhounds, though they're a little lighter and racier – and passions run high on the day of the race. 'It is very, very exciting – you can hear people shouting up to ten miles away when the dogs are coming home! Apart from anything else, there's quite a lot of betting on the outcome!'

Although the counties of Cumberland and Westmorland officially disappeared a few years back when 'Cumbria' was created in their stead, the names are preserved in a unique style of wrestling. 'It's different from what you see on the television. You put your arms round each other, and grip behind your opponent's back. You've got to keep your hands behind each other's backs. If you lose your grip you've lost, and if your opponent forces you to touch the floor you've lost, too!'

One of the most spectacular and gruelling events is the fell-race from the sports field where the Games take place right up to the top of Buttercrag – almost one thousand feet high. 'I think the record is thirteen minutes and so many seconds. It takes then roughly eleven minutes to get up there, and about

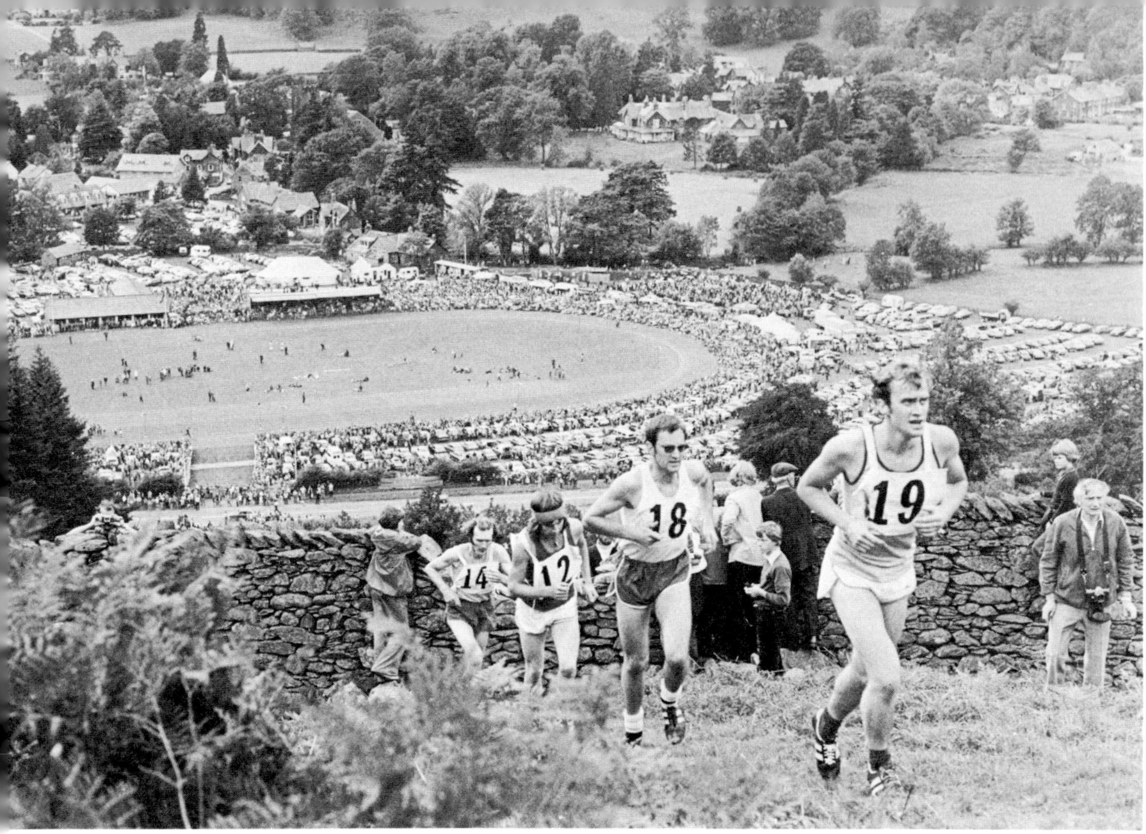

Two of the most exciting events in the Grasmere sports. *Above:* The fell-race, in which the runners climb the 1,000-foot Buttercrag in about eleven minutes. *Below:* Hound trailing, in which the hounds follow an aniseed trail over ten miles, and there's plenty of betting on the outcome.

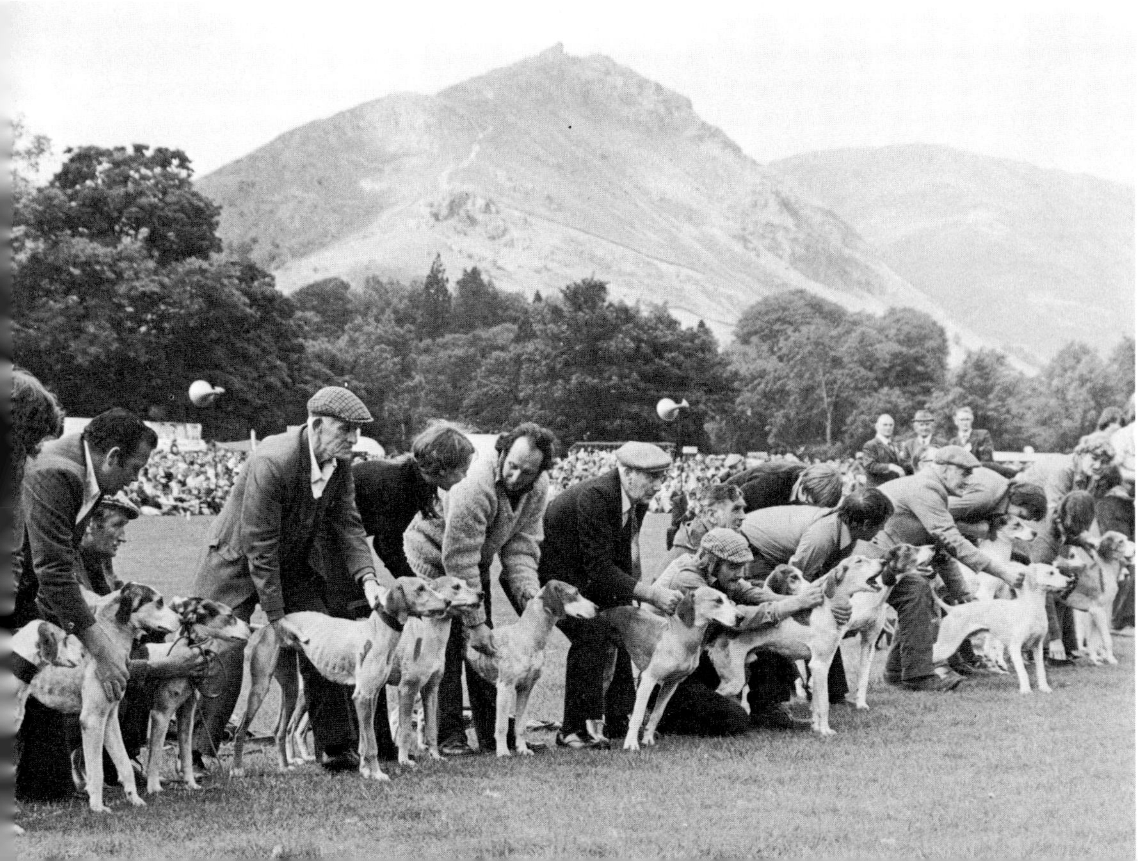

two minutes, so many seconds, to come down! They come down at a tremendous rate – they'll jump eight or nine yards at a time, and I've never yet known anyone break a leg. I've known one sprain his ankle the odd time, but I've never known a breakage!'

The running race up Ben Nevis, and the Glen Nevis river race, Inverness-shire

Not surprisingly, fell runners from the Lake District tend to do very well in the annual running race up Britain's highest mountain, Ben Nevis. George McPherson, chairman of Fort William's community council and of the town's tourist association, and also president of the committee that organizes the race, explained it to us.

'The record at the moment is one hour twenty-six minutes and fifty-five seconds, and it's held by David Cannon from the Lake District. The best runners do seem to come from that area because they do a lot of fell-running. We did have the Gurkhas running at one time, and they seemed to do very well on the mountain with their short little legs, but then they lost out on the flat!'

George told us a little about the race's history. 'The first record of an attempt is in 1895 and it was run occasionally up until 1937, when it was decided to run it on an annual basis, but then two years later war broke out. They did run one or two races during the war to raise funds for "Wings for Victory" and "Salute the Soldier" and what have you. But it was really set properly in motion in 1951, and has been run regularly ever since.'

On the first Saturday in September some four hundred runners begin the gruelling five miles up the mountain, and marginally less gruelling five miles down again. 'To make sure that every competitor does go right up to the top we have people up there with discs, and we insist that each runner collects a disc from the summit and brings it back to prove that he has been there. The scene at the top is quite unbelievable! In fact some of the runners, especially the tail-enders, look almost as if they were drunk, and in many cases they have to be taken by the shoulders, turned about, steered in the right direction and pushed back down again, otherwise they would just carry on and run right over the precipice!'

Even so, the race is potentially dangerous for a number of reasons, and the race committee gratefully accepts the help of many local organizations. 'We get assistance from the Royal Air Force, and the local mountain rescue teams, the Army, and the police who'll be on duty on the hill. We get the Royal Army Medical Corps – that's the Territorials – who are doctors working in the bigger hospitals in Glasgow, and we'd have something like thirty-five or forty doctors on the hill on the day. We have to take special precautions because of the dangers of exposure.'

Apart from the glory, there is a challenge cup for the winner, plus a gold medal, and a prize worth about £25. 'And probably the first twenty home will get an award of some kind.'

Although the Ben Nevis race is entirely amateur, it is a serious business, unlike the annual Glen Nevis river race, held on the middle Sunday in August. 'This is a race on anything that will keep you afloat – mattresses, rubber tyres, anything – and it's run over a course of about a mile and a quarter, but it includes a jump over the waterfalls, the lower falls, and this is quite spectacular because they have to leap about thirty feet into a small pool. All kinds of craft have won the race – this year, for instance, it was an airbed!'

The Running of the Walls race at Berwick-upon-Tweed, Northumberland

A sporting event doesn't necessarily have to be old to be well established as a tradition, as we discovered when *Down Your Way* visited Berwick-upon-Tweed and asked Norma Campbell, who at the astonishing age of forty-nine won a gold medal at the World Marathon Championships in Berlin in 1978, about the Running of the Walls race.

'About eight years ago my late husband and a group of other young men decided it would be a good idea to have this race around the town's walls. As he was a coach he was very interested in promoting an event in this area because we didn't have anything previously, and it would give the people of Berwick-upon-Tweed the opportunity to see top-class athletes in action.'

Apart from the first two hundred yards, which are run on the road, the whole race is run around the top of the town's Elizabethan walls, and has become so popular that there are now eight different events, ranging from the race for girls between eleven and thirteen, who run just one lap of the walls – a mile and a quarter – through women and men, who runs six and a quarter miles – five laps – to the veterans of both sexes.

'A man becomes a veteran when he's forty,' Norma said, 'and women become veterans when they're thirty-five. Some people think that women should also become veterans when they're forty because you get some extremely fit women of thirty-five!

'Last year we had a thousand competitors entered for the races overall. The biggest race is the men's race, with between three and four hundred runners. It always attracts top-class distance runners – previous winners have included David Black, Mike McLeod, and Nat Muir who won it in 1980 in a record time of thirty-two minutes, twenty-seven seconds.'

It looks potentially quite dangerous since the walls are fifty feet high, and the

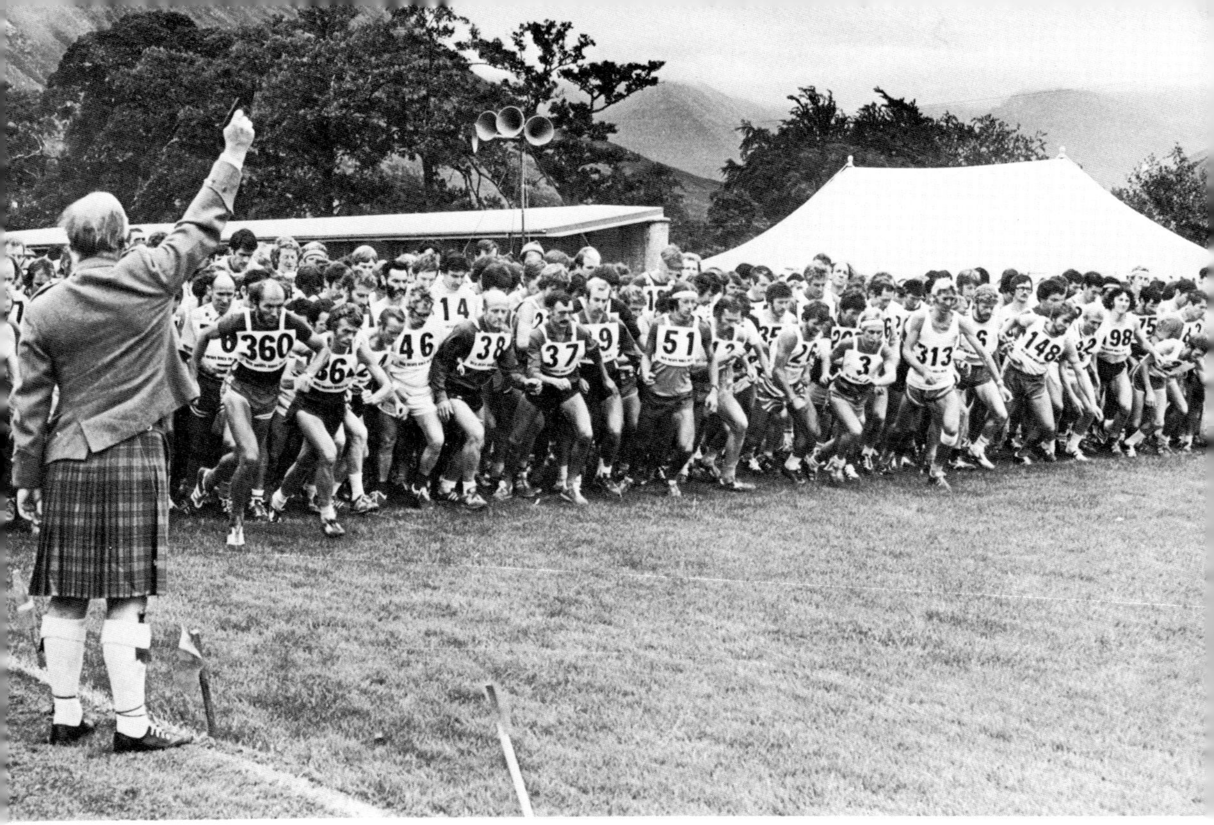

Russell Johnston, MP, starting the 1978 Ben Nevis race. It's a gruelling five miles to the summit – and then back down again.

The start of the Isle of Wight marathon, which finishes on the Esplanade in Ryde, twenty-six miles away.

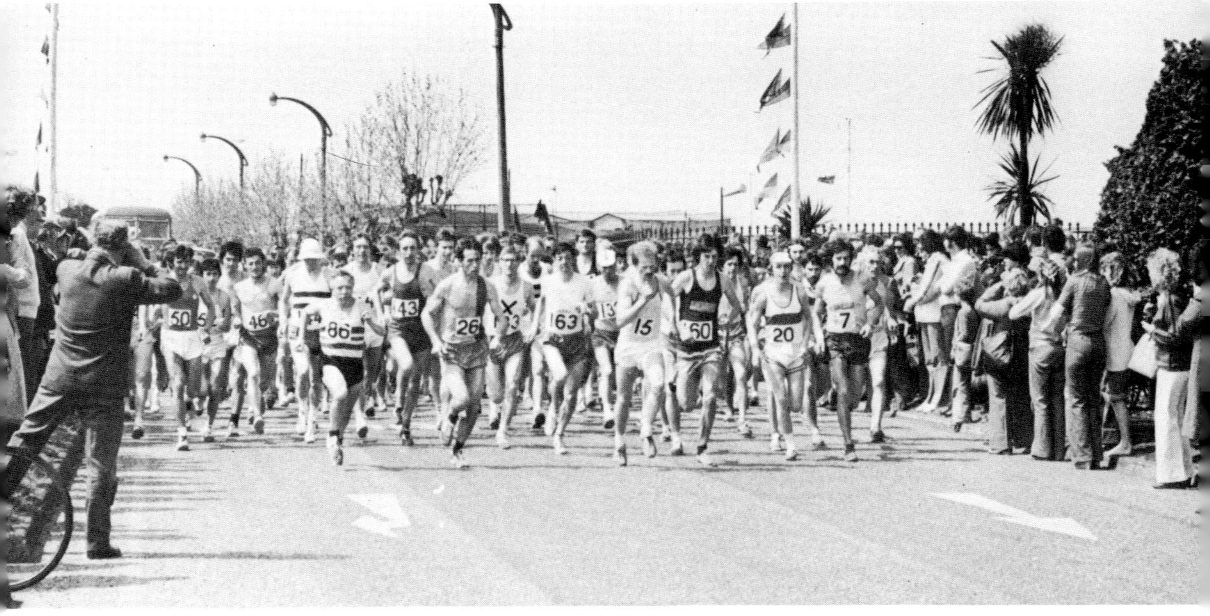

wind sometimes comes howling in off the North Sea, but Norma assured us that it really wasn't. 'The only thing that makes it hard is if the wind is against you when you're coming up Bank Hill. That makes the run very hard, but apart from that it's not bad at all. It's very scenic, one of the most pleasant road races in the country, in fact.' The race is held on a Sunday in September. 'It's not possible to hold it on a Saturday because this is a market town, and the streets are too busy then, and so the police wouldn't be able to help us with directing the traffic.'

Norma, who didn't take up running until she was forty, has run in the race herself, though the highest she has ever finished in the field is sixth. 'I'm a marathon runner,' she said, 'and the walls race is just too short for me! I'm not going to enter this year – I'm really bushed with all the organization this year and I intend to retire from competition this season anyway!'

The Isle of Wight marathon

In the Isle of Wight, Eddie Leal is not only treasurer and coach to the Ryde Harriers, and organizer of the Isle of Wight marathon which he instigated in 1957, but still manages to take part in it himself. The race is over the official marathon distance, twenty-six miles three hundred and eighty-five yards, set after the 1908 Olympic Games in London, and takes the three hundred or so men and the handful of women who enter through half a dozen of the island's villages and four towns, finishing on the Esplanade at Ryde. Eddie knows the route well. 'I had many painful hours pushing a surveyor's wheel over various routes until we finally settled on the one we now have.'

Running the marathon itself can also be a painful experience, as Eddie explained. 'I always find it begins to pain at about eighteen miles, but all you have to say to yourself is "It's only pain!", and if you can grit it through twenty-two miles, then you can make it to the finish. I find that at about the eighteen-mile mark I get visions of lovely food. It becomes an obsession, and when you finish you feel as though you want to fall on a heavy meal, but you daren't. In the early days I made the mistake of coming in and feeling ravenous and falling on a lovely meal of salad and trifles and jelly, only to suffer for it about an hour later!'

Road bowls at Armagh, Northern Ireland

In Armagh, Northern Ireland, they use the public highway for quite a different purpose – playing road bowls or 'bullets'. The obvious question to put to John Gribbon, chairman of the Northern Road Bowls Association, was how they managed to avoid hitting – or being hit – by passing cars or buses while play was in progress. 'It very seldom happens that they hit a bus or any other traffic, for the simple reason that the officials are out in front to keep the road clear, and so the bowl is only played when the road is free of traffic.'

The game started in Northern Ireland in the seventeenth century. 'There are some people who say the game came with the Normans,' John Gribbon told us, 'and others say it came from Holland, where it is still played, incidentally, but the most likely explanation is that it was originally an English game that came with the linen workers from Yorkshire way back, about 1680. In Ireland, actually, it is only played in the two counties, Armagh and Cork.'

The players use a bowl made of lead and steel that is about the size of a boy's cricket ball, but weighs a pound and three-quarters, and the game is played over a distance of about three miles. 'Basically, whoever covers the distance in the least number of throws wins the competition – something similar to golf. The average throw is approximately two hundred and fifty yards. The bowl bounces on the road, and wherever it stops that's where it's marked on the road with a bit of grass, and that mark – we call it the "butt" – is where you play your next bowl from. So it goes on, and you get about twenty throws in a competition.'

Most games have an umpire or a referee, but road bowls has both. 'The referee stays back at the butt and makes sure that the player delivers the bowl from the butt and not from in front of it. The umpire is the man who stands out in front and marks accurately where the bowl stops.'

Styles of throwing vary, it seems, on a regional basis. 'In Armagh they all bowl underarm, but the Cork people now, they bowl overarm, and obviously they can get a better lift at corners, and that type of thing, whereas our players try and spin or pull the bowl, whatever's necessary to get round the corners!'

The game has tremendous support locally, according to John Gribbon. 'In the 1979 All-Ireland Championships, played in Armagh, there were about five thousand people out on the road to watch. At the moment, up in the North here, we have the All-Ireland Senior champion, Patrick Mullen, and naturally we're very proud of him!'

Carpet bowls at Otterburn, Northumberland

At Otterburn, Northumberland, they also play bowls, but it could hardly be more different. For a start they play indoors, on a pitch a mere thirty feet long, which is covered in what looks like the green baize they use on billiard tables. 'It's a slightly heavier material than that,' Bert Rogerson, chairman of the Otterburn Indoor Carpet Bowls Club, told us, 'but it has ordinary carpet underlay beneath it. Because the floor was uneven we built a platform that was perfectly even and covered that with carpet.'

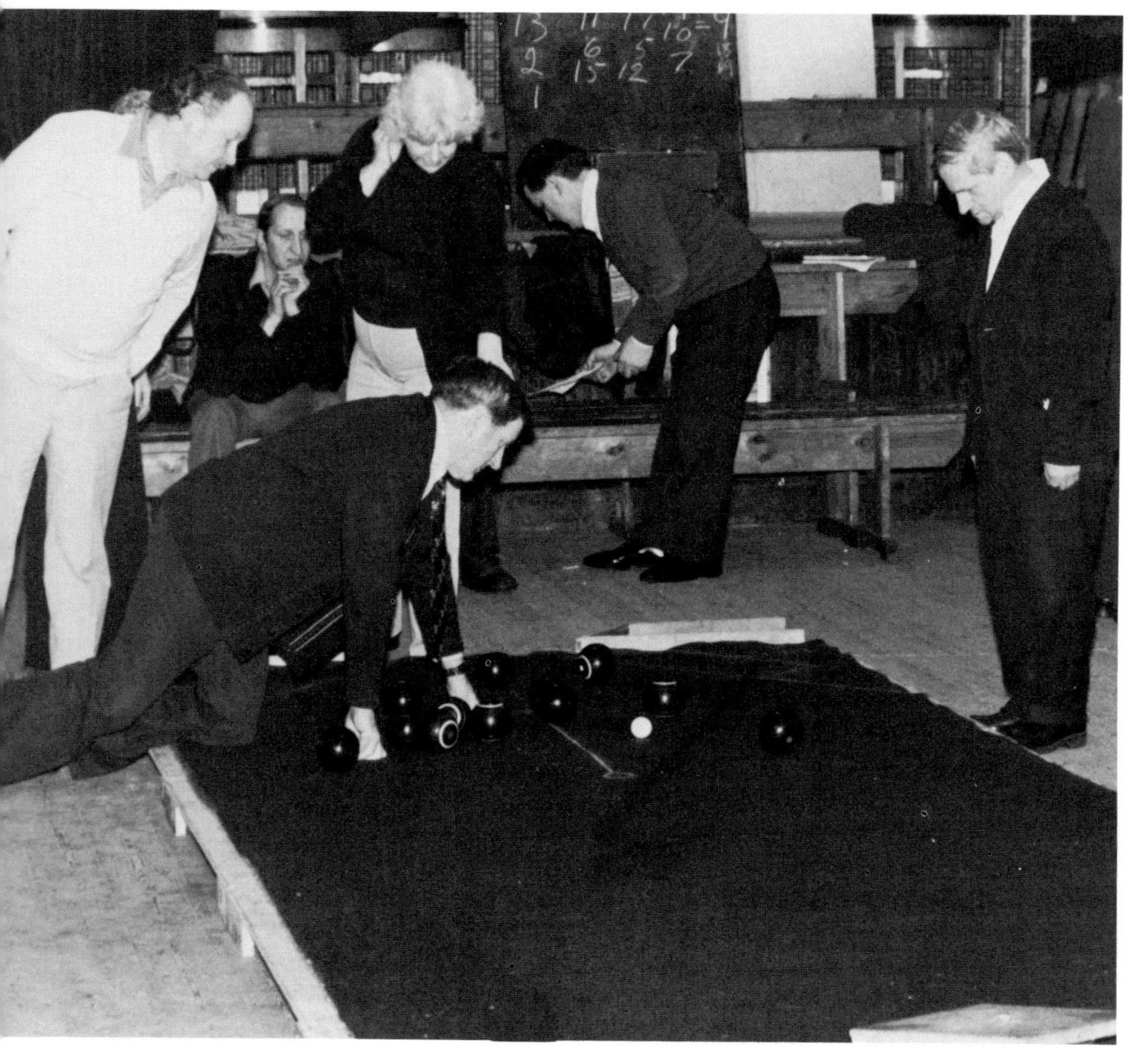

The unusual game of carpet bowls. Any bowl which touches the wooden diamond is out of the game.

The game bears much more resemblance to the sort of bowls Sir Francis Drake played on Plymouth Hoe than to road bowls. It's played with biased woods, half the standard size, which are carefully rolled towards the "jack" at the far end of the green. But there is one enormous difference – a wooden diamond in the middle of the green, which the bowls must not touch, and which leaves only a couple of feet clear on either side. 'The diamond is sprung so that, if a bowl does touch it, it is knocked to one side, and that bowl is then out of the game.' It's removed from the green with an extra-long walking stick they keep specially for the purpose. 'The idea is to stop people from moving on to the mat to remove the bowls, because anyone moving on to the mat makes dimples in it, and that makes it uneven for the other players.'

In outdoor bowls keen players like to follow their woods down the green, as if their mere presence behind the wood will help it end up in the proper place. In carpet bowls, though, you have to keep your enthusiasm under control. 'If you have a wood in your hand, and you follow the one you have played down alongside the mat, if you pass the diamond that wood in your hand is blown!'

There are four players in each team who all have two bowls apiece, and the aim is to get them as close to the jack as possible, but if another player's woods are already covering it you need real skill, especially as you also have the wooden diamond to negotiate. 'You've got to get as near as possible just by running along the backs of the ones that are placed. If you get your bowls nearest to the jack, you score two points.'

Quiz leagues at Standish, Lancashire

Perhaps the most unlikely new game we have come across was in the small town of Standish, Lancashire, where they have come up with the unusual combination of a quiz and darts, as retired police sergeant Harry Sawyer explained. 'In 1972 people put their heads together and thought it would be a good idea to introduce darts into a quiz. I know this sounds unusual, but the idea was to throw darts to set the value of the questions. We have a bag with numbers 1 to 20 in, and before each question is asked a number is drawn from that bag. Let's say it was number 5 – the darter then throws three darts at number 5 (doubles and trebles count as singles), and if he puts three darts into it he gets an extra point to make it four in all. If he gets two darts in, the value is two points and one dart, only one point.

'There are four members in a team and two of them are designated darters. One throws for the first half of the contest and the other throws for the second half. They can also answer questions, and we often find, if it's a sporting question, it's the darter who knows the answer!'

There are ten teams from local pubs and clubs competing in the league, and the method of scoring in the league is the same as in football – two points for a win and one for a draw. 'There is just one proviso to that, though. There are thirty questions for each side, and if a team answers more than twenty questions correctly they get an extra point, so a win can be worth three points, while even a loss can be worth one.' The questions, which cover a wide range of topics, are set by Harry. 'I collect them and set them, and we have all sorts – historical, biblical, geographical and sport. The difficulty I find is not so much collecting them, as making them balance evenly, so that they are fair to each side.'

The Speakers' Club at Buckingham

Coming up with subjects is also one of the main problems facing an official of another club – the Speakers' Club in the former county town of Buckinghamshire. 'We have an official called the "topics chairman" said John Murray, a past chairman of the club, 'and his task is to think up themes and present them to anybody at random at the meeting, and they then have to speak off the cuff on that subject for two minutes without flannelling. The topics could be anything – a typical one would be the journey between here and a nearby town, or hedges, or road-sweepers – anything.'

The Speakers' Club in Buckingham was founded twenty-five years ago as an offspring of the Toastmasters' Clubs of America. 'We now have clubs all over the country, and their purpose is to provide companionship and the chance to practise for people who want to do public speaking in any form. We have about eighteen members, and they're a fair mix, too – policemen, farmers, factory workers, office people, postmen. . . .'

They meet once a fortnight, apart from a summer break, and as well as topic sessions they have debates and set speeches on a subject they've been given in advance. 'The subject could be one you've chosen yourself, or one that we all have to speak on. Recently we all spoke on our choice for Idiot of the Year, and why!'

The object of the exercise, apart from the sheer fun of it, is to help members improve their techniques. 'We elect our own criticizers – "evaluators", we call them – on an *ad hoc* basis before each meeting.'

Once a year the Club holds a competition, the winner of which goes on to represent them, first at area level, then at district, and finally national level. In fact the Club has a former national champion among their number – Dennis Haward, who won the national competition in the mid-seventies with a speech on how different people respond to listening to music. Naturally John Murray is hoping that it won't be too long before they have another!

Made in Britain

*Some expected industries –
and some unexpected ones*

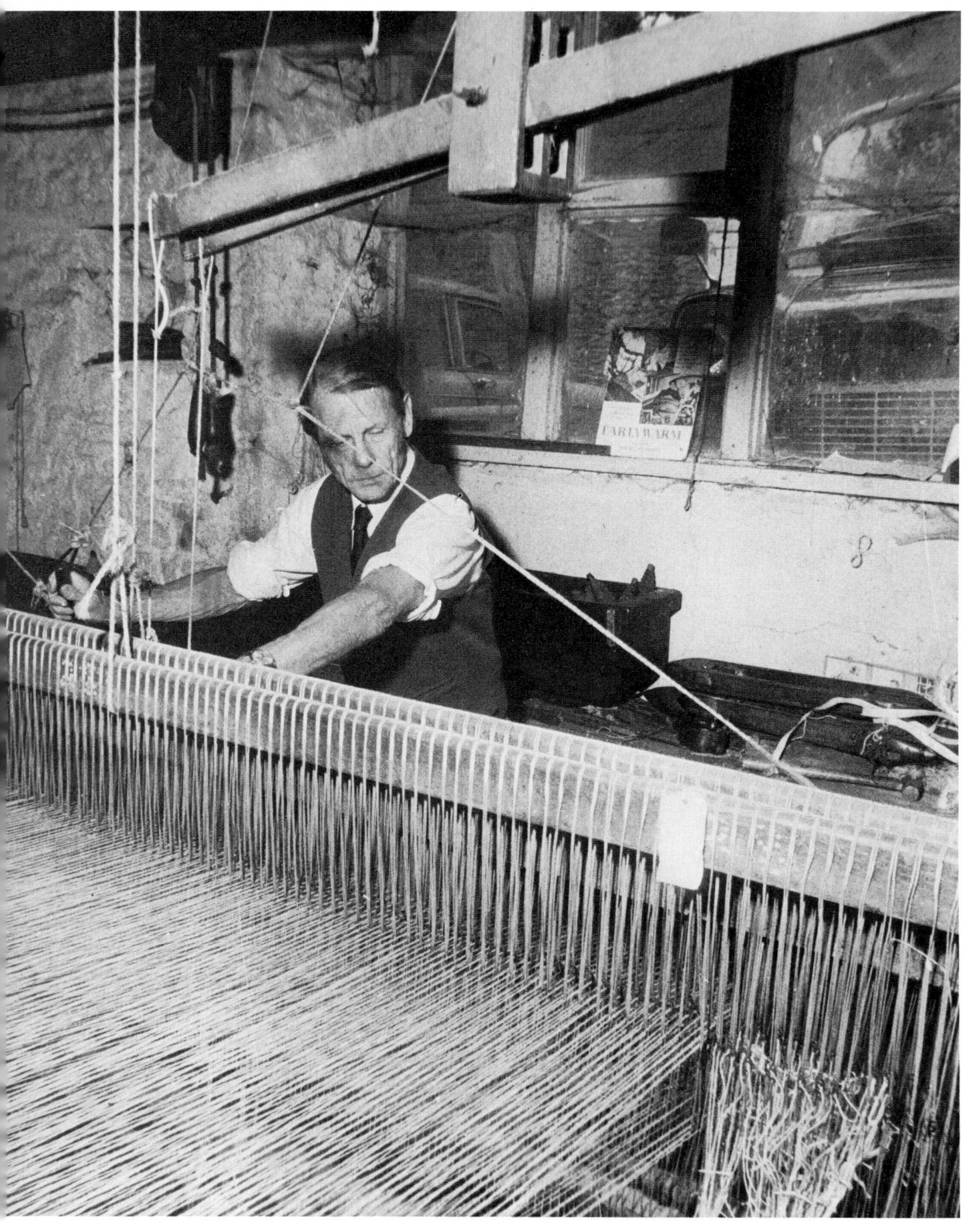

Richard Early's family have been making blankets in Witney for over three hundred years.

Blankets at Witney, Oxfordshire

In recent years many of Britain's great, traditional industries – steel, shipbuilding, car-making – have been facing major problems, as anyone knows who reads the papers or listens to the news on radio or television. It is extremely encouraging, then, to find on our travels to towns and villages all over the country any number of small industries – some traditional, some revived, some new – which are flourishing.

Perhaps the most striking factor they all seem to have in common is the very evident satisfaction that everybody involved gets from their work, much of which is very highly skilled. It is no coincidence that many of the people we met had been with the same firm all their working lives. Many of the businesses were family affairs, going back for generations. Take for instance the Early family, in Witney, Oxfordshire, on the edge of the Cotswolds, which has been involved in blanket-making for over three hundred years.

'My five times great-grandfather', said Richard Early, 'was apprenticed to blanket-making in 1669, and the family have made blankets, father to son, ever since!' But blanket-making in Witney goes back even further than that, as Richard Early explained.

'"Duo molini" – two mills – are mentioned in Domesday Book in 1085, though we don't know for certain that they were woollen mills. But in 1179 there is a mention in local records of a weaver from Witney being fined six shillings and eightpence for some offence. He obviously wove something, and it's likely that it was blankets.

'Before the Industrial Revolution there were sixty master weavers with a hundred and fifty looms all over the town. The master weaver, like Thomas Early, was the kingpin. He bought the wool, then blended it in his own house with the help of his family, and then took it out to the spinsters round about Witney, in the Cotswolds, and even in Wiltshire, and they would spin the wool. It would take a lot of spinsters to keep one loom going. Then he would bring the spun yarn back to his own house and his family would weave it on handlooms.

'When the Industrial Revolution came, the more go-ahead master weavers bought up the little mills on the River Windrush, worked by water power, where the blankets were washed and shrunk after they'd been woven, and introduced into those mills the new machinery, like Hargreaves' Spinning Jenny, and Crompton's Mule and so on. So that was the beginning of the factory system.'

Shrinking the blankets is a crucial part of the process. 'A blanket that is woven one hundred inches square will shrink to about sixty inches square – the better quality the wool, the more it will shrink, and the thicker and warmer the blanket will be. 'After that the blanket is put on a rack and stretched out to its correct size, and then "raised" – made fluffy – by teasing the surface. In the old days the tuckers, as they were called, used natural teasels to do it.'

The fact that Witney stands on the River Windrush, Richard Early believes, was one reason why the blanket trade developed there. 'It would provide the power for the little fulling mills, and some people say that Windrush water has special properties that make the blankets washed in it so good. Indeed Dr Robert Plot, in his *Natural History of Oxfordshire* written in the mid-seventeenth century, said that it was the "nitrus abstersive" properties of the Windrush. I don't know what that means, and I suspect he didn't either, but I certainly don't deny it!'

In 1981 Richard Early celebrates fifty years with the firm, and qualifies for the 'Half Century Club', founded by his father in 1945 for all employees who have served more than fifty years. 'Originally there were twenty-five members. Since then we have had to relax the rules a little because of the higher school-leaving age, so now women who've served over forty-five years and men who've served over forty-eight qualify, and we now have sixty-four members.'

The day we visited the factory we met one of them, Mrs Barbara Madden, who was retiring that very afternoon after forty-six years. 'I've been here all my working life, like my mother before me. She was here forty-eight years.' Mrs Madden told us about Witney blankets, and especially about the thickest blanket they make – the Hudson Bay.

'That is a "Points" blanket that goes out to Hudson Bay for the trappers and the Indians. It's called a "Points" blanket because years ago, when the trappers couldn't read or write, the points in the blanket showed them how many furs they'd got to give for a blanket – three and a half points, four or five. These days I expect they know more about it, but we still put the points in and they're still called Hudson Bays.'

The quickest blankets Barbara Madden has ever seen made were finished in a matter of hours. 'The sheep were sheared here in the morning, the virgin wool was spun and the chain made, we wove the blankets, they were washed, finished and put on a helicopter to London Airport and they were in New York, London and all the capitals on the same day!'

Although she was never involved in making any of the firm's special blankets for a celebrated customer, her mother was. 'She made one for Princess Marina when she was going to marry the Duke of Kent. She picked out the colour she wanted, and it was called "Marina Green". Very nice it was, too!'

A woollen mill at Nailsworth, Gloucestershire

Further west in Gloucestershire, the Nailsworth valley was also once famous for its woven woollens, particularly 'West of England broadcloth'. But where there were once some twenty-eight mills in operation, today there is just one – Longford Mill.

'The reason the industry started in the Nailsworth valley,' said Bill Smith,

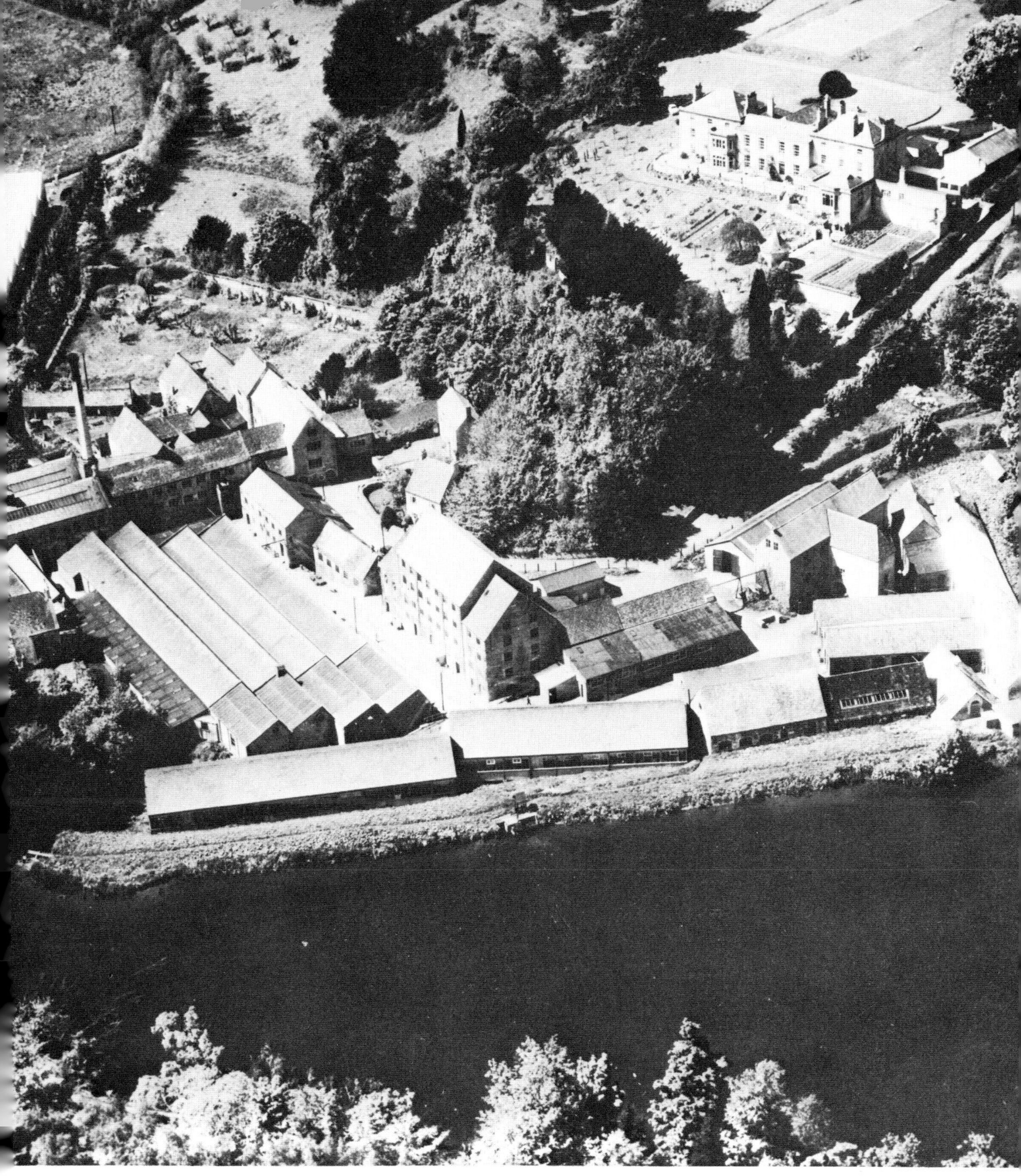

The Nailsworth valley once boasted twenty-eight mills, but now only Longford Mill remains. Here they make the cloth for covering tennis balls.

managing director of Longford Mill, 'was that the raw material, the Cotswold sheep, were very near at hand, and one of the most important things was, of course, the abundance of water in the valley, both for power and for washing the wool and also scouring the cloth.

'The industry went into decline here for a number of reasons. One of the main ones, I think, was that the West of England clothiers were very slow to adapt themselves to the demand for new types of cloth, and of course industrialization took place much more quickly in the north, particularly because of the Yorkshire coalfield which meant that cheap coal was readily available. The other main reason was that there had been such an expansion of the industry in this area in the early nineteenth century that there was a great degree of over-production.'

The decline continued well into the early seventies, so Bill Smith and his colleagues decided to stop making all other sorts of cloth and concentrate on just one – the cloth that covers tennis balls. 'We decided on it for two main reasons. First of all, the explosion of the game of tennis, world-wide, had become such that we were just unable to meet the demand if we were making other types of cloth as well. This was obviously an expanding market and we wanted to make the best use of it, both from the company's point of view and for the security of employment for our workpeople.'

When we visited Longford Mill they were producing enough cloth to cover a staggering one million, two hundred thousand tennis balls a week, and sending it all over the world – '. . . with the exception of America where, unfortunately, there is a prohibitive tariff area against us.'

As the game of tennis has changed over the years, so the tennis ball cloth has adapted to suit it. 'Up to the twenties the balls were covered in a very smooth cloth, made from fine Merino wool. As the game got faster and faster, and the balls were hit harder and harder, they became very difficult to control through the air, and they also wore out very quickly, so we developed a very much rougher, coarser cloth, using wool from a special cross-bred New Zealand species, which made the ball easier to control through the air and off the ground, and gave it a much greater resistance in wear.'

Of course, these days tennis balls don't just come in white. 'The fluorescent yellow colour was developed mainly when indoor play became more general, because the yellow fluorescent dyestuff is much sharper to the eye under conditions of artificial light and also in conditions of poor daylight. In sunlight, though, the white colour is better.'

Although Bill Smith and his colleagues don't actually put the covering on to the tennis balls, he explained to us just how it's done. 'The ball itself has to be made first – it's composed of two half-spheres which are joined together. Then it is coated with adhesive, and the back of the cloth is coated too, and the two pieces, cut in the shape of a figure-of-eight or an hourglass, are stuck on. No machine has yet been developed to do it automatically. I think it will come, but it hasn't yet.'

Glass-making at Great Torrington, Devon, and at Tutbury, Staffordshire

When the *Down Your Way* team visited the pretty Devon town of Great Torrington, the obvious question was why Dartington glass, since the village whose name it bears is some miles away, near Totnes?

'Well,' said Tony Easton, the firm's financial director, 'Dartington, near Totnes, is the home of Dartington Hall, which is an organization set up some fifty years ago, and I suppose it could be the largest commune in the world, where everyone works for everyone else's benefit. In 1963, when they realized that nobody else had really copied what they had started, they decided that they would have another go, and they chose Torrington because there was a depopulation rate of about six per cent, high unemployment, and very little industry. They decided that making glass was a craft that would be beneficial to the area and they also decided that they would base it on the Swedish style of making glass, which is simple, clean lines, not cut in the traditional English way. They therefore went ahead and set up the factory in 1967. Originally we had eighteen Swedish glassblowers, all highly skilled, brought over, and we took on five local boys straight from school.'

Since then the operation has grown rapidly, and they now have about ninety-five glassblowers. 'Eighty of those will be trainees who are taken straight from school, and the rest of the workforce is made up of local people – fifty or so in the processing departments, the packing rooms and the office. Because we do take on school-leavers we are a very young factory. The average age is twenty-nine!'

The factory is run very much on Swedish lines, with up to ten men working in a team. 'Our production rate is very, very high, and we like to think we have a closely knit team of men, working for each other, and this runs right through the factory. Although people are working with molten glass very close together, touch wood, we have never had a serious accident in the glassblowing shop, and this is because the discipline within the team is such that if a lad is not in the right place at the right time, not only is he causing danger to his fellows, he is also upsetting production!'

All the glass at Dartington is hand-made, although perhaps 'mouth-made' would be more accurate because it is all blown. It's done by blowing down a hollow tube into a dollop of molten glass on the end, which is then shaped by the mould inside which it is being blown. Throughout the whole process the glassblower is twisting the rod to keep the object even, and he has to judge when the glass inside the mould has reached the required shape. Needless to say it is a technique that takes anything up to ten years to acquire. 'It is very skilful. Right from the word go you have to learn how to judge the right amount of glass to take from the pot. If you take too little, you won't have enough to finish the product. If you take too much, you're just wasting money. It has to be just right, and this is what takes the time and the learning!'

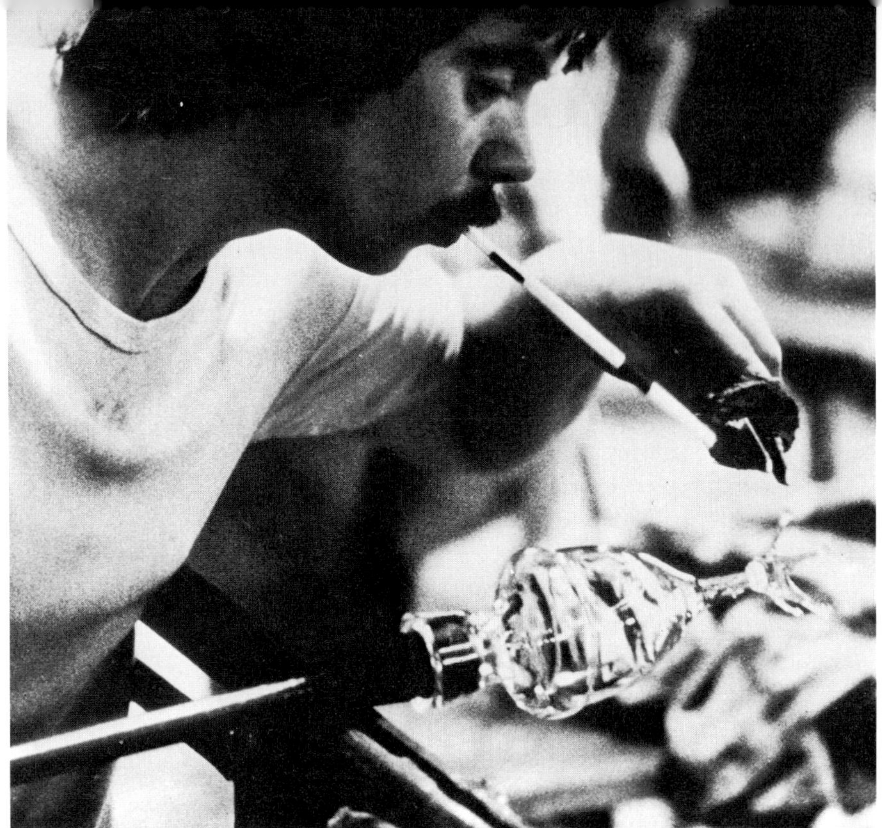

The immensely delicate art of glass-making. Dartington glass is made in the Swedish style, with clean, simple lines.

At Tutbury they have not departed from the traditions of English glass-making, and still produce fine cut glass like this.

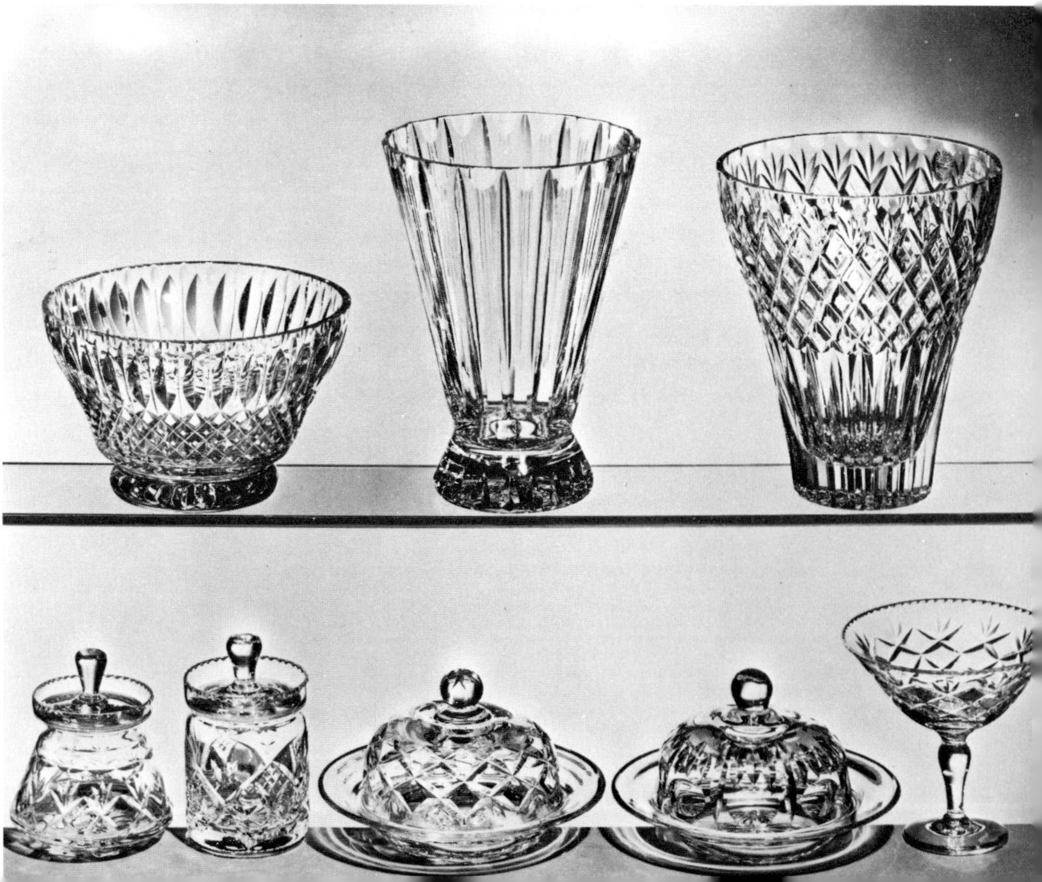

As Tony Easton explained, Dartington glass is a departure from the traditions of English glassmaking, because it isn't cut. When we visited the Tutbury Crystal Glass Factory at Tutbury in Staffordshire we discovered the additional skills involved in producing the beautiful wineglasses, decanters, jugs and fruit bowls which sparkle like diamonds, and along with the polished silver and starched white linen set the seal on any formal dinner table.

'At Tutbury the glassblowers work in smaller teams, of four. 'It's actually a team of three, 'Roy Bailey, the firm's production manager, told us, 'with a fourth man who takes the article away to a lehr – where the glass cools down from about 500 degrees to room temperature over about two and a half hours, which "anneals" it, takes the strain out of the process as much as possible!' The main body of the glass or jug that is being blown is made in a mould. 'From there the rest of it – the handle of a jug, or the foot and leg of a wineglass, is cast on freehand, for want of a better word.'

Once the plain glass is finished it goes upstairs to be cut. To the outside eye that looks like the most skilful process of all, since the cutters actually cut the glass by holding it against a hard stone wheel revolving at two thousand, eight hundred revolutions a minute! 'Before they start they have some faint markings on the glass to aim at, but once they've committed the article to the wheel, that's it. They can't slow it down, and straighten it up or anything like that. It's a skill that takes years of practice to develop.' But of course even the most skilled cutter makes the occasional mistake. 'There are rejects. Some can be repaired, others go out and are sold as "seconds", or they go back into the furnace to be recycled.'

With some justification Roy Bailey is very proud of what the factory produces. 'I mean, I've been here forty-two years, and I don't think you'd stay that long if you weren't proud of what you're doing.' He believes, understandably, that Tutbury crystal is the finest you can get, though even he found it hard to say precisely why. 'It is difficult to put a finger on it really, but when we speak of "colour", in fact we mean "no colour". We don't want any tinge of colour at all – it's icy cold, icy to look at. Then you know you've got a good piece of full lead crystal, which has over thirty per cent red lead in it.'

If you want to be sure that you're buying the genuine article, Roy told us, the thing to do is give it a good knock. If you get a deep, ringing sound, you know you've got real lead crystal.

A bell foundry at Loughborough, Leicestershire

Another man who knows everything there is to know about deep, ringing sounds is Paul Taylor, whom we met when *Down Your Way* visited Loughborough in Leicestershire. He is the fifth in line of the Taylor family which owns the largest

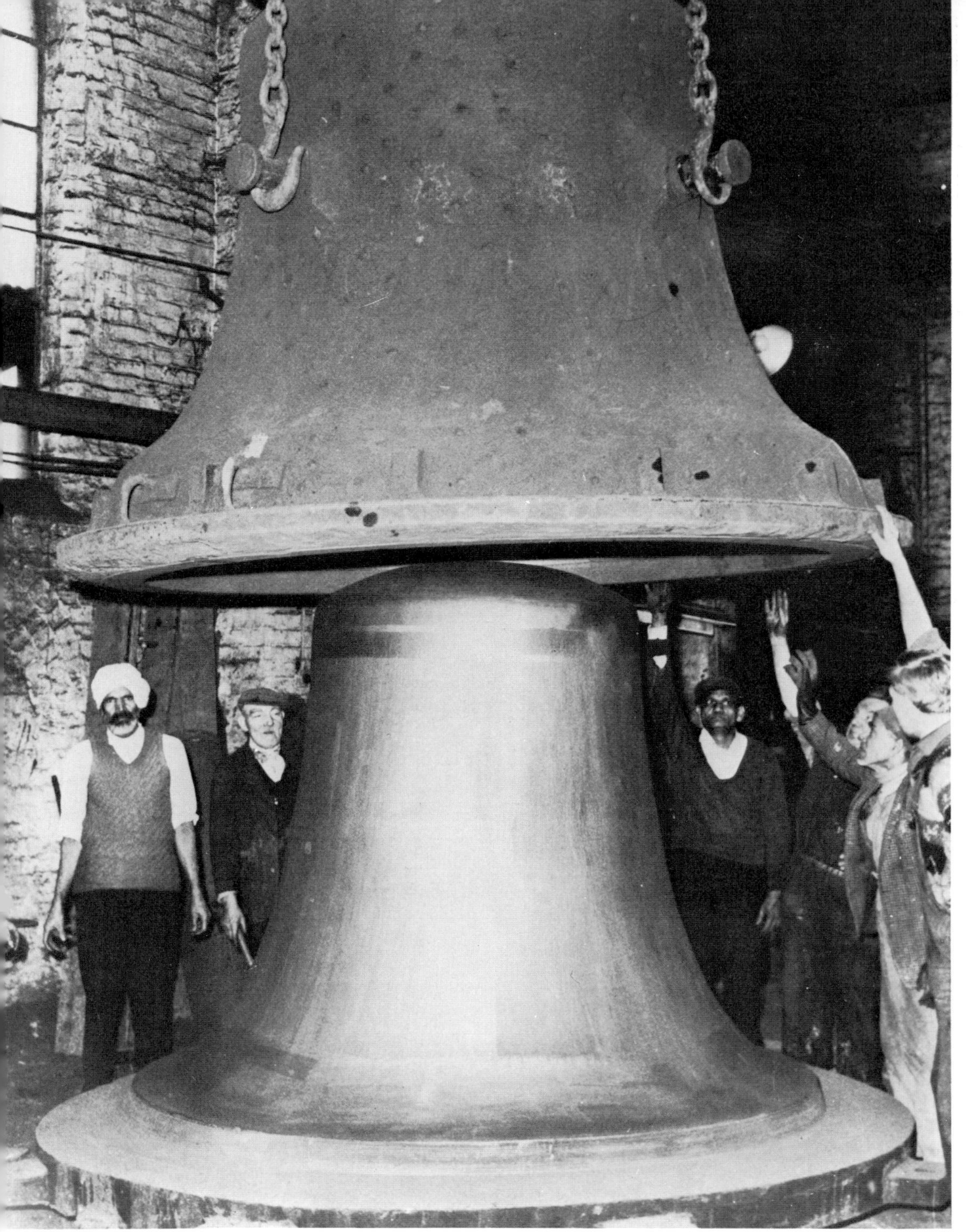

The Taylors' bell foundry at Loughborough is the largest in existence, and Taylor bells can be found all over the world.

Right: The Canberra Carillon is tested before it is shipped to Australia.

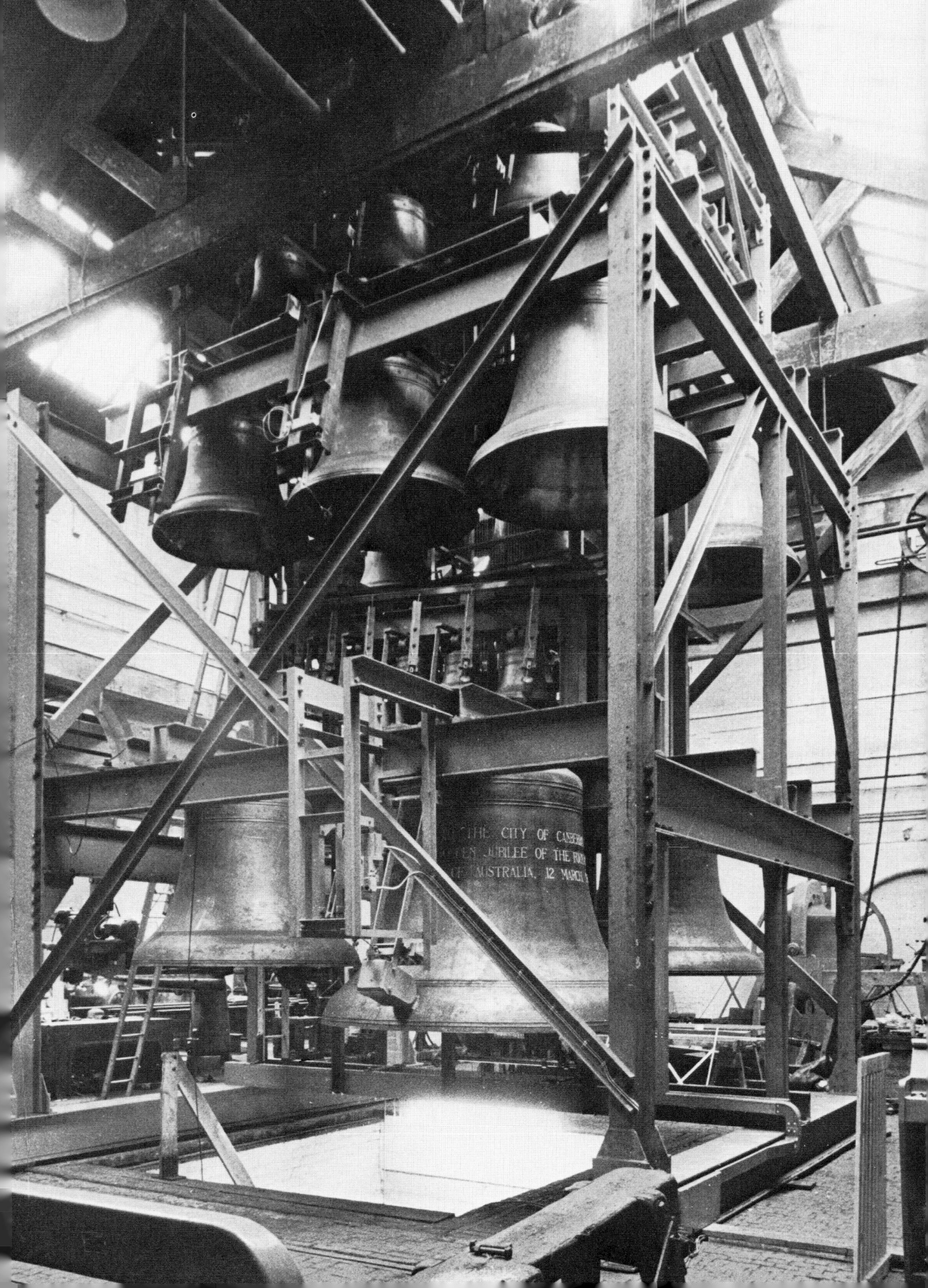
CITY OF
OF THE
STRALIA, 12

bell foundry, not just in England, but in the entire world, turning out about one hundred tons of bells every year.

There are, Paul Taylor told us, Taylor bells pretty well all over the world. 'One of the spoils of the last war was a bell which is now, I'm told, in Moscow, and there are quite a few Taylor bells in America. There are also Taylor bells in pretty well every county in England, too. "Great Paul" in St Paul's Cathedral, which at seventeen tons is the biggest bell in the Commonwealth, was made by my grandfather in 1881. The biggest bell I've made was a fifteen-tonner, and that is in Liverpool Cathedral. His name is "Great George".'

Since there is no immediately obvious reason to connect Loughborough with bells, Paul Taylor told us just how the firm came to be there. 'Well, bell founders are a peculiar lot, and years ago they used to go to the place where the bell was wanted and made it there, because obviously transporting heavy weights in the old days was a real problem. That's why you get "Bell Lane", "Bell Field" and so on in lots of villages. Anyway, the second Taylor came to Loughborough because the rector here wanted his bells doing properly, so he packed his trappings and moved from Oxford to Loughborough about 1840. By that time you began to get transport – you got railways, you got canals, and then roads, and since Loughborough is pretty central this is where he stayed.'

The bells are made from bell metal, which is in fact bronze. 'That's an alloy of copper and tin, what the textbooks call a "superior metal", not to be confused with brass which is copper and zinc, an "inferior metal".' The size of the bell determines its tone, and the bigger the bell, the deeper its tone would be. 'You can't get a low note out of a small bell, so that if you want a middle C, say, the bell will be roughly five feet across the mouth – that's the open bit – and will weigh the best part of two tons. We have got all sorts of instruments to check the tone of a bell, but it comes down eventually to your ear. If you haven't got a musical ear, you really shouldn't be a bell-maker!'

To make sure the clapper is working properly, the bells are tested on the sort of rig on which they will eventually be hung. 'We in England ring our bells in a way peculiar to us, in which each bell swings on its own weight in almost a complete circle. You have a light wooden wheel round which the rope goes, and when you see the bellringer pulling the rope, it goes through to the top of the tower round the big wheel, and that swings the bell. Nowadays we go and hang the bells in the churches and cathedrals ourselves. Years ago, bell founders and bell hangers were different men, but these days the same bloke does it.'

Needles at Alcester, Warwickshire

If a seventeen-ton bell is at one end of the size scale, then a minute needle no thicker than a human hair, which is used for eye surgery, is at the other. It is just one of a range of surgical needles manufactured in the old Warwickshire town of Alcester, where it is a traditional industry. It began, we learnt from Derek Payne, manager of the Stainless Surgical Needle Company, back in the early eighteenth century.

'Monks came from Long Crendon, and brought the secret of the process with them. They began manufacturing needles here primarily because I think some of the local mills could provide the machinery to point the needles, and draw the wire to size and things like that. It was a very, very slow job in the old days. The wire had to be cut and straightened by hand, each needle had to be hammered to a straightness, and then a hole had to be punched in by hand, and the whole thing ground, again by hand, so the needle was a very expensive item!

'It wasn't a very healthy job either, because they passed the needles over a stone, the dust got into the atmosphere, they breathed it in, and got pneumoconiosis or some similar ailment, and they usually died at about thirty or thirty-two. Of course they were well rewarded – they got about £7 a week, those men, and enjoyed a good life until they died. But then the owners brought in dust extractors, and played water on to the stones, and this made it a clean job, so that the men lived till they were sixty or sixty-five. But of course the owners wanted to cut wages at the same time, so the whole lot rioted, and there was quite a to-do, and some of the old needle factories even had their own small police forces!'

These days the two surviving small needle factories in the town are happy places. 'It's a family business largely,' Derek Payne said. 'We've got twelve people here and three married couples among them. Everybody does all the various processes, so there are no demarcation disputes.'

Although there is some machinery in use these days, the basic techniques haven't changed in two hundred years. 'What we do is bring in the stainless steel wire, and cut it into straight lengths. Then we point both ends, because we made two needles on one wire. Then we press the wire and put in the eyes, and then it is broken into two needles and the two heads are ground. That makes an ordinary needle, but to make surgical needles the thing is flattened and a triangular section is put on the shaft. Then we heat-treat them up to one thousand degrees to get them hardened, and then they're polished and the cutting edges are ground. They have to be very sharp because obviously they've got to go through muscles. Then they are polished again, inspected and then sent out all over the world.'

They produce about one hundred and thirty thousand needles a week, which sounds like an awful lot of needles. 'Don't forget that they're all used only once, and then thrown away, and in any one operation you could use up to twenty needles.'

They produce a different needle for almost every surgical process you can imagine. There is a curved one for tonsil operations: 'If the surgeon is operating in a constricted space he needs a curved needle to get round.' Then there are the tiny ones used in eye surgery, which cost anything between £1 and £2, and one rather large, ugly-looking brute. 'That is for post-mortems. When they've done a post-mortem on you, and you've got to be sewn up again, they use a piece of string and one of these needles!'

Seeds at Torquay, Devon

With the increased leisure time many of us have these days, gardening has been enjoying a boom. *Down Your Way* went to visit one of the biggest and best-known seed companies, Sutton's, although we were somewhat surprised to find them in Torquay and not in Reading, where their miles and miles of flowerbeds alongside the railway line were a sure sign to seasoned travellers that they were approaching Reading station.

'We moved here in 1977,' Peter Coxhead, joint managing director, told us, 'mainly because in the Reading area we couldn't take on the very large numbers of temporary staff that we need from November to April in any year. Down here, of course, there is quite high unemployment, so we are able to take on a very large number of people during the winter period who work in the tourist industry in the summer months.'

Although Torquay is certainly milder than Reading, and known for its warm weather, the climate had nothing to do with the move. 'It used to be a fairly popular misconception with the public that we grew a lot of our seeds at Reading, whereas of course we grow our seeds all round the world. We tend to grow them where there is the best climate at harvest time for that particular crop. For instance we grow sweet peas in California, mainly because the desert air out there doesn't harden the shell too much, so that the customer gets a better result. We also grow seeds in Italy, India, Australia, Holland and we've been looking at the Nile delta in Egypt. We send out a "mother" seed to our growers all over the world, which then becomes the next season's crop. From that crop we select the best plants, which then provide the "mother" seed for the next crop, and we've been doing this for a number of years.'

The seeds are tested in two ways – in the firm's laboratories, and outdoors on their trial grounds at Stoke Gabriel near Totnes, alongside the River Dart, and at Gulval near Penzance. 'We test them to make sure, if they're flower seeds, that the variety comes true to type, that the flowers do not fade, and that it does everything we say of it.'

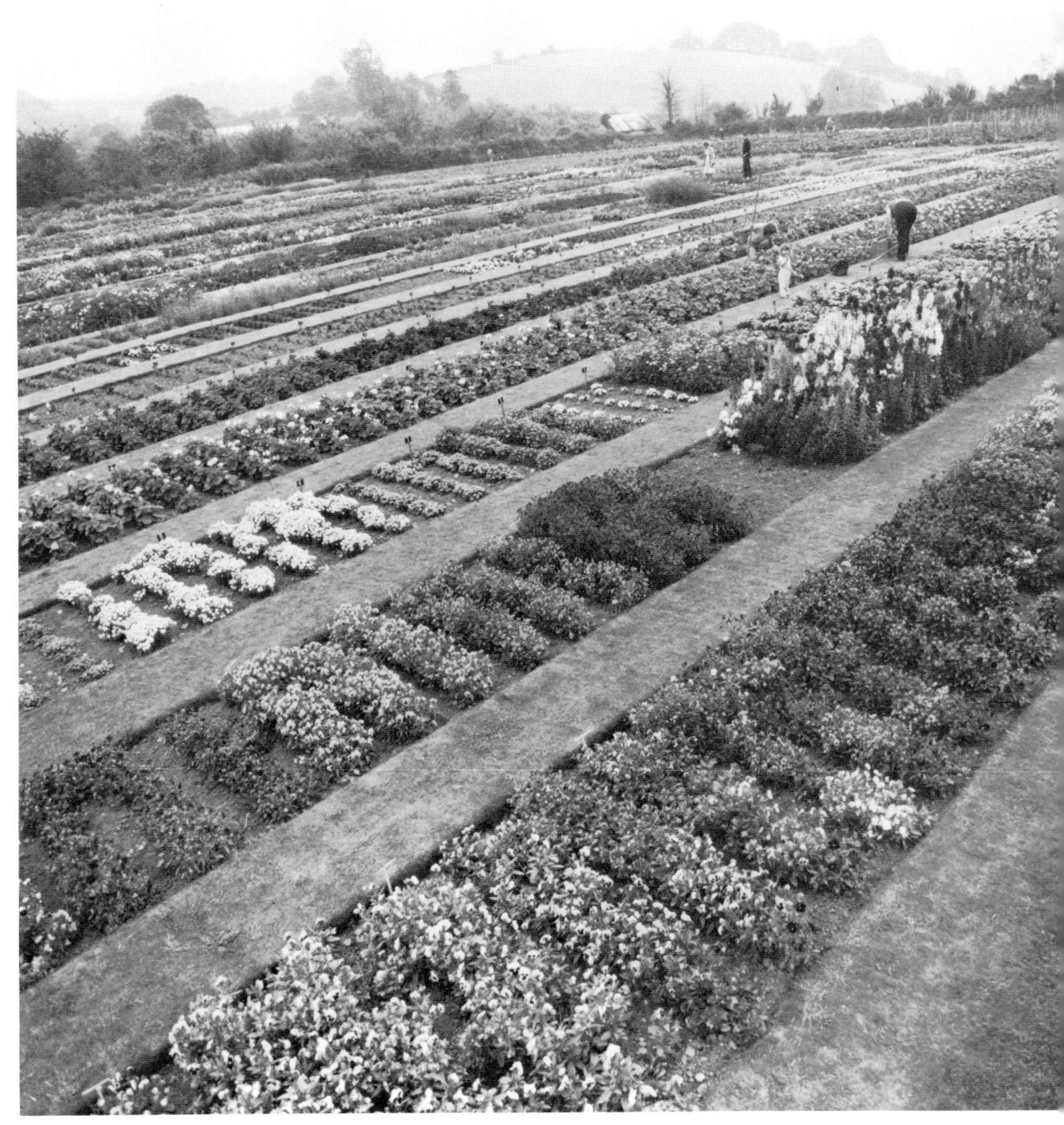

The nurseries of Sutton's Seeds at Torquay. They sell thirty-two million packets a year.

They sell an astonishing thirty-two million packets of seeds a year. The most popular flower seeds, Peter Coxhead told us, are nasturtiums and sweet peas, and the most popular vegetable, surprisingly, beetroot. 'The reason is that our sales of beetroot are of one variety and we pack around three quarters of a million here at one go.'

Although many of us grumble these days about excessive packaging the fact that the seeds are double-wrapped – in a foil packet inside the traditional paper one – is for our benefit. 'We started using the foil packaging about twelve years ago. We dry down the seeds, and then store them in special moisture-proof rooms where the seeds are then packed into foil and sealed. The seeds then should not age until the foil is broken, so it is double insurance for the customer, keeping the seeds at absolutely peak performance.'

Growing willow for cricket bats at Bungay, Suffolk, and making cricket bats at Robertsbridge, East Sussex

One extremely obliging plant that you don't need to grow from seed is the willow. Just stick a piece in the ground and without more to-do it will take root and start to grow – extremely vigorously into the bargain! There are of course, many different kinds of willow – weeping ones, creeping ones, minature ones – but with Brian Johnston among our number it would have been very perverse to look at any kind other than that wielded by young men in white on summer afternoons – cricket-bat willow.

We visited the firm of Edgar Watts, which has been growing willow at Bungay, Suffolk, for almost seventy years now, as the founder's grandson, Toby Watts, explained. 'He began this about 1912. He started off really as a furniture dealer and had a friend who came up from Essex, who said he knew a bit about splitting willow out to make bats, and he started growing these and cutting the trees down at that time.'

The willow they grow is the ideal timber for cricket bats. 'It's very light, and it's got a very long fibre which gives it its strength when hitting a cricket ball. There is no other tree which has that long fibre. We have tried poplar, and though it is heavier it will not stand up to a ball striking it.' They export wood for bats all over the cricketing world – India, Pakistan, Australia and New Zealand – since the best willow grows only in England, and over seventy per cent of it in East Anglia.

The trees take an average of fifteen years to reach maturity, but as they grow at different rates the only way of knowing when a particular tree is ready for the chop is by measuring it. 'To make a man's cricket bat it's got to be fifty-four inches round at roughly chest-height. 'When we get the trees into the works, we

A stack of 'clefts', which are about to become cricket bats.

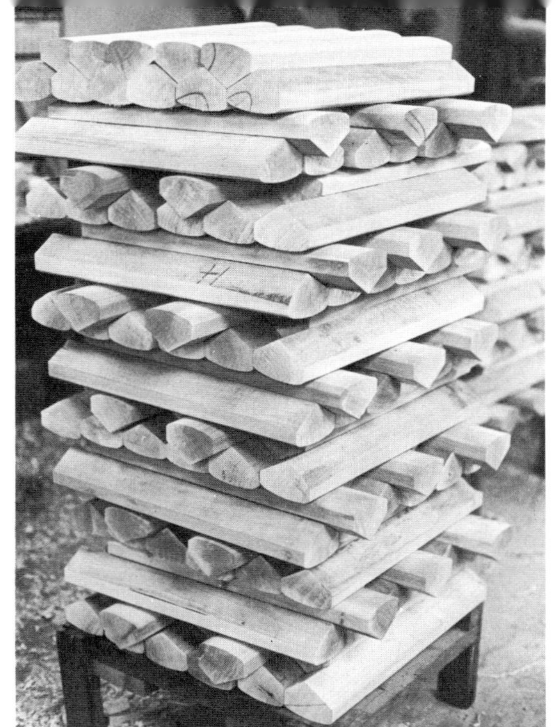

Matching the handle with the splice in the bat. The handle may consist of up to twenty pieces of cane.

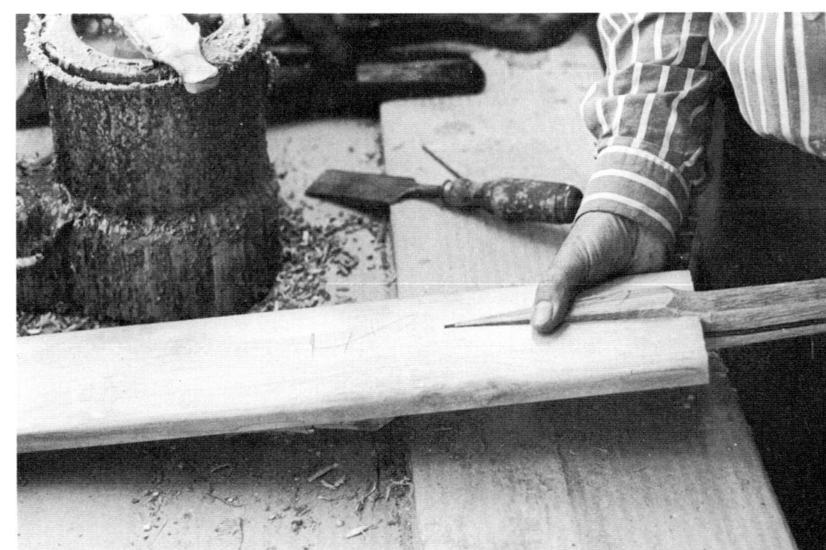

The shaping of the blade of the bat is still done by hand.

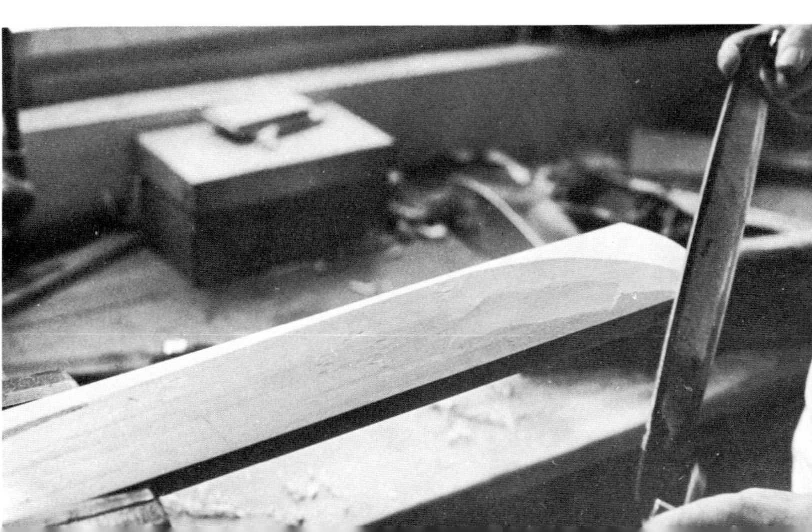

cut them into two-foot-six lengths. Then they are taken into the mill, and they're split as though you're cutting a cake, straight to the centre, and these are split with mallets and wooden wedges. From then on they are sawn normally, and we are left with a shape rather like the old-fashioned haystack, with a face, two flat sides, and going to a point at the back.'

The ideal 'cleft' – as the roughly hewn blocks are called – is as straight-grained as possible, Toby told us, because that gives the finished bat its strength. 'If the grain starts to run off at one edge, and the ball strikes that edge, the piece is likely to break away. The next thing you look for is colour. Everybody likes the look of a nice white cricket bat, but as soon as a bit of colour comes in it's down-graded, and if you get slight blemishes caused by insects or knocks or anything like that, it's down-graded yet again.'

They grow enough willow to produce some eighty thousand 'clefts', some of which could well find their way to Gray Nichols' factory in Robertsbridge, East Sussex, where they turn out some twelve hundred and fifty finished bats a week. We talked to the firm's sales and promotions director, better known to cricket-lovers as Jock Livingstone, the Australian-born batsman who scored so many runs for Northamptonshire in the fifties, and he told us a little of the firm's history.

'We are now in our one hundred and fifth year. The present site came into being in 1943, and any cricketer will be interested in how we came here. Because of our need to expand, it was decided that we needed a new site, and as the war was still on our managing director, the late Len Newbury, wrote to the requisitioning officer to see if it was possible to get a new site. He found that the requisitioning officer was, in fact, none other than the great Maurice Tate, with whom Len Newbury had played a few games of cricket whilst an amateur batsman with Sussex!'

Once the willow arrives in Robertsbridge, they get to work on it right away. 'Willow is a very wet substance – in fact, it is a reed and not a timber – so what happens is that the ends of the clefts are waxed to expel all the fluid because willow is very, very porous. They then go into the kiln to be dried out, and in about six weeks they lose something in excess of half their weight, with the moisture being expelled.'

Apart from using machinery to cut away the rough surplus willow, the rest of the operation is done by hand. 'The whole shaping of the bat is done purely by the skill of the bat-maker himself. The only measurement he uses at all is a width gauge, because we are not allowed to make the bats too wide!'

Brian Johnston was curious to know why the handle of a bat stayed in place when it was only glued. 'It's the accuracy of the fit,' Jock said. 'The bat-maker tries the handle in place, and if he's not quite satisfied, he takes a little more off. And when he's satisfied that it's a perfect fit, and he's matched it up with the splice in the bat itself, he then glues it, and that's it.' And there is far more to the handle than meets the eye, as Jock went on to explain.

'We use anything between twelve and twenty pieces of Sarawak cane, which comes from the island of Borneo. It's the best cane for handles, but we also insert a steel leaf – a tempered steel leaf. The idea is that, when the shots are played, the steel leaf forces or springs the canes back into position.'

A number of famous cricketers come to Gray Nichols for their bats – England's golden boy David Gower, and up-and-coming young batsmen like Chris Tavare and Paul Parker, and the captain of the hugely successful West Indies team, Clive Lloyd. Jock offered to show us the bat being made for him – provided someone helped him pick it up! 'Around two pounds five ounces is the normal weight for a bat these days, but this particular one weighs three pounds three ounces, and has got five grips on it. Clive's got huge hands, and as I say, only someone like Clive could even carry a bat like this, let alone use it!'

Like bells, cricket bats are tested for quality by sound. 'We have a lignum vitae mallet, and by striking the bat with it we can tell from the mellow sound that the ball will come off it at a fair rate of knots.'

Needless to say, Jock had not a single good word to say for the aluminium bat which was introduced by Dennis Lillee amid a good deal of ill-feeling during the MCC's 1980 tour of Australia. 'As far as we're concerned, it didn't look like a cricket bat, didn't feel like one, and it certainly didn't play like one, 'Jock said firmly. 'We had a bat sent over from Australia and tried it out and we did find that it scuffed the cricket ball.' It is now banned by the laws of cricket and all bats must be made of willow, so that marvellous summer sound of leather on willow has been preserved for generations to come.

Glove-making at Woodstock, Oxfordshire

In the beautiful and historic town of Woodstock in Oxfordshire we met Lance Clothier, who is a glove-maker – not cricket gloves, but leather and sheepskin ones. Lance is one of only two glove-makers left in Woodstock, although it was one of the town's traditional industries, and he explained why it had developed there in the first place.

'The Manor of Woodstock was a hunting lodge long before the Battle of Blenheim and the building of the Palace, and deerskins from the forest were brought to Woodstock tanneries for tanning. When the Huguenots arrived in this country with the sheep, and the wool trade arrived in the Cotswolds, these skins were brought to Woodstock, too, for tanning. There used to be something like twenty thousand pairs of gloves made here, with about a thousand people employed. But now I suppose there aren't more than a thousand pairs a week made, with not more than fifty people employed in the industry. They are cut out here and then they go out to be sewn up in people's homes. Then they are brought back here for finishing.'

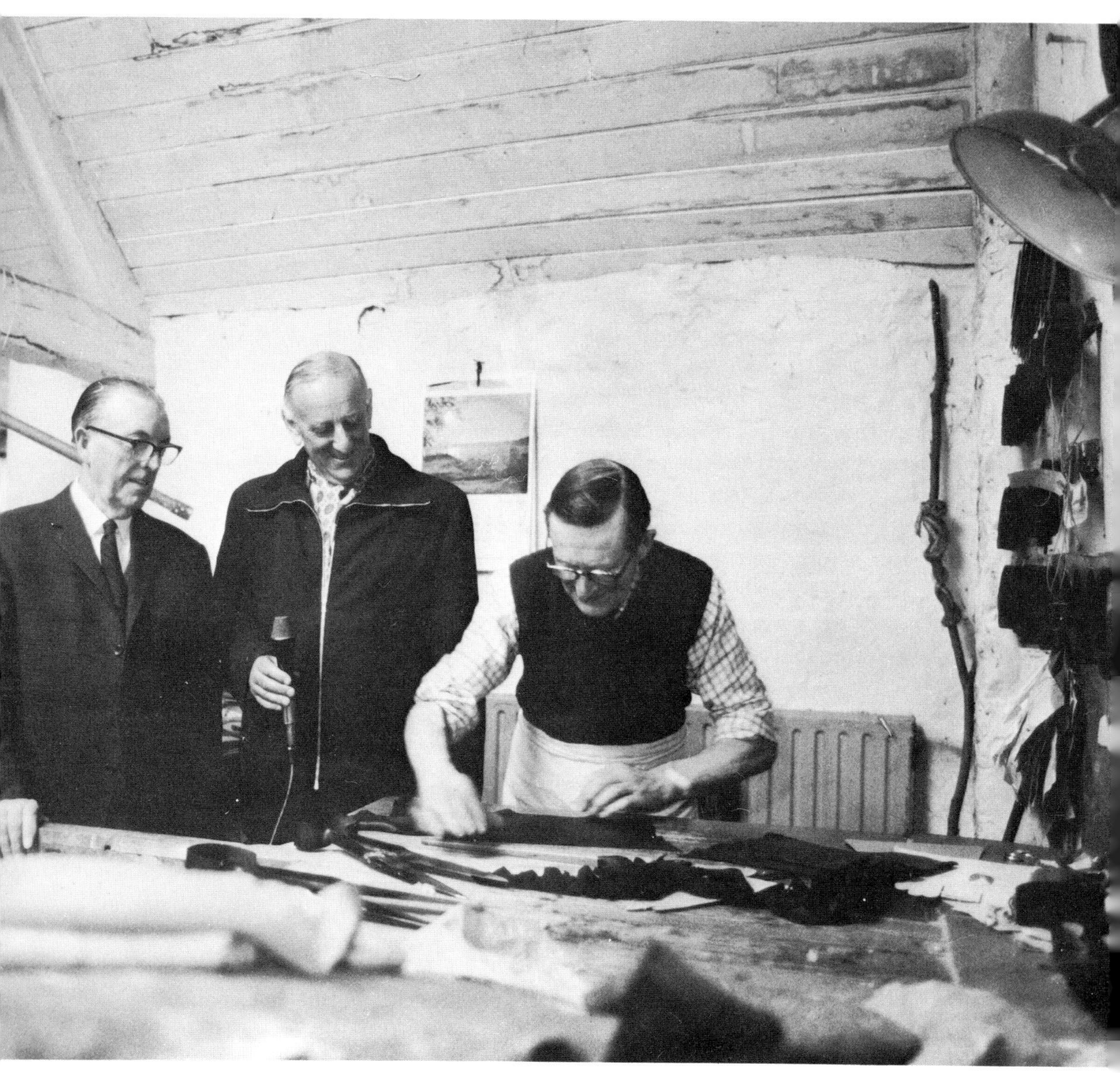

Brian Johnston interviews Lance Clothier, glove-maker at Woodstock, and watches a colleague at work.

As a reminder of Woodstock's past there is a tradition that royalty passing through Woodstock are presented with a pair of gloves. 'Queen Elizabeth I was presented with a pair of gloves which are now in the Bodleian Library in Oxford, and the present Queen was presented with a pair a few years ago, outside here on the Town Hall steps.'

Knitwear at Glendale, Isle of Skye

They also make gloves on the Isle of Skye, along with sweaters, hats and scarves, at Skye Venture Knitwear in Glendale, which is run by Sue and Barry Everson. The Eversons conduct their business from a small, stone house called the Black House, which is a traditional Skye building, as Sue explained. 'The animals lived at one end and the people lived at the other. Every winter, around October, they brought the animals in, and they stayed in there the whole winter, with just a wooden partition between them and the human inhabitants. Then, in May, they let the animals out for the summer, and barrowed out all the manure. The smell must have been frightful! It's called a "black house" because there was no chimney for the smoke from the peat fire to escape through, so everything inside turned black!'

The Eversons produce a wide range of knitwear in a number of different yarns. Sue picked up a garment to show us. 'This sweater is done in wool from the Outer Isles, and it's hand-knitted. The wool we use for the majority of our sweaters and so on is Cheviot wool, which is spun in Scotland. We also have some speciality wools because we find that a lot of people like undyed wool, so we use the natural wools of Swaledale and Herdwick and Welsh Mountain black sheep, which gives the different shades of cream, brown and grey without being dyed.' Most of the sweaters are knitted in fisherman's rib because it is warm and virtually windproof, which makes it ideal for gardening, golfing and especially fishing, for which you stand still for long periods of time.

They have about twenty hand-knitters working for them locally, and they also have a few domestic knitting machines. 'We have two in the Black House,' Sue said, 'one for our mentally handicapped son who does scarves and hats now that he's left school, and one for Barry because he does all the designing and he creates the new patterns, and works out how things go.

'We've also got a few machines in people's homes in the Glen. We've found that people prefer to work in their own homes, to suit their own hours, and they'll give us a guarantee of a weekly quota. One person might say they'll knit eight garments, someone else will knit twelve or sixteen. When they're done, they'll ring up and say "Come and fetch them." My husband then goes and fetches them, pays them and gives them more wool.'

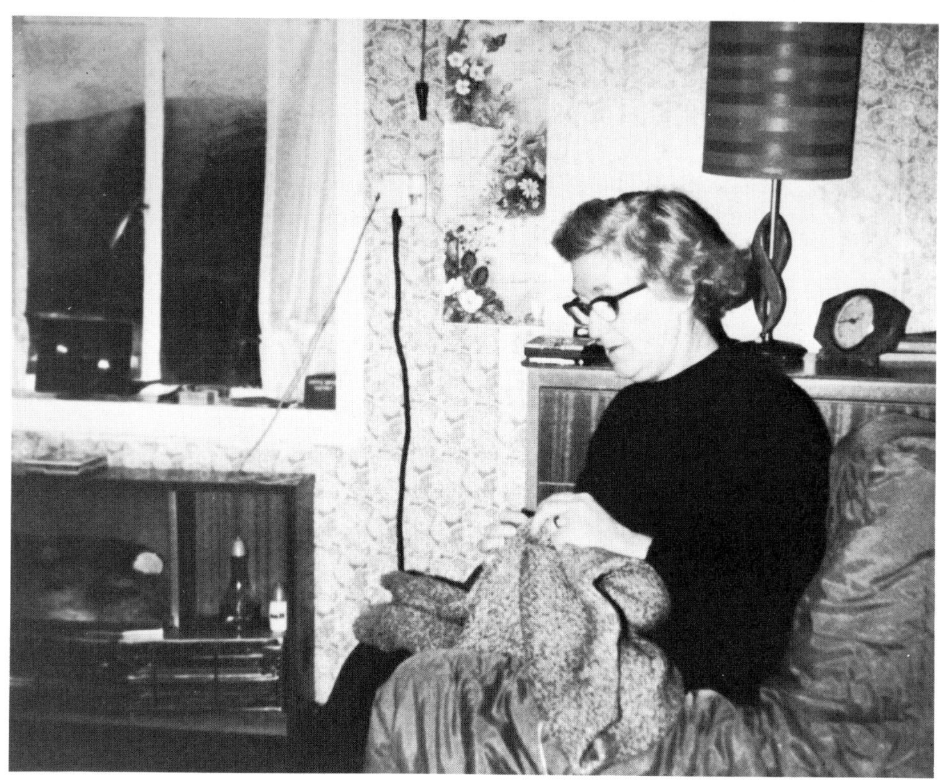

Twenty home-workers are employed by Skye Venture Knitwear. Most of the work is done by hand, but for some items machines are used.

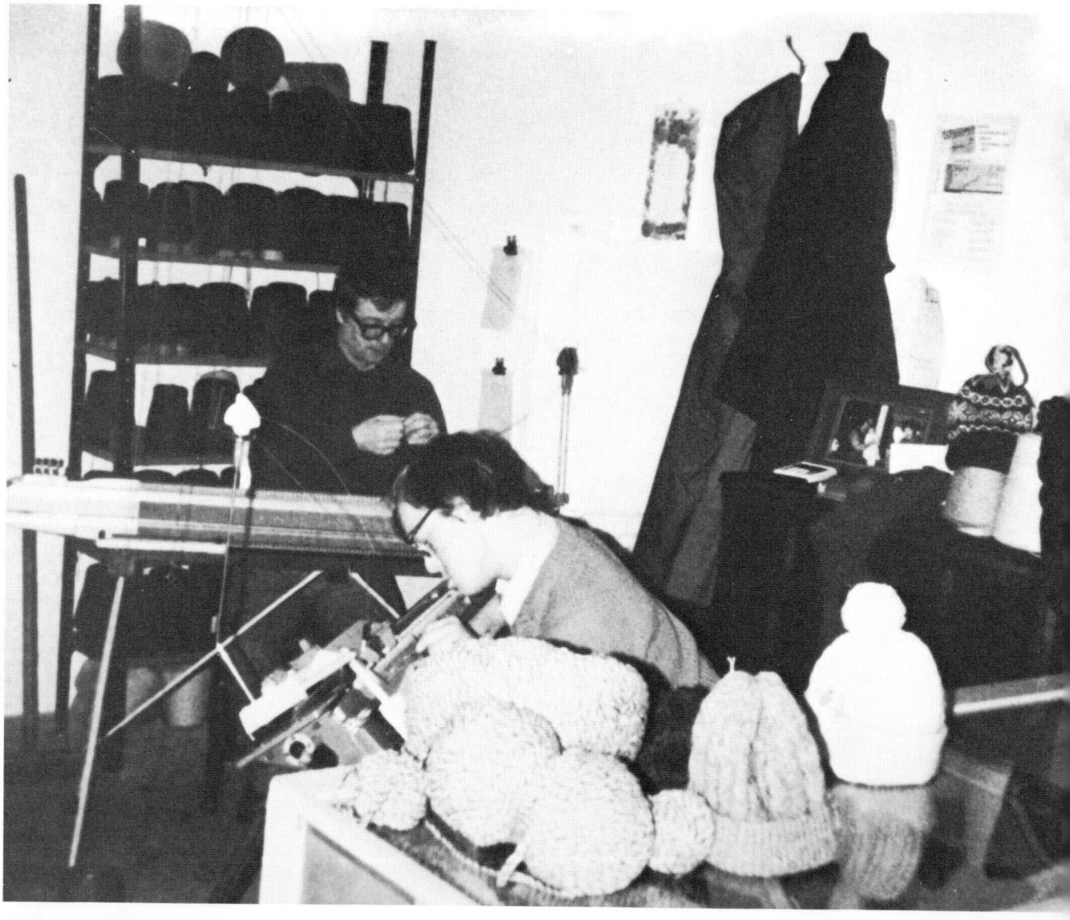

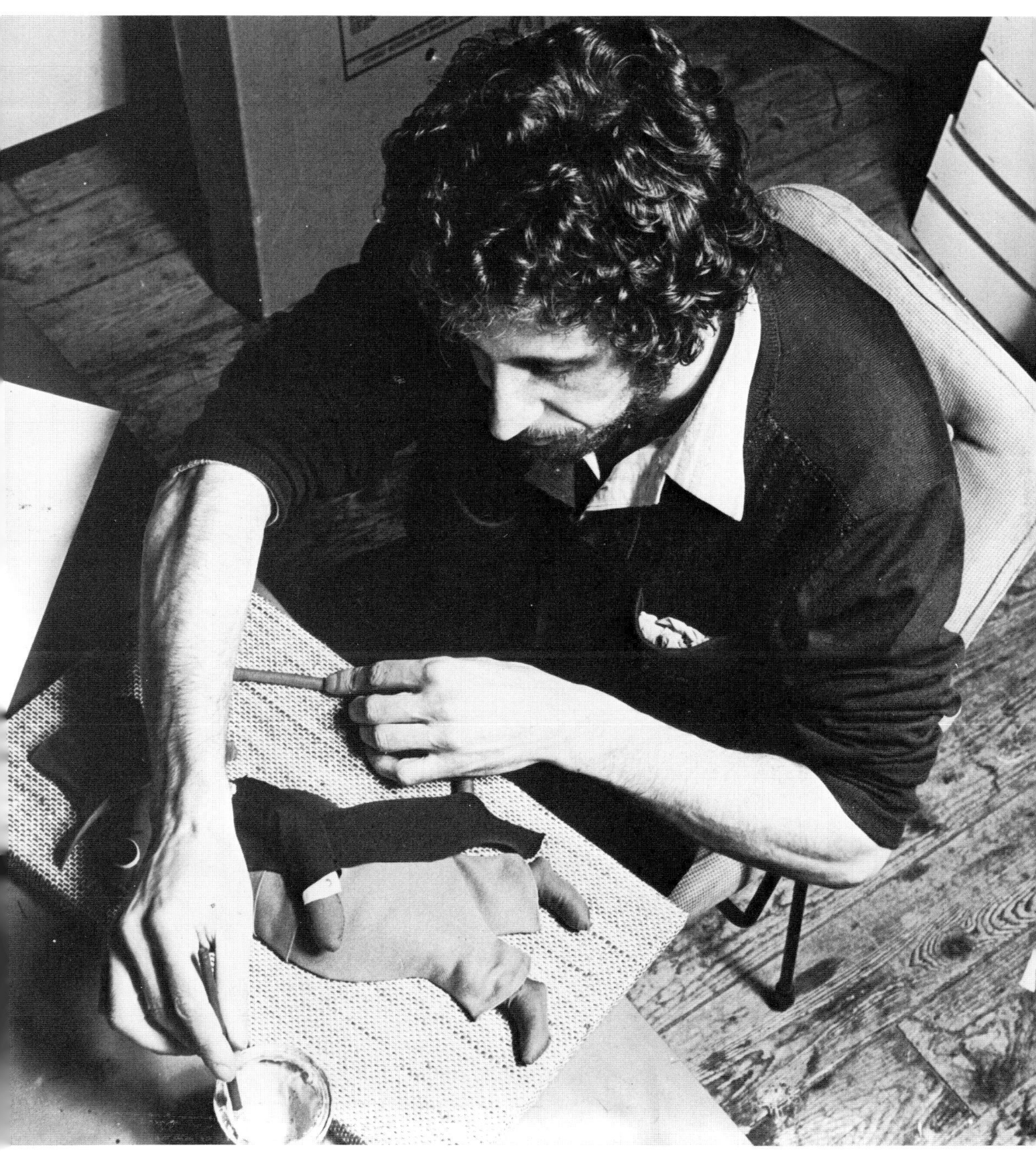

Jonathan Products is an unusual firm: the toys are for looking at rather than playing with, and the employees are paid according to their needs.

Soft toys at Rawtenstall, Lancashire

Skye Venture Knitwear is obviously very much a part of the local community, but in the town of Rawtenstall, Lancashire, we found a firm which really is not so much a business but more a way of life. It is called Jonathan Products, and its speciality is beautiful, half-model toy mice called Elsie and Hubert, dressed in exquisitely detailed costumes and mounted on hardboard so that they can be fixed on the wall and admired. Craig Hewitt, who founded the firm, explained just how the idea came about.

'We were making different kinds of soft toys and some 'hard toys' too, but I wanted to produce something really different, something beautiful and original. The only problem is that, if a child plays with a toy like that, it soon gets destroyed, so I thought, "Well, if we could cut one in half, we could put in all the detail that you require and mount it on the wall, so that the child can enjoy the picture without necessarily playing with it." It was cheating a bit, but we feel it's good.'

The first clue to the unique nature of Jonathan Products is a sign outside which reads, 'Makers of Toys to the Lord's Children'. Craig Hewitt and his colleagues are all committed Christians, and members of the Sunshine Fellowship. 'We were led to start the business through prayer. One night at a prayer meeting we got a vision of a factory, and so we said, "What do you want us to make, Lord?" Because I'd been unemployed, I had been making toys for my little boy, and so we said, "Right, we'll make toys." And so we started off in our hallway, and in the vicarage, making toys between us, and it just grew from there. We soon got a little retail shop, but that wasn't big enough, so we've moved now into this factory.

'There are six full-timers, six part-timers and a couple of outworkers. We all take a regular wage because we feel that people should be paid for their labours, but we all take different rates of pay because we each take only what we need. If someone needs more - if they have, say, more children - then they take more money, and the others don't mind because we're all working towards one end.'

Craig and his colleagues all share a remarkable faith in God and demonstrate it in all sorts of ways. 'We didn't feel it was right to be in the house we were in, so we sold it because we were heavily mortgaged and so on, although we didn't have enough money to buy another one. So, after prayer, we felt we should give everything we had to the Lord. I mean, obviously, it's difficult throwing the stuff up to heaven, but we just said, "Right, Lord, it's yours to take."

'The following day He returned it all with a blank cheque. The telephone rang about lunchtime and someone said, "I've got a blank cheque here for you to buy the house you've been looking at outright, without any mortgage, to put everything in, do all the alterations, and make it fit to live in." I know who it was, but he wanted to remain anonymous because he wanted the glory to go to God, not to himself.'

The day in the factory begins every morning at nine with prayers. 'We all meet together and we pray about the happenings of the previous day, the people we have met, and for the people we're going to meet today. We commit everything in prayer, because what's important is not so much what God is doing with the factory as what He is doing with the people here. It's our relationships that he's concerned about.'

Puzzles at Nether Wallop, Hampshire

Down in the Hampshire village of Nether Wallop is another toy-making venture. Perhaps 'toy' isn't quite the right word, though, since it conjures up hours of gentle amusement, whereas what James Dalgetty and his colleagues produce at Pentangle Puzzles provides hours of frustration, perplexity and bewilderment, as the letters they receive in the office testify. One that arrived from Wales read: 'To whom it may concern. In the interests of sanity, I would be eternally grateful if you would forward me a solution to your puzzle, The Gordian Knot. In the event of the solution not reaching me during the next fortnight, please redirect your reply to the nearest asylum. Thanking you in anticipation....'

'We don't normally send out solutions,' James Dalgetty said. 'We're selling puzzles, not the answers, but if we get a doctor's certificate, or a letter like that one, we usually oblige!'

They make a wide variety of puzzles at Pentangle, with names like Blockbuster, Lunatic, Woodchuck, and the Ball and Chain. The last-named is a simple-looking puzzle involving a wooden ball and various bits of metal, including a metal ring on a black thread, but it is in fact fiendishly difficult! 'Actually, like Archimedes, I thought of that one in the bath, but most of them aren't that easy, and take many weeks of work. About half the fifty puzzles we make are the product of our twisted imaginations, and the other half are equally divided between traditional puzzles, and the designs of other people.'

The puzzles are made by the dozen or so staff at Pentangle, and are assembled by housewives living in Over Wallop, Middle Wallop or Nether Wallop. 'Some of the bigger ones, like our Grandpa Chuck, have up to ninety-six pieces, and they can put them together in ten minutes.' The biggest puzzle, which stands in the company's hall, has no fewer than one thousand and thirty-seven pieces. 'If you were to stand the pieces one on top of the other they would be two and a quarter times the height of Salisbury Cathedral spire!' What if, Brian Johnston asked boldly, he were to take it quickly to pieces – how long would it take James Dalgetty to build it up again?

'I don't think you would take it to pieces very quickly,' he replied honestly. 'It takes forty man hours for two people who know what they're doing to put it together again!'

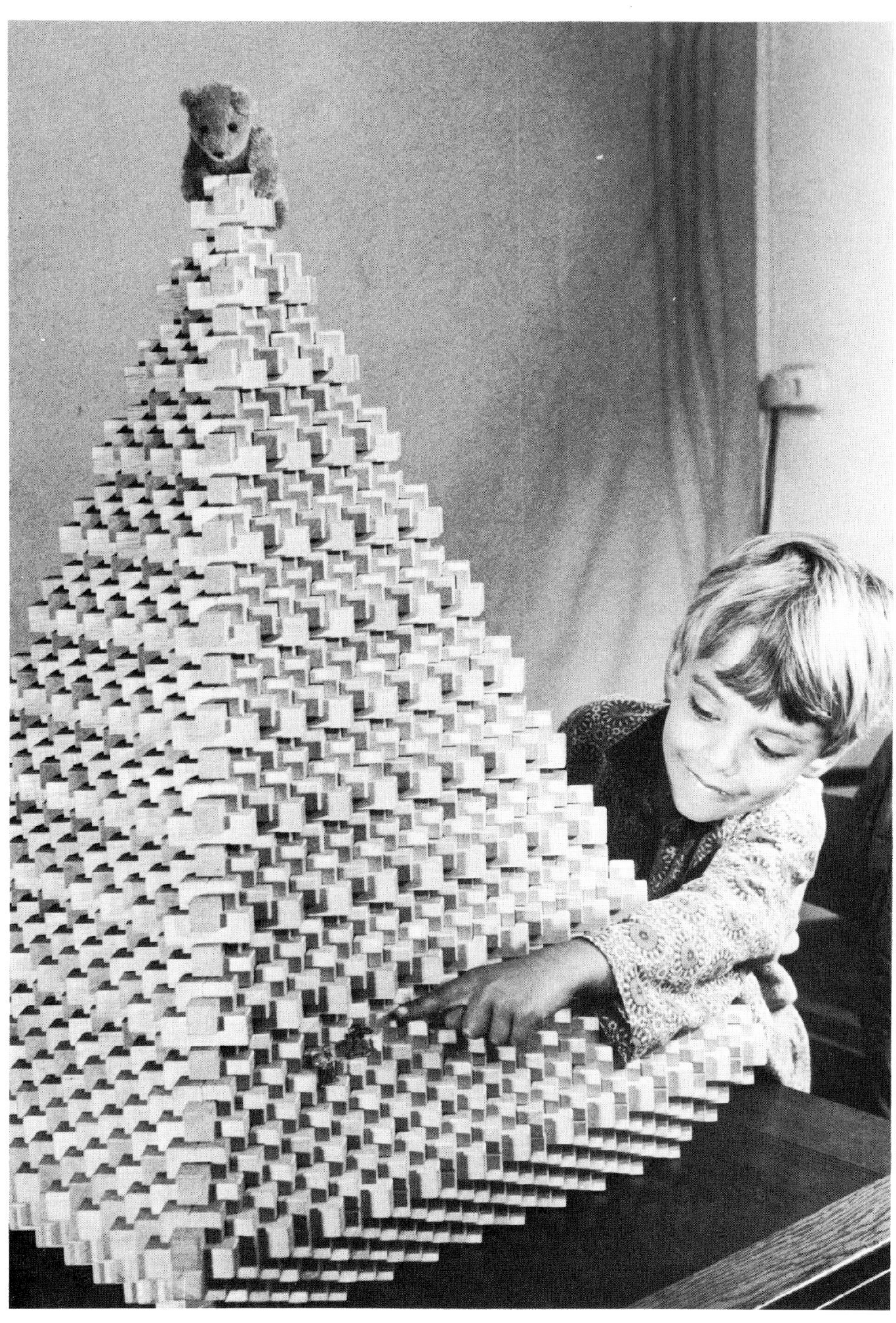

Brian Johnston wanted to know how long it would take to rebuild this puzzle if he took it to pieces. It looks as if someone else may have the same idea!

James Dalgetty has been fascinated by puzzles ever since he was a boy. 'I was given an ivory puzzle as a child, and then found I could buy them in junk shops for five shillings in the good old days, and this started my enthusiasm.' As an addict, he was able to tell us something of the history of puzzles.

'They start with recorded history, just about – Samson's riddle in the Bible, "Out of the eater came forth meat, out of the strong come forth sweetness." Unfortunately there was something very disreputable going on in puzzledom, and his wife was threatened for the answer. He was so angry that his resulting rage ended with the death of thousands of Philistines!

'And then there was Oedipus, who answered the riddle of the Sphinx. He would have been eaten had he failed to do so. Alexander the Great is perhaps the first recorded person with a puzzle object, but of course he cheated by cutting the cord!

'Then there is the Chinese Rings, which is quite a famous puzzle – it has nine rings on a long, U-shaped loop, and it takes two hundred and fifty-five moves to get them off – and which was invented in AD 181, supposedly by a gentleman called Hung Ming, who gave it to his wife to keep her busy while he was away at the wars!

'The first real puzzle craze in this country started in about 1880 and lasted till 1920, when people went mad inventing puzzles and patenting all sorts of marvellous puzzles. It died out with the Depression, though, and the second puzzle craze was started by Pentangle in 1970, and hopefully it will go on to the year 2500!'

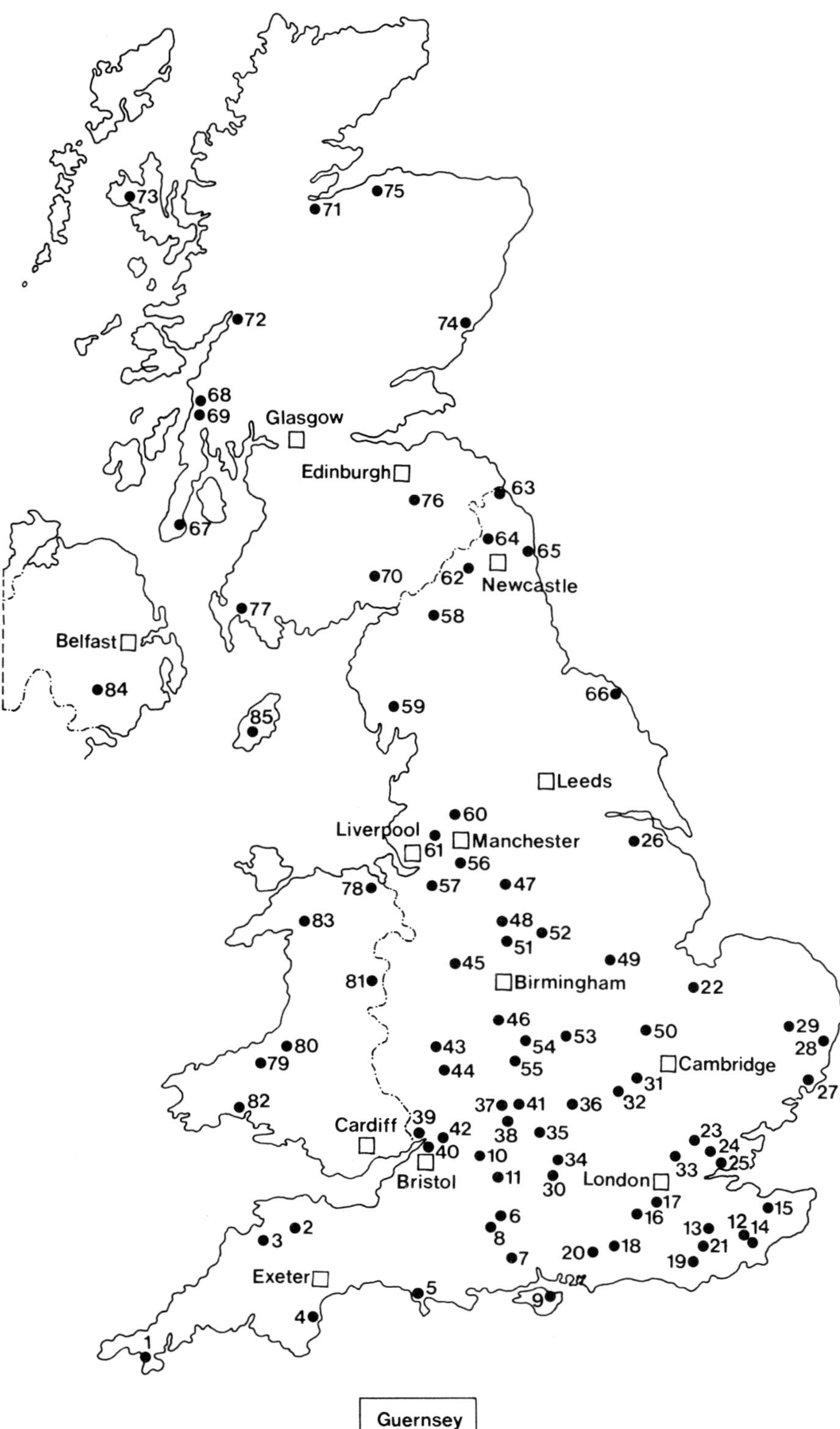

Glasgow
Edinburgh
Belfast
Newcastle
Leeds
Liverpool
Manchester
Birmingham
Cambridge
Cardiff
Bristol
London
Exeter
Guernsey
1
2
3
4
5
6
7
8
9
10
11
12
13
14
15
16
17
18
19
20
21
22
23
24
25
26
27
28
29
30
31
32
33
34
35
36
37
38
39
40
41
42
43
44
45
46
47
48
49
50
51
52
53
54
55
56
57
58
59
60
61
62
63
64
65
66
67
68
69
70
71
72
73
74
75
76
77
78
79
80
81
82
83
84
85
86

Guide to the Regions

(*The figures in brackets refer to the map*)

South-West England

South England

South-East England

North-West England

North-East England

Scotland

Wales

Northern Ireland

Isle of Man

Channel Islands

Queenie Newcombe's honey cake

3 oz butter
2 oz medium colour brown sugar
2 eggs
3 oz honey
1 oz golden syrup (level tbs)
8 oz self-raising flour
1 level tsp ground cinnamon
1 oz flaked almonds
A little milk to mix if needed

Cream together butter and sugar. Beat in honey and syrup. Fork the eggs and gradually add these to the mixture. Sieve the flour and then carefully fold it into the mixture using a light figure-of-eight movement. Add cinnamon and flaked nuts (chopped a little if you like). Now add enough milk, if necessary to make a moist consistency, that is one which drops easily from the spoon when lifted. Do not make it over-moist. Turn the mixture into a well greased seven-inch cake or loaf tin and bake in the middle of the oven at No. 4 or 350° F for about 1–1¼ hours. Test for readiness with a knitting needle. Do not allow it to become too brown. It is advisable to lower the oven to No. 3 or 325° F during the last half hour of cooking.

Marie De Garis' Beanjar

1 lb haricot beans
1 pig's trotter or piece of shin beef
1 onion
Salt and black pepper to taste
Parsley, and bay leaf optional
Stock

Soak beans overnight. Place all ingredients in a stone jar or deep earthenware dish, cover well with good stock. Fit a tight-fitting lid and cook in a slow oven for about five hours. The beans, when cooked, should be whole and not 'mushy'.

Marjorie Cashmore's recipes

Groaty Dick (*Grauty Pudding or Grauty Dick*)

½ lb groats
1½ lbs shin of beef
1 lb leeks
2 medium-sized onions
Bay leaf (optional)
Hot water to cover
Salt and pepper

Enough for four servings. Simply put all ingredients into a stew jar or casserole dish and bake slowly for at least four hours, longer if possible.

Fillbelly (*Fill Bally or Bread Pudding*)

1 stale loaf of bread
½ lb shredded suet
1 lb brown or granulated sugar
1 lb sultanas or raisins
3 eggs
2 oz butter
About 2 tsp mixed spice

Soak bread and then drain and squeeze out excess moisture. Flake with a fork and then add other ingredients. Mix well together and spread mixture in greased baking tin. Dot with butter and bake in a moderate oven (No. 2/3 or 325° F) for about two hours until nicely browned.

Faggots and Peas (*Faggits and Pays*)

1½ lbs pigs fry
2 medium sized onions
1 tbs dried sage or
½tbs fresh sage
1 cup white breadcrumbs
Salt and pepper
1 tbs plain flour or cornflour for
thickening

Enough for four servings. Thoroughly wash pigs fry, leaving caul (kell) which forms the outer coating of the faggots in warm water as this makes it easier to handle. Mince the fry and onion and mix thoroughly with breadcrumbs and seasoning. Form into eight portions and wrap each portion in a piece of the caul. Place in baking dish and cover with water. Bake in a moderate oven (No. 2/3 or 325° F) for about three hours, basting frequently until nicely browned. More hot water can be added if needed, during basting. Thicken juices about half an hour before serving. Usually served with 'mushy' peas – dried peas soaked overnight and then steamed or slowly boiled while faggots are cooking.

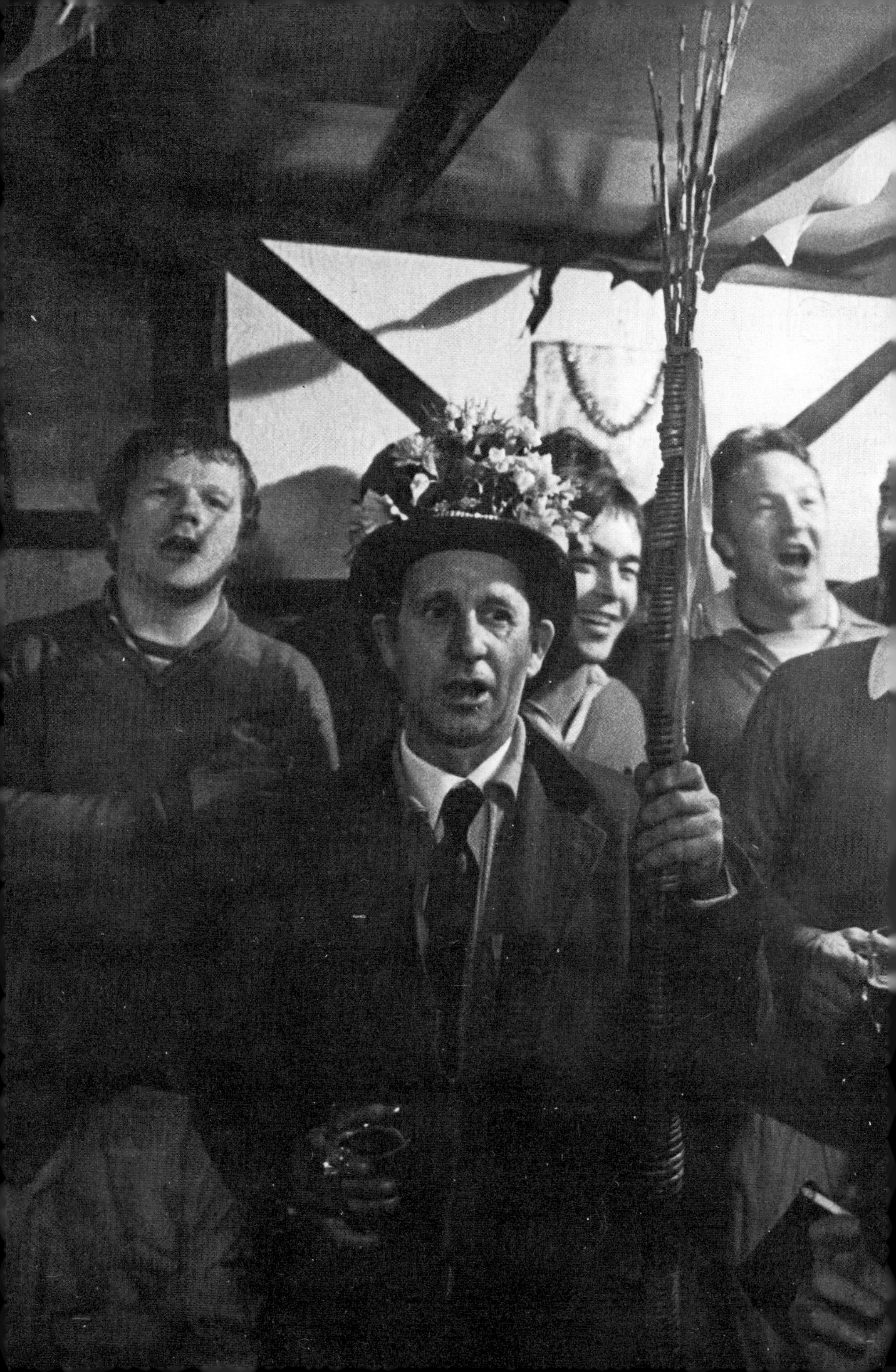